BEYOND THE BAC

Higher Education in France and Abroad

Second edition

Editors:

Helen Shavit

Jude Smith

AAWE: Association of American Women in Europe
Paris, France

Published by AAWE: Association of American Women in Europe
34 avenue de New York, 75116 Paris
www.aaweparis.org / +33 (0) 1 40 70 11 80 / aawe@orange.fr

AAWE is a non-profit association *(association régie par la loi du 1er juillet 1901)* and a member of FAWCO, an NGO with Special Consultative Status to the UN Economic and Social Council.

All rights reserved. No part of this book may be reproduced in any form or by any means without the written consent of the Association of American Women in Europe (AAWE).

The Association of the American Women in Europe (AAWE) cannot be held responsible for any information contained in or omitted from this book. AAWE does not guarantee the competence of, or endorse the opinions of any person, firm, company, or organization listed herein and does not take responsibility for any transaction or agreement you may enter into with them.

Director of Publication: Helen Shavit
Education and Bilingualism Committee Chair: Jude Smith
Cover Design: Missy Leiby
Graphic Design and Layout: Josh O'Donovan
Dépôt légale: février 2020

Copyright © 2020 AAWE
ISBN 978-2-9518326-7-1

Table of Contents

Acknowledgements 4
About the Editors 5
Preface 6

Thinking Ahead
Thinking Ahead – Keeping Your Options Open 10
The Gap Year 14

Higher Education in France
Introduction to the French Higher Education System 24
University Studies in France 36
Classes Préparatoires aux Grandes Écoles: CPGE or Prépas 57
Grandes Écoles 70
Becoming a Doctor in the French System 79
Becoming a Lawyer in France 85
Specialized Schools/ Écoles Spécialisées 89
Undergraduate Study in English in France and the EU 100
Graduate Study in France for the International Student 107
Glossary of Terms 123

Higher Education Opportunities Abroad
Undergraduate Study in the United States 134
Financing Your Education in the US 147
Graduate School in the US for International Graduates 158
University Study in Canada 166
Undergraduate Study in the UK 173
Higher Education in the Netherlands 186
Higher Education in Australia 196
About the Authors 204

Acknowledgements

This publication is the result of the volunteer efforts of numerous contributors, from chapter authors and reviewers to copy editors and student participants. We wish to thank, first and foremost, our chapter authors who generously donated their time and expertise and graciously accepted our editorial comments and suggestions. We would also like to express our appreciation to the chapter reviewers, and in particular, Colette Guillopé, Professor Emerita of Mathematics at the Université Paris-Est Créteil, for her review of chapters addressing the French university system.

Graphic designer Missy Leiby created a beautiful cover and AAWE Office Manager, Josh O'Donovan, worked skillfully and tirelessly on the layout. They have our deepest appreciation and thanks for their patience and perseverance.

We heartily thank AAWE President, Clara Siverson, for her enthusiastic support throughout this project. We also extend our heartfelt gratitude to former AAWE presidents and editors of prior AAWE education guides, Carolyn White-Lesieur and Sallie Chaballier, for their ever-ready assistance and encouragement. Last but not least, we wish to express our sincere thanks to all the individuals acknowledged below for their important contributions in bringing the second edition of this publication to fruition.

Lee Aderet	Ines Kouidri	Robynne Pendariès
Alex Audi	Aimée Lahaussois Bartosik	Vanille Plume
Chiara Barone-MacDonald	Heloise Lambert	Iris Ritter
Chloé Cabantous	Nicole Leopoldie	Daniel Rubinstein
Jennifer Chauveau	Zöe Lillian	Anne-Sophie Saverino
Samantha Csenge	Céline Lim	Andreas Schiefer
Sophie Dimich-Lovet	Amélie Matisse	Jack Souami
Loren Duchene	Maïa Matisse	Riley Simmington
Mariamne Everett	Caroline Nguyen	Quentin Tang
Emilie Foyer	Nathalie Nguyen	Alex Tcherdakoff
Linda Goldfarb	Philippe Oster	Caroline Texier
Edouard Hargrove	Corinne Ott	Charles Torron
Syriash Kishorepuria	Adrien Pendariès	Lauren Wyman

About the Editors

Helen Shavit earned Bachelor and Master degrees in Speech Pathology from Boston University and Rutgers University, and practiced as a Speech-Language Pathologist in New York City before moving to France in 1991. She chairs the Publications Committee at AAWE where she co-edited the first edition of *Beyond the Bac – Higher Education in France and Abroad* and the 8th edition of the *AAWE Guide to Education in France* (for *maternelle* through *lycée*), along with Jude Smith and Denise van Veen. Prior to these publications, she directed a survey of the education paths followed by AAWE member children, *Education and Franco-American Children*. Helen has two sons, who after earning the *baccalauréat général,* pursued their undergraduate and graduate studies in Italy and the US.

Jude Smith moved to France in 1996, weeks after receiving her Master of Education degree from the Harvard Graduate School of Education. Previously, she worked as the *directrice adjointe* for the United Nations Nursery School, and then served for nearly five years as coordinator of the Education Directory for the Message parent support group. Jude co-edited the 8th edition of the *AAWE Guide to Education in France* and the first edition of this publication, and currently serves as Chair of the AAWE Education and Bilingualism Committee. In addition, she is an active member of the American School of Paris' Board of Trustees. Most importantly, she is the mother of two daughters, both born and educated here in France, and attending universities in the US.

Preface

Beyond the Bac – Higher Education in France and Abroad is a publication of the Association of American Women in Europe (AAWE), a non-profit organization *(association 1901)*, based in Paris. The organization has published eight editions of the *AAWE Guide to Education in France* (for *maternelle* through *lycée*) and is now pleased to present the second edition of this handbook on higher education, destined for the French, bicultural, and international Anglophone student.

Higher education has become an international arena from which the young person stands much to gain, and opportunities abound. However, determining the path to follow, or school to target, can be daunting. Taking the time to investigate the possibilities while keeping an open mind, and to earnestly reflect on one's capacities, interests, and goals, will lead to a well-informed choice.

The rapidly changing vista of higher education across the globe, and the pace of the numerous reforms in France in particular, demand that the student be proactive in seeking information that is current. We have endeavored to ensure the accuracy of the information dispensed at the time of this printing, however, as information becomes outdated rather quickly, the reader is advised to also consult the references and official websites provided at the end of each chapter.

Beyond the Bac – Higher Education in France and Abroad is divided into three sections, the first of which is geared to the younger *lycée* student who is just beginning to consider his or her options. The first chapter concerns thinking ahead with an eye to keeping one's options open, while the second delves into the gap year option and deferred admission.

The second section of the handbook encompasses nine chapters devoted to the higher education system in France, including one devoted to studying in English in France and other EU countries. This section concludes with a glossary of terms relevant to higher education in France.

The third section covers the education systems and study opportunities available to students in selected Anglophone countries. Three chapters address university studies in the United States, including one on financial aid, followed by individual chapters devoted to higher education in the United Kingdom, Canada, and Australia. New to the second edition is a chapter on undergraduate studies in English in the Netherlands.

Wherever possible, chapters have been supplemented with pertinent student anecdotes. We selected these comments from responses to a questionnaire sent primarily to AAWE member children, who are either currently enrolled in or have recently graduated from higher education programs.

We hope this book will help the reader understand the different higher education systems, their unique characteristics, and the respective application procedures. This knowledge will help the student gain the clarity and confidence necessary to choose a learning path that is best suited to his or her ambitions and desires. The future holds new horizons and endless possibilities; honest self-reflection, diligence, and thoughtful planning will undoubtedly bring success.

Helen Shavit and Jude Smith

Thinking Ahead

Thinking Ahead – Keeping Your Options Open

Catherine Godard

Broadening Horizons

Thinking about higher education may seem rather daunting to a student who is entering *troisième* (US 9th grade) in France, and yet it is really not too early to start investigating options and preparing for different eventualities. It is a great time to enjoy summer programs for high school students that are offered in the UK, Canada, the US, and here at home in France. Many young people may have already benefited from summer camp experiences and are happy to have the opportunity to actually study a subject they might be interested in during the summer. It is a time to explore, to take subjects that are not found in the French curriculum, to meet other students from around the world, and to understand what it is like to live in a dorm and have a roommate. Dedicating one summer month to such a project is very enriching and still leaves time for students to enjoy a family vacation. Attending summer school also acts as a catalyst for students in their regular course work here in France. Different viewpoints, varying pedagogical methods, cultural enrichment, and scholastic friendships can often help students to see the point of their studies and to focus on the essential.

Students considering going abroad for higher education should keep in mind that they may be judged on their report cards from *troisième* through *terminale* (US 9th–12th grades). This process of responsibility for students' own results is important not only for admissions, but represents a step toward the necessary maturity for university-level work, when there will be no parents to look over their shoulders to ensure their work is done.

Troisième is also a wonderful time to develop a student's passion and time should be allocated for the pursuit of interests outside of school. Even though secondary school in France consists of long days and hard work, parents should do their best to find a way to help their teenagers channel their energy into productive and consistent extracurricular activity. Scouts, sports, music, dance, and volunteering can all be enriching for students. Although France has nothing comparable to the US hospital volunteer system of "Candy Stripers", students interested in medicine may want to find another way of helping out in a hospital or geriatric center. Students interested in law can watch legal proceedings or "shadow" a lawyer. Take advantage of the *stage de troisième* to direct your student toward the causes and interests he/she holds dear.

Academically, the year of *troisième* in France is the last year of *collège* (US middle school), culminating with the *brevet* exam. For those considering the possibility of a US, UK, Canadian, or English-language university studies offered worldwide, *troisième* is a good time to start preparing for the tests of English language proficiency that are usually required of international students, such as the TOEFL, IELTS, or the Duolingo English Test. Test preparation is essential for the SAT and the ACT, often required for students aiming for university study in the US, or even some of the English-language programs throughout Europe.

Anglophone parents can be active players in broadening their teenager's English vocabulary base. Talk about articles, read books, and help your teenager to think about issues that concern everyone. There are smartphone apps that can be helpful in expanding English vocabulary and developing math skills. Students also need to read in English to build the sort of skills necessary for university study and for the SAT, ACT, and English language proficiency exams, particularly if the student is coming from a French-only *lycée*.

Decisions, Decisions

In France, *seconde* (US 10th grade) is the year that students determine which speciality classes in the *bac général* program they will follow in *première*. It is a year fraught with many decisions and often frustration as students face numerous demanding courses covering the range of subjects offered for the baccalaureate. Students are being solicited on all fronts and are not necessarily ready to make such important decisions as to higher education choices; which subjects they will follow, which system of higher education, and which country to pursue further study. The scope of information and the decisions to be made can often be daunting. The French *conseiller d'orientation* can provide excellent advice. This government service is provided in most high schools and the office will often distribute Onisep (Office national d'information sur les enseignements et les professions) publications and advise students about university fairs in their area. The CIS International University Fair Paris[1] for information on North American, European, and worldwide universities offering programs in English takes place early each autumn, and is an excellent start for all students considering going abroad for their undergraduate studies. The experience of looking at brochures, consulting with representatives from these universities, and becoming informed helps students to take control of their own decision process.

Première (US 11th grade) is an especially intense year, as not only does much hinge upon the academic performance of the student, but the pressure is on as the student prepares for his/her first baccalaureate examinations at the end of the school year.

Selective higher education programs will look closely at the student's grades and teacher evaluations. For those undecided about where or what they will study upon graduation, it is advisable to keep options open while researching the possibilities. This means taking at least the SAT or ACT test (needed for applying to most American schools and some European schools with international English sections). The PSAT, administered in October is also advised, as it is good practice for the SAT test and can qualify an American citizen for the National Merit Scholarship program. Attending the CIS International University Fair Paris is a must, and the student should also attend the French *salons de l'éducation* organized throughout the year where students can learn about their options in the French higher education system and meet with school representatives. The online student magazine, *l'Étudiant* (www.letudiant.fr), can also be very helpful for understanding and learning about the different study options in France as well as study opportunities abroad.

> *Students should take the SAT or ACT exams to keep their options open.*

By the time students are entering *première* they should be keeping a journal. Journal writing provides a wealth of inspiration when it comes to drafting the personal essay required for many university applications. Photos, sayings, quotes, heroes, issues – all can be jumping-off points for a student's own personal input. While this is a particularly good idea for those planning on attending college in the US, it is a very useful exercise for all students, aiding them to clarify their preferences.

As students enter *première* and in some cases *terminale* (US 12th grade), they should be aware that their applications may be heavily influenced by two of their teachers and one school administrator, as recommendation letters may be required. It is important to earn the respect of ALL teachers and administrators, given the system of *conseils de classe* in France, in which they, along with student and parent class delegates, meet to discuss the performance and progress of each student and assign an overall evaluation. When students start off on the wrong foot it is difficult to shed a less-than-perfect reputation. Students should understand that they are responsible for getting along with others, and for their own education, not just for their applications, but, for their entire life.

A Note About the SATs and ACTs

It would be folly to think that students need no preparation for the SAT or ACT tests. There are courses given in Paris and online that can help with basic vocabulary and test-taking techniques. The official SAT College Board website and Khan Academy[2] offer free online options to prepare for the exam. Often students raised abroad are caught up on little words such as "integer", "cob", or "imp", but they do have an advantage with cognates in French and English. The French system favors long developed answers, while the SAT is based on rapidity and short answers. Students need time to adapt to the different process and may take online practice tests and even a PSAT in October of *seconde*, as a way to prepare.

It is best to have taken one SAT/ACT exam before *terminale*, either in May or June of *première*. If the results are satisfactory, then it is one less thing to worry about in the application process during the very demanding final year of *lycée*. Many American universities also require at least two SAT Subject Tests (see chapter "Undergraduate Study in the United States"). It may be a good idea to take an SAT Subject Test in

French in January of *première*, just to get used to the test and to gain a bit of confidence. SAT Subject Tests may be taken up until November of *terminale* for early admission applications and through January for regular applications, depending on the university.

Although many excellent US universities are now "test optional" in their admissions decisions, it may still be best to take the SAT or ACT exams to keep your options open. However, I would caution against spending huge amounts of time and money preparing for standardized tests, then taking and retaking the exams, while sacrificing time spent on ideas and passions that make the student an interesting individual.

The Deciding Year

The admissions process starts in earnest at the beginning of *terminale* with application deadlines looming in the early part of the year for universities in the US, Canada, and the UK. The application process for French schools begins in November with online applications starting in January and continuing through the spring. Due to an academic year that starts in February, Australia's deadlines are later. Please check country specific chapters in this publication for deadline details. Prospective students must inform themselves of deadlines, preferably during the summer preceding their *terminale* year, to avoid losing the opportunity to attend their university of choice.

Whether or not students apply to an American university, another Anglophone institution, or finally decide to stay in France, all of this preparation will have been helpful. Their level in English will have improved and they will have gained self-awareness and built self-confidence, readying them to face the demands of any educational system. Bicultural students are so fortunate to have so many options. They can decide to stay in France for a first degree and go abroad for a master's. They can opt to earn a first degree abroad and then return to France to pursue study at a *grande école*, other specialized school, or university. Some universities like Cornell and Columbia in the US, and other reputed schools elsewhere, such as the London School of Economics, offer joint-degree programs with prestigious institutions in France. Whatever they choose, these students will have benefited enormously from their multicultural outlook and their steady preparation for all eventualities.

All options are viable and worth considering, but the best ally in such a situation is a solid understanding of what each system has to offer. The advice of higher education professionals and college counselors can help students to see more clearly and to make the best possible choice.

Endnotes

1. Organized by the Council of International Schools with logistical support from AAWE. See www.cois.org
2. www.khanacademy.org/test-prep/sat

The Gap Year

Sallie Chaballier and Jude Smith

The term "gap year" has gained currency over the last decade among American high school students. A generation ago, students "took time off" between high school and university or during their college years to work and/or travel, but this phenomenon was relatively limited and organized programs for this purpose were non-existent. In contrast, British students have long favored taking a gap year before college, and the concept has spread more widely to Australia, Canada, and New Zealand. Though students taking a gap year are still the exception rather than the norm, particularly in France, more and more young people are taking a break after the stress of the college application and admissions process and before matriculating at the school of their choice.

In France, an "official" gap year, referred to as *l'année de césure*,[1] was introduced in 2015. It allows students to defer matriculation at the school to which they have been accepted (pending approval from the institution). The *année de césure* may also be taken mid-studies or following a first degree and before matriculating into an advanced degree program. However, should the student choose to postpone committing to tertiary studies or prefer to wait a year in order to reapply to a program to which admission was denied, a traditional gap year or *année sabbatique* may still be taken. In this case, the individual would apply (or reapply) to schools when he or she is ready, though guaranteed admission to a public university would no longer apply.

A gap year can take any form – work, travel, community service, family time, introspection, adventure, or some combination of the above. It is *not* to be confused with an additional year of secondary school, during which a student repeats or augments his or her high school studies in order to improve university admission prospects. The gap year may entail study of some kind, but it is more for personal enrichment than remedial purposes. Students may also simply want or need to work in order to save money for university tuition.

Why Take a Gap Year?

A gap year allows a young person to take a break from academics, to gain perspective on himself or herself and on the world, to work in the "real world", to travel, or pursue an extra-academic interest, and, most of all, to gain maturity and autonomy before embarking on university studies. A US college administrator recently remarked that "the 19-year-old brain is very different from the 18-year-old brain" – an observation that holds true neurologically and psychologically for many young people.

> *More and more young people are taking a break after the stress of the college application and admissions process and before matriculating at the school of their choice.*

For a young person unsure of which path to follow after high school/*lycée*, a gap year can provide a buffer of time and experience. Even for a student who knows what he or she wants to study, a gap year still brings maturity and focus. Some students elect to take a gap year after an initial year of university, and resume their studies with renewed enthusiasm. Others take a gap year after receiving their undergraduate degree in order to ponder their options for a career, professional school, or postgraduate study. There is even a recent phenomenon of "mature" gap year takers – adults who interrupt their careers for a year or who take a pause before changing careers.

More and more American universities take a favorable view of a gap year experience, and some, such as Harvard University, actively encourage accepted students to take a gap year before matriculating. Princeton University, for example, has their Novogratz Bridge Year Program for admitted students that allows them to defer their enrollment; they first undertake nine months of volunteer community service abroad, along with immersion in a foreign culture to give them experience and maturity. Today, as French institutions of higher education recognize the benefit of students taking a gap year, the *année de césure* or *année sabbatique* is an option that appears to be gaining ground among young people.

The Gap Year and University Admissions

There are advantages both to applying to university while in high school/*lycée* before taking a gap year, and to waiting to apply during the gap year itself. Applying to university during the last year of secondary school, being admitted but then deferring admission, gives peace of mind to students who have a clear idea of their college preferences or who are admitted to their university of choice. They can then go off on their gap year with a light heart and concentrate fully on the experience. On the other hand, waiting to apply to university until after finishing high school, with a diploma in hand plus the initial experience of a gap year, can bolster a student's credentials. This second option could boost the chances of admission to a student's university or universities of choice. Since no two students are exactly alike, this choice depends on the young person's preferences as well as on the vagaries of the college admissions process. A gap year may emerge as the best option for a student who is disappointed by his or her offers of university admission.

In France, pursuing a gap year in the form of an *année de césure*, is possible under one of the following conditions:

- Working in France or abroad
- Study or training in a concentration other than the one the student will pursue

at university
- Pursing an entrepreneurial endeavor as an *étudiant-entrepreneur*[2]
- Volunteering for French government-approved community and social service opportunities:
    - Service Civique, in France or abroad, as detailed further in this chapter
    - Volontariat de Solidarité Internationale (VSI)[3]
    - Volontariat International en Administration (VIA)[4]
    - Volontariat International en Enterprise (VIE)[5]
- Other volunteering opportunities in a non-profit, such as Service Volontaire International — SVI
- Volunteer service as a fire fighter

Detailed websites for these options are offered in the "Resources" section at the end of this chapter. Be advised that your volunteer program may require approval from your institution prior to commencing the *année de césure*.

Students must strictly adhere to the parameters set out by the school they plan to attend, whether it's a *université* or even a *prépa* or *grande école*. Not every institution offers the opportunity for a *semestre* or *année de césure* (6 or 12 months), and the student must request this option, rather than assuming that it's possible without prior consent. In order to take a gap year, students need to provide the institution with a letter of motivation, which clearly states the proposed activity during the requested *césure*. In turn, an internal committee will review the request. If approved, students retain student status in France and may use their student ID card (*carte étudiante*) during the period of *césure*. Financial stipends are available during this period and/or ECTS (European Credit Transfer System) credits may be earned towards a degree program. Detailed information on *l'année de césure* (in French), is available on the French government student websites.[6]

A caveat: Some universities that encourage non-academic gap years, explicitly forbid admitted students from enrolling in another academic institution during their year of deferral. Students who do enroll at another college or university during a gap year may forfeit their admission to the university where they intend to eventually matriculate; hence, they are advised to find out their university's policy on the matter. In addition, regulations for deferring admission vary from university to university, so a student must find out the policy of his or her university of choice before requesting a deferral.

Gap Year Options

Work, travel, community service – the sky's the limit for activities during a gap year for students deferring enrollment or holding off applying to an American institution of higher learning. Some students combine several different elements during the year, while others embark on one sustained project. Students planning to pursue higher education in France may choose from numerous options as well; however, they must first obtain approval from the institution to which they have been accepted if it concerns an *année de césure*. A student taking an *année sabbatique*, on the other hand, may choose any activity, including enhancing skills or building a portfolio in order to reapply to a school to which he or she had been rejected. The following are a few factors to consider when contemplating a gap year.

First, how much structure does a young person want or need? At one extreme, there are gap year programs that, for a substantial fee, provide food, lodging, project direction, and supervision similar to a summer travel program. At the other end of the spectrum, some young people simply want to set off with a backpack with no set itinerary, hoping to finance their travels through odd jobs along the way. Alternatively, others may simply live at home and work, or stay with friends or family in another country while working. A structured program may be reassuring for parents, and helpful for students who are focused on a specific project. On the other hand, the experience of fending for oneself, finding lodging, shopping for food, cooking, cleaning, and living away from home can provide valuable lessons in life skills.

Financial considerations play a key role in deciding whether to take a gap year and how. It should be said that even a supervised gap year could still be less expensive than a year of full US college tuition and fees. The experiences and growth afforded by a gap year literally are "priceless", and a protracted trip or period of living abroad does not have to be a prohibitively expensive luxury. Learning to live on a budget is an important lesson for any young person. Parents of gap year takers who are not part of a supervised program will need to set firm guidelines with their child as to what they will and will not subsidize during the year, and agree on a monthly budget. In France, the EU, and the US, there are programs in place for volunteers to receive small stipends for their efforts, with some programs even covering travel, lodging, and food expenditures.

Supplemental health insurance is absolutely essential for any travel outside one's home country, and is required for some structured gap year programs. French *sécurité sociale* alone will not suffice for most gap year plans.

Where to go?

Many structured gap year programs focus on developing countries in Southeast Asia, Africa, or Latin America, though the entire world awaits an intrepid young person who wants to travel. Australia and New Zealand are popular destinations for young people who want to work during their gap year, or combine work with travel on a Working Holiday visa. EU and US citizens are very welcome in those countries, and the visa formalities can be completed online. Visa recipients will need to have a minimum level of financial resources, health insurance, and a round-trip plane ticket.

What about being a volunteer either locally or around the globe? A French government sponsored program, the Service Civique (civic service), offers 6-12 month volunteer opportunities in France and abroad for young people between the ages of 16 and 25. A variety of areas are targeted, including education, sports, culture, relief work in developing countries, and emergency aid. The program, inaugurated in 2010 with 15,000 volunteers, has proven hugely popular; there were 140,000 participants in 2018 and about 200,000 in 2019. A monthly "compensation" of nearly 500 € is paid to the volunteer for a minimum of 24 hours of work per week, with an additional meals allocation of about 100 €, and another stipend of just over 100 € to cover the costs of student housing. The program is open to French citizens and other EU nationals as well as to non-EU citizens who have maintained regular residency in

France for at least a year.

Volunteer service opportunities exist throughout the European Union. Instituted in December 2016, the *corps européen de solidarité*,[7] a volunteer initiative of the European Union, is gaining ground. Similar in scope to the Service Civique, this program targets young people between the ages of 18–30, who are EU residents or residing in select partner countries. The program duration is from two to twelve months, and can be initiated in the student's home country or another part of the EU. Contrary to the small stipend offered by the Service Civique, the *corps européen de solidarité* does not offer any financial compensation for work; however, travel, lodging, insurance, and a small stipend for meals is offered.[8]

In addition, there are numerous opportunities internationally for French citizens, including working for the French government in embassies, Alliances Françaises, research institutes, or economic missions. This is known as Volontariat en Administration — VIA.[9] Students receive a work stipend of 1,200 € to 2,800 € per month depending on the country; however, students will likely have to cover their travel and living expenses. Similarly, a young person may gain professional experience by volunteering in a business abroad, (Volontariat en Enterprise — VIE).[10] A stipend of between 1,200 € to 3,000 € per month is provided under the same conditions as the VIA. Other programs recognized by the Service Civique for volunteer opportunities in administration and business may be found through Civiweb,[11] where students can search by geographic area throughout the world.

Similarly, the US government offers numerous civic volunteer programs for young and dynamic citizens. Founded in 1961 by President John F. Kennedy, the Peace Corps remains a beacon of American civic service and volunteerism worldwide. Since its inception, more than 230,000 volunteers have worked on projects throughout the world, and in the process discovered new cultures and fostered the doctrine of peaceful coexistence. Today, Peace Corps volunteers work on programs in six different domains: agriculture, community economic development, education, environment, health, and youth in development. Volunteers must be at least 18 years old and hold US nationality. They receive a small stipend in addition to air travel costs, living expenses, and medical and dental care throughout the duration of their service project. Volunteers must commit to a project duration of 27 months.

While a Peace Corps commitment requires an over two-year duration and international travel, there are US domestic government sponsored service programs with a shorter time span. In 1988 the City Year education program was initiated in Boston. With educational achievement as its cornerstone, City Year assigns teams of 10–15 "near-peer mentors" to schools with high populations of "at-risk" students. Today this successful program serves 29 US cities. During their 11-month period of service, volunteers tutor students, teach English to non-native speakers, help with extracurricular activities including local service projects, and provide homework assistance. To qualify, volunteers must be US citizens, between 18–25 years of age and be at least a high school graduate. Volunteers receive a twice monthly, pre-tax, living stipend ranging from $630 for most cities and up to $955 for New York City. Other benefits include health insurance, local transportation passes, a relocation stipend of $500 if you're moving more than 50 miles from your home, and college scholarship opportunities.

City Year is now part of the larger US federal service program, AmeriCorps, which counts over one million "members" (volunteers) since its inception in 1994. Annually, 75,000 AmeriCorps volunteers serve throughout the US working on projects in six domains: Education, Economic Opportunity, Veterans & Military Families, Disaster Services, Healthy Futures, and Environmental Stewardship. AmeriCorps volunteers work with numerous organizations including City Year and other state and local networks, and the well-established federal government program to combat poverty, VISTA. The AmeriCorps NCCC (National Civilian Community Corps) engages regional volunteer teams of 18–24-year-olds who may clear trails in national parks or build houses for those in need. Disaster relief projects are through the FEMA Corps in conjunction with the Federal Emergency Management Agency. All programs last from one to twelve months, and may include summer positions. Volunteers must be US citizens and in some cases require specific levels of education and skill sets. Benefits include a living allowance for basic expenses, money for college or trade school, scholarships, professional development, and networking opportunities through their extensive alumni community. Some programs also provide healthcare, while others may offer a stipend for the volunteer to purchase insurance.

Conclusion

While most young people are eager upon completion of their secondary school studies to embark on the grand adventure of higher education, some may need or want a year or more to "de-stress" from the demands of the final year of high school/*lycée*. A gap year is a wonderful option for students who are not ready to delve into the demands of university and could use to mature a bit prior to this step in becoming an adult. Global adventures to travel, work, or volunteer are all on offer. Options abound for worldwide programs, through private organizations or government-sponsored programs in France, the EU, and the US. Independent travel/work visas in Australia and New Zealand offer a chance for students to explore a region of the world often too far to visit. Social service volunteerism offers the option to explore new places or even connect locally, while meeting interesting people, and growing as a person, all while making the world a better place. As they say, "The sky's the limit."

References and Resources

Gap year websites and programs have proliferated, making it impossible to provide an exhaustive guide or make specific recommendations. While we cannot endorse any particular program, here are a few suggestions to help initiate a search for more information on taking a gap year.

- Founded in 1980, *The Center for Interim Programs* is the first and longest-running, independent gap-year counseling organization in the United States: www.interimprograms.com
- Useful list of programs and books from a top US liberal arts college that endorses the idea of a gap year: www.middlebury.edu/admissions/apply/gapyear/bibliography

- Rustic Pathways is an established specialist in adventure and service travel for young people, with language/cultural immersion home-stay programs and on-going community service projects around the globe. www.rusticpathways.com
- British website, clearinghouse for ideas, countries, and programs: www.gapyear.com
- Australian government website detailing visa options for young people (18-30 or 18-35, depending on nationality) seeking to travel and work in Australia.
    - French passport holders: https://immi.homeaffairs.gov.au/visas/getting-a-visa/visa-listing/work-holiday-417/first-working-holiday-417#Overview
    - US passport holders (only): https://immi.homeaffairs.gov.au/visas/getting-a-visa/visa-listing/work-holiday-462/first-work-holiday-462
- New Zealand equivalent of the above with travel/work options for those 18-30 years of age: https://www.immigration.govt.nz/new-zealand-visas/options/work/thinking-about-coming-to-new-zealand-to-work/working-holiday-visa
- French website offering comprehensive health and travel insurance for long trips (more than three months abroad) as well as for shorter trips. www.allianz-voyage.fr
- Global health and travel insurance providers:
    - (In English): https://www.worldnomads.com/travel-insurance
    - (French website for students with documentation in French and English) www.allianz-voyage.fr/assurances/sante-jeunes-a-l-etranger
- French and EU programs:
    - French Ministère de l'Éducation Nationale et de la Jeunesse offering volunteer programs in France and abroad (Service Civique): www.service-civique.gouv.fr
    - EU citizen volunteer programs (European Solidarity Corps): https://europa.eu/youth/solidarity
    - International social volunteering programs: www.france-volontaires.org
    - French Ministère de l'Éducation Nationale et de la Jeunesse website *(Découvrir le Monde)* to find volunteer programs abroad: www.decouvrirlemonde.jeunes.gouv.fr
    - Fonjep (Fonds de coopération de la jeunesse et de l'éducations populaire) list of approved social volunteer groups: www.fonjep.org/solidarite-internationale/volontariat-de-solidarite-internationale
    - Service Volontaire International (SVI): www.servicevolontaire.org
    - Volunteer opportunities for VIA and VIE: www.civiweb.com
- US Citizen Government programs:
    - Peace Corps: www.peacecorps.gov
    - Corporation for National & Community Service: www.nationalservice.gov
    - AmeriCorps: www.americorps.gov
    - City Year: www.cityyear.org

Endnotes

1. www.etudiant.gouv.fr/cid136530/la-cesure-comment-ca-marche.html
2. www.etudiant.gouv.fr/pid33854/entrepreneuriat-etudiant.html
3. www.etudiant.gouv.fr/cid136384/les-volontariats-de-solidarite-internationale.html
4. www.etudiant.gouv.fr/cid136430/le-volontariat-international-en-entreprise-ou-en-administration.html
5. Ibid.
6. www.etudiant.gouv.fr/cid136530/la-cesure-comment-ca-marche.html; www.etudiant.gouv.fr/cid136541/cesure-la-faq.html#q21
7. https://europa.eu/youth/solidarity
8. www.service-civique.gouv.fr/page/qu-est-ce-que-le-service-civique
9. www.etudiant.gouv.fr/cid136430/le-volontariat-international-en-entreprise-ou-en-administration.html
10. www.etudiant.gouv.fr/cid136430/le-volontariat-international-en-entreprise-ou-en-administration.html
11. www.civiweb.com

Student Anecdotes

I took a gap year after finishing *lycée* because my application to the specialized school that I wanted more than anything was not accepted. So during this year I tried to reinforce every subject that could help my application to the same school the following year. I had time to focus on what I really wanted to do and study the things I wanted to but didn't have time to study before the bac. Specifically, I deepened my knowledge of the arts. My application to the school was accepted the next year. …If I could give advice to someone wondering how the future will look like, I would just recommend to trust himself/herself and his/her inner voice. I think a gap year is interesting to get to really know what we want.   – *Lucia*

I took a gap year after my bachelor's to build my own startup. During this time, I gained a lot of practical experience about business like finding partners and suppliers, building my own website or marketing a product online and offline. I learned how to be resourceful and independent. For example, I taught myself how to use graphic design software when there was no designer on our team. I believe this experience was beneficial because I learned a lot in a short amount of time and the experience contributed to me getting into my master's program and the jobs I wanted later on.   – *Chloé*

I took a gap year before starting university in the US to study Mandarin Chinese in Shanghai. I improved my language skills and got to travel throughout China and Asia.   – *Daniel*

I took a year off between completing my Bachelor's degree in the US and beginning my Master's degree in France. During this year, I returned to France to prepare my application for the program. I enrolled in a few classes at the university to which I applied and worked with my thesis advisor to prepare the application. I also worked at various jobs, including at a study abroad office, at a non-profit for arts events, and babysitting for a French family. The gap year allowed me to define the path I wanted to pursue at the university and also to gain work experience in different fields.   – *Samantha*

I did not do a gap year but I regret it because unless you are certain of your path it is interesting to have a couple of experiences and take the time to think about what you want to do and how you want to do it.   *– Heloise*

I left for England right after the *bac* and spent a year as a nanny for a French/Anglo family in Portsmouth. I turned 18 three months after my arrival. The gap year was beneficial for me in several ways. I took English lessons with grown-ups (the teacher was more interesting than in high school), I met multi-cultural people (Spanish, German, Polish, Italian) and we had to speak English among us. As this was the first time out of my family house, I had to do my own groceries and the cleaning and stuff. I also spent time with children and we really have to learn from them!   *– Vanille*

I was out of school between my BA and my MA and taught English in Japan. Taking a year out really helped me decide what I wanted to do and what I wanted to focus on in my MA.   *– Emilie*

Higher Education
in France

Introduction to the French Higher Education System

Fred Weissler

All public institutions of higher education in France are governed by French law and must adhere to the rules and regulations set by their governing ministries. For the most part, higher education falls under the auspices of the Ministry of Higher Education, Research, and Innovation (Ministère de l'Enseignement supérieur, de la Recherche et de l'Innovation – MESRI). However, many of the specialized schools and *grandes écoles* fall under the auspices of other ministries.

Higher education in France is currently undergoing substantial re-organization. Major reforms enacted over the past decade and until very recently are being put into place, resulting in significant re-structuring and re-organization. These changes concern both the public face of higher education and research in France, as well as its internal workings.

The student wishing to pursue higher education in France has several options: university studies, the *grandes écoles* and their associated preparatory classes, specialized schools, and various less academic, more job-oriented, two or three year programs. The purpose of this introductory chapter is to explain these options so that the reader can then consult the appropriate chapter(s) in this guide for more information. Procedures for applying to higher education programs at the entry level, i.e., following high school *(lycée)*, will also be described, both for students in France and the European Union, as well as for students elsewhere. In addition, at the end of this chapter, certain aspects of the overall organizational structure of higher education in France will be described so that the interested reader can see how the various options fit together. This information could also be helpful in choosing an academic program, both at the entry and advanced levels.

French Universities

The French universities award the following three basic academic degrees, which are accredited by the French government: *licence* (the undergraduate degree obtained after successful completion of a three-year course of study), *master* (obtained after two additional years of study), and *doctorat*. The three degrees together are often referred to as LMD. One important feature of the French *universités*, which distinguishes them from the other types of higher education institutions, is that any student who has passed the French *baccalauréat* exam has the right to enroll in an entry level program at a French *université*. However, as will be explained later in this chapter (and in more detail in the chapter on French universities), certain entry-level programs have the right to select students on the basis of their academic record.[1]

An important difference between the French and American universities is that entrance to a *université* is always for a specific academic program, and the degree will reflect this choice. In other words, a student must select an area of specialization in order to enter a university. For example, one would not apply to Université XYZ, but to a *licence de sciences économiques et de gestion*, at Université XYZ. In a given academic area there might be options available starting in the second, or more likely, third year. For example, in a *licence de sciences économiques et de gestion*, a third-year student may be able to choose between a concentration in economics and one in management. In a mathematics *licence*, there could be a choice in the third year between a concentration in pure or in applied mathematics, and then even a choice among various areas of application of mathematics. In the context of a given program, including a chosen concentration or option, there is little choice of specific classes. The course of study is the same for all students in that program/option. This is unlike the American system, where a student can choose from a whole catalog of courses and declare a major as late as the end of two years of university study.

Transferring from one program to another, even at the same university, is difficult after the first year or if the programs are in substantially different academic areas. A student who wishes to change academic area at the end of the first year might have to repeat the first year of studies. However, it is always possible to move between two different programs at the same university at the end of the first semester without any penalty.

Also, unlike in the US, one generally begins medical or law school right at the first year of university studies, rather than in the context of a graduate or professional school. In particular, thanks to the open admissions policy of French universities, any student with the high school *baccalauréat* may enroll in medical studies. However, in the event there is greater demand than capacity, individual universities may select students based on their academic profile. For students who are enrolled, the real selection occurs at the end of the first year. Since the organization of medical and law studies is so different in France as compared to the US, this guide contains a specific chapter for each of these two professions. In particular, other avenues to enrollment in medical school made possible by recent reforms will be described.

Most universities are named by the city where they are located, but in many cases have an additional name. For example, Université de Tours is also Université François Rabelais. If a city has several universities, they are often numbered. For example, the three public universities in Lyon are called, combining their numbers and names, Université Claude Bernard Lyon I, Université Lumière Lyon II, and Université Lyon III Jean Moulin. The Université de Lyon without any other designation is in fact a consortium of universities and other institutions, or a *Communauté d'universités et établissements* (ComUE), which will be described in more detail near the end of this chapter. In recent years, universities in close proximity have been merging together. For example, the Université de Bordeaux[2] was created in 2014 by the merger of the Universités de Bordeaux I, II, and IV, and so Bordeaux today has two public universities, Université de Bordeaux and Université Bordeaux-Montaigne (Bordeaux III). Also, in 2012 the Université de Metz and the Universités de Nancy I and II all merged and became part of the much larger establishment, the Université de Lorraine[3] which includes many other institutions of higher education. The Université de Lorraine has the status of *grand établissement*, an official designation which will also be discussed near the end of this chapter.

In the Paris area, the university landscape is also evolving, and can perhaps be best understood in an historical context concerning the Sorbonne. The Collège de Sorbonne was founded by Robert de Sorbon, chaplain to Louis IX, in 1253, and was one of the colleges of the Université de Paris at the time. Jumping ahead, the Sorbonne became the administrative center of the "new" Université de Paris created in 1896.[4] After the events of 1968, the Université de Paris was partitioned into the various Universités de Paris, numbered 1 to 9 (later expanded to include 10 to 13), four of which retained affiliation with the Sorbonne: Université Paris 1 Panthéon-Sorbonne, Université Paris 3 Sorbonne-Nouvelle, Université Paris 4 Paris-Sorbonne, and Université Paris 5 René Descartes.[5] In 2018, the Université Paris 4 Paris-Sorbonne merged with Université Paris 6 (Pierre et Marie Curie) to form the Université Sorbonne-Université.[6] In 2019, Université Paris 5 René Descartes merged with Université Paris 7 Paris Diderot to form the "Université de Paris".

Grandes Écoles and *Classes Préparatoires*

The *grandes écoles* are highly selective schools for which admission, usually after two years of post-*baccalauréat* study, is predicated on a competitive exam, called a *concours*, and for which a specified number of places are available *(numerus clausus)*. This competitive exam is most often taken after an intensive two-year preparatory program called *classes préparatoires aux grandes écoles* (CPGE), commonly referred to as *prépa*. Admission to a *prépa* after high school *(lycée)* is also competitive, based mainly on the student's overall academic record. These preparatory programs often take place in a *lycée*, but some *grandes écoles* incorporate them directly, which is referred to as *prépa intégrée*. A student who has completed one or two years of *prépa* can usually transfer to a *université* at an appropriate level instead of going to a *grande école*, for example, if admission to the desired *grande école* is not attained. (See the chapter "*Classes Préparatoires aux Grandes Écoles*".)

The well-known École Normale Supérieure (commonly referred to as Normale Sup or ENS), as well as the three other Écoles Normales Supérieures (Paris-Saclay, Rennes, Lyon), École Polytechnique, and HEC, are among the most prestigious of the *grandes écoles*. From a cultural perspective, the best of the *grandes écoles* are similar in prestige to the Ivy League and similar schools in the United States. Most of the political, engineering, and business leaders in France studied at a top *grande école*. In fact, most of the *grandes écoles* are either engineering schools or business schools *(écoles de commerce)*. In recent years, many *grandes écoles*, in an effort to shed their reputations of elitism and to seek out a more diverse student body, have begun to open their admissions process to students who have pursued paths other than *prépa*, such as an IUT *(institut universitaire de technologie)* or even two years at a *université*. The duration of the program at a *grande école* is generally (but not always) three years. There are both public and private *grandes écoles*.

While there does not seem to be an official definition of *"grande école"* or an official list of the *grandes écoles*, a confederation of *grandes écoles* called the Conférence des Grandes Écoles (CGE),[7] founded in 1973, includes over 200 public and private *grandes écoles*. Not all *grandes écoles* are members of the CGE, but the most reputed ones generally are. The notion of which school is considered a *grande école* seems to evolve over time. We emphasize that in the context of the French system, a *grande école* is not a *université*, even if from an outside perspective, a *grande école* seems like a university in its activities of teaching and research. If a *grande école* wishes to offer one of the LMD degrees, it must do so through a formal agreement with a *université*, unless it has the status of *grand établissement*. Most of the *grandes écoles* award their own degree, incorporating the name of the school or institution. For example, École Normale Supérieure offers several *master* degrees in cooperation with universities in Paris as well as its own degree, *le diplôme de l'ENS*.

Member schools of the Conférence des Grandes Écoles (CGE) may award two other post-graduate degrees, an MS (*Mastère Spécialisé*, spelled this way, as opposed to *master*) and an MSc (Master of Science). These degrees are accredited by the CGE itself. The MS degree is a high-level degree, requiring an additional year of study following five years of post-*bac* studies (*bac*+5). The MSc degree follows four years of post-*bac* studies (*bac*+4) and requires 18 months minimum to obtain, including at least four months of professional training outside the classroom. Furthermore, the classes in an MSc program are given at least 50% in a language other than French.

There are more than 200 engineering *grandes écoles*. In order to be qualified to grant an engineering diploma, the school (more precisely, the course of study) must be certified by the CTI (Commission des Titres d'Ingénieur). The successful student receives a degree called *Ingénieur diplômé de XYZ*, where the name of the engineering school is inserted at the end. While not a *master* degree, this diploma is officially recognized by the French government as the same level as a *master* degree. In French parlance, the *titre d'ingénieur diplômé* confers le *grade de master*.

A complete list of all the institutions accredited to grant an engineering diploma in France can be found at an official government website.[8] Some of the most famous ones, in addition to École Polytechnique, are in the ParisTech[9] network created in 1991. Its member schools have appropriately changed their names, or added names, to be part of ParisTech. For example, École nationale supérieure de chimie de Paris (ENSCP) is now (also) Chimie ParisTech; École nationale supérieure d'arts et métiers (ENSAM) is now Arts et Métiers ParisTech; and École des Mines is now Mines ParisTech. Another group of engineering *grandes écoles*, the INP (institut national polytechnique) is comprised of four public institutions, Bordeaux INP, Grenoble INP, Lorraine INP, and Toulouse INP. Each INP is itself a grouping of several engineering schools, with a total of more than 30 in the entire network. The group of engineering schools called Écoles Centrale includes the Écoles Centrale de Lille, de Lyon, de Marseille, and de Nantes. The former École Centrale de Paris merged with the École supérieure d'électricité (Supélec) and the new engineering school is called Centrale-Supélec. Finally, there is a group of engineering *grandes écoles* that is university based and is called the polytechnic network, or Réseau Polytech. Created in 2017, it includes 15 schools of which 14 have a common admissions procedure, as well as *prépas intégrées*.

France has more than 200 business schools, or *écoles de commerce*, the vast majority of which are private. Many are also *grandes écoles*.[10] The best known are HEC Paris, ESSEC Business School, EDHEC Business School, and EMLYON Business School. These schools award various types of degrees, including Bachelor, Master, and MBA, as well as PhD in some cases. There is a government commission that decides which of the *bac*+5 degrees are equivalent to the French degree *master*, i.e., *confère le grade de master*.[11] In addition, those business schools which are members of the CGE may award the two degrees: *Mastère Spécialisé* and MSc.

Of special note is INSEAD, which was established in 1957 as a European business school for graduate level studies and historically has attracted an international student body.[12] It is a member of the Alliance Sorbonne Université.[13] The *alliances*, or *associations*, of institutions of higher education will be discussed in the last part of this chapter.

Another group of *grandes écoles* worthy of special mention are the ten *instituts d'études politiques* (IEP), or institutes for political science, usually referred to as Sciences Po with the name of the city, such as Sciences Po Bordeaux, or Sciences Po Rennes. Seven of the IEP: Aix-en-Provence, Lille, Lyon, Rennes, Saint-Germain-en-Laye, Strasbourg and Toulouse, have a common *concours*, or entrance exam, which is taken during the last year of high school or after one year of post-*bac* studies, such as a *prépa*.[14] There is a common *prépa* for this *concours* offered at the Institut National Universitaire Champollion (INU Champollion), as part of its first year *licence* program.

The IEP of Paris is called simply Sciences Po.[15] With a double governing structure as both a public and private institution, Sciences Po models itself more as a US university, and awards an undergraduate Bachelor of Arts degree after three (not four) years of study. It offers dual undergraduate degrees with several universities outside France, including Columbia University and the University of California, Berkeley, as well as universities in Germany, England, Hong Kong, and Australia. The undergraduate programs are open to students with a high school degree, with different application procedures for students coming from France or abroad, and for the dual degrees. The procedure for applying is specific to Sciences Po and explained on its website. Its graduate program offers both master's and doctoral degrees, with some of their master's programs taught entirely in English.

Specialized Schools

The French system of higher education includes many specialized schools *(écoles spécialisées)* of higher education. One good example is the École nationale supérieure des Beaux-Arts (ENSBA), otherwise known as Beaux-Arts de Paris, the premier school for fine arts in France. The school begins directly after high school, and admission is highly selective, based on the applicant's high school record, an artistic portfolio, and a series of tests and interviews. Less than 10% of applicants are admitted. In addition, there are more than 50 other fine arts schools throughout France. As another example of specialized schools, there are 20 Écoles nationales supérieures d'architecture (ENSA) in France. These schools also begin right after high school and admission is competitive, based primarily on the applicant's high school record. Specialized schools exist in a very wide variety of areas, including performing arts, fine arts, museum studies, architecture, communication, and journalism. It should be noted that the specialized schools cover areas that, in the US system, are more integrated into the universities. In most cases, the specialized schools will come under the auspices of a ministry other than higher education, research, and innovation, such as the Ministère de la Culture in the case of the fine arts and architecture schools. The specialized schools award degrees that are specific to the area of specialization.

Formations Professionnelles

The last option for post-*baccalauréat* studies mentioned at the start of this chapter, are the *formations professionnelles*. As opposed to the academically-oriented programs described above, the *formations professionnelles* are specifically designed to prepare a student to enter the job market. These programs often involve a significant portion of internships *(stages)* in partnership with private industry. A number of professional and technical programs and degrees are offered at universities and elsewhere. For example, the BTS *(brevet de technicien supérieur)* and the DUT *(diplôme universitaire de technologie)* are degrees conferred after two years of post-*baccalauréat* study in such areas as telecommunications, administration, material science, fine and applied arts, and other areas related to engineering and business, as well as the paramedical professions and others. The BTS program usually takes place in a *lycée* and the DUT is offered by an *institut universitaire de technologie* (IUT), which is a component of a *université*. Both the BTS and DUT programs are selective, i.e., admission depends on a student's record and is not guaranteed by having the *baccalauréat*, even though an IUT is part of a *université*. The spectrum of BTS and DUT programs is a mirror, at a lower level, of the types of programs available in the more advanced *écoles spécialisées* and *grandes écoles*.

In addition, the *licence professionnelle* is a degree conferred after a one-year program designed in partnership with specific companies, meant to follow the DUT, the BTS, or the first two years of a *licence* program. A *licence professionnelle* is explicitly designed to train the student for a specific profession. Interestingly, the *grande école* Arts et Métiers ParisTech offers a three-year Bachelor de Technologie degree, designed for students having completed a *baccalauréat technologique*. This seems to be a unique example of such a degree.

Students who have completed a BTS, DUT, or *licence professionnelle* could, depending on the specific program, continue afterwards in a general *université* program. Even though the *licence professionnelle* was created as a terminal degree, leading directly to employment, about 20% of students with a *licence professionnelle* continue on to further studies.[16] Also, many of the *grandes écoles* accept applications for admission from students with a DUT or BTS degree.

The reader wishing more detailed information on these programs should consult the chapter on specialized schools, as well as the chapter on university studies.

Private Institutions

As already noted, not all the institutions of higher education are public. According to a government website, 18% of students in higher education in France are enrolled in private institutions.[17] In addition to the many private engineering and business *grandes écoles*, there are about a dozen private universities in France, about half of which are Catholic. For example, the Université Catholique de Lille - Fédération Universitaire Polytechnique de Lille,[18] the largest non-profit private university in France, is a consortium of more than 20 different university faculties and *grandes écoles*.

General Information and Application Procedures

As an indication of the relative sizes of the various constituent parts of higher education in France, during the 2017-18 academic year, there were a total of 2,680,400 students enrolled in all programs combined. Of these, 56.9% were enrolled in a French public university (not counting those enrolled in an IUT), 4.3% were enrolled in an IUT, 3.2% were enrolled in a CPGE, 9.6% in a BTS program, 5.9% in an engineering program, 6.5% in business school, and the rest, 13.5%, in other programs.[19]

The cost of higher education at a public institution in France has always been very modest, tuition being of the order of several hundred euros per year. Also, at least for the first two years of post-*baccalauréat* study, most students live at home and go to school nearby. Some of the more prestigious public *grandes écoles,* however, charge tuition of the order of several thousand euros per year.[20] Tuition at private schools, generally 3,000 € to 10,000 € per year, is much less than the very expensive private universities in the US.[21] More recently, there is a government proposition to charge non-European students an increased tuition for the standard *licence* and *master* degrees (2,770 € at the *licence* level and 3,770 € at the level of *master*). This measure is being challenged under French law and it is not clear, as of this writing, if these tuition increases for non-European students will be maintained, and if so at what amounts.

Universities and other institutions of higher education in France are increasingly aware of the difficulties faced by students with disabilities. In addition, many have policies to promote equality (for example gender equality) and diversity among the student body. Most have pages on their websites devoted to these various issues.[22]

A prospective student should use all available online tools and websites to research possible programs of interest. The primary resources are the online platforms Parcoursup,[23] and for students outside France, Campus France.[24] Both platforms have extensive online tools for finding post-*baccalauréat* programs of study. In addition, the websites of the various educational institutions all have guides to the programs they offer. Once a preliminary selection of possible programs of interest has been made, it is advisable to consult the website of the institution offering that program to obtain as much information as possible. Finally, there are many private, student-oriented online publications that can provide additional information and guidance.[25] These can easily be found by an online search for *"formations supérieures"* or *"études supérieures".*

The application itself is usually completed online. Students in their last year of high school in France must apply via the website, Parcoursup. This platform is also used by students who have started a university-level program, but wish to change and start anew at the first-year level. Through the website, students can learn about the application process and the different programs to which one may apply. The information for the coming academic year usually becomes available for examination in December. In addition, there may be important complimentary information about application procedures on the websites of individual programs. This is especially true when a group of programs share a common entrance exam. While a great many, if not the vast majority, of websites in higher education have an English version, it is recommended insofar as possible to consult the French version. Mistranslations and omissions in the English version may occur.

The Parcoursup online application procedure must be completed by the deadlines indicated on the website, generally within the first three months of the year. The specific application deadlines **must** be strictly respected. Keep in mind that the Parcoursup application will be reviewed by high school teachers, and a favorable recommendation is essential. It is therefore advised to meet with teachers and discuss choices ahead of time. It is important to note that while the vast majority are, not every first-year program in higher education is included on the Parcoursup website. As an example, first-year admission to many of the specialized schools is not available via Parcoursup.

Students outside the French system can consult the Campus France website for instructions on applying to higher education programs in France. In many cases, such as for students in the European Union, it is necessary to use the Parcoursup website. Outside the European Union, the application procedure might depend on the country of origin.

Finally, to ALL prospective students, the procedures described herein may have changed since publication of this book, as modifications are common. Students in the French system will be directed toward the appropriate online platform and be given the current procedure. Other students should definitely consult the website, Campus France. Again, it is highly recommended to consult the website of the programs of interest.

International Studies

There is an increasing effort underway in France to recruit international students, and a parallel effort to prepare French students for international careers. The website Campus France mentioned above has a wealth of information for foreign students and researchers. Most institutions of higher education in France provide information on their websites devoted to guiding foreign students, as well as information about international partnerships. Usually, a student at a given university in France can spend part of the time (one or two semesters) at one of the official foreign partner institutions. The Erasmus+ program organizes both student and faculty exchanges among European institutions of higher education, but active partnerships and exchange programs worldwide are also common. The European Credit Transfer System (ECTS) facilitates student mobility between institutions of higher learning across Europe. Moreover, many French *universités* offer combined programs and degrees *(doubles diplômes)* with foreign institutions. Such programs are exempt from the requirement of automatic acceptance based on having earned the *baccalauréat*. Additionally, a number of foreign universities are opening branches in France. For example, Georgia Tech - Lorraine, is a branch of Georgia Tech in Atlanta and has a partnership with CentraleSupélec.[26]

A student graduating from a US university wishing to pursue graduate work in France will find a large spectrum of programs available. (See the chapter, "Graduate Studies in France for the International Student".) While a good knowledge of the French language would be helpful, and for many programs a necessity, that is no longer universally true. Campus France lists approximately 1500 academic programs taught entirely in English.[27] At the doctoral level, one should note an important difference between the US and France. At a US university, a doctoral program includes course work and qualifying exams, followed by the doctoral thesis. In France, that coursework is typically found in the second year of a *master* program. Admission to a doctoral program at a French *université* is conditioned on having both a thesis advisor and a thesis project, as well as financial support. In practice, this means that a student with an undergraduate degree from a US university who wishes to pursue a *doctorat* in France might be oriented first toward a *master* program.

Consortiums of Institutions and *Grands Établissements*

Finally in this chapter, we give more information about the structure and organization of higher education in France. While this information is not directly needed by the prospective student, it could help orient someone in the face of what could seem like a labyrinth of choices.

Essentially all the institutions of higher education under the aegis of the Ministry of Higher Education, Research, and Innovation, as well as many of those depending on other ministries and many private institutions, belong to a consortium *(regroupement)* of institutions. The purpose of these consortiums, created by law in 2013, is to take advantage of economies of scale in both teaching and research, to increase international visibility of French higher education and research, and to reinforce and coordinate the activities of higher education and research in a given region in France.[28] It is to be emphasized that the landscape of these consortiums is currently in flux. The configuration today is not the same as five years ago, and will likely be quite different five years from now.

As described by an official document dated September 2019,[29] these consortiums take the form of a *Communauté d'universités et établissements* (ComUE), of an *établissement public expérimental* (with component institutions), or of an *association* (or *alliance*) with a public institution of higher education. As of this writing, there are 19 ComUE, four *établissements publics expérimentaux,* and seven *associations* in France. To this list, one must add a fourth category of consortiums given as "under construction" on the government document.

One confusing aspect of the ComUE is that many of them are called *université*, even though in fact they are consortiums of *universités* and other institutions. For example, the ComUE Université Paris-Saclay[30] includes three *universités*: Université Paris Sud (Paris 11), Université de Versailles-Saint-Quentin-en-Yvelines, and Université d'Évry, as well as four *grandes écoles,* such as CentraleSupélec, and Agro Paris-Tech. The ComUE Université de Lyon comprises four universities: Université de Lyon I, II, and III, as well as Université Jean Monnet - Saint-Étienne plus several *grandes écoles,* such as ENS de Lyon, École Centrale de Lyon, and Sciences Po Lyon. Not all the ComUE are called *université*. The ComUE d'Aquitaine comprises four universities: Université de Bordeaux, Université Bordeaux-Montaigne, Université de Pau, and Université de la Rochelle, as well as three *grandes écoles*, Sciences Po Bordeaux, Bordeaux INP, and Bordeaux Sciences Agro.

Some ComUE are more integrated with their component institutions than others, for example, in terms of awarding academic degrees, or coordinating research laboratories and projects. Indeed, in many cases, the academic degrees are awarded in the name of the ComUE, either in place of or jointly with the awarding university. A typical situation is that the *licence* degrees are awarded by the member *universités* of the ComUE, some of the *master* degrees are awarded by the member *universités* and others are awarded by the ComUE or jointly with the ComUE, and that the doctoral degrees are all awarded at least jointly with the ComUE. This is the case for example with the ComUE Université Paris-Saclay and with the ComUE Université de Lyon. Also, many of the ComUE websites have a guide to all the degree programs offered by their various member institutions, at least at the level of *master* and *doctorat*. They sometimes give a listing of all degree programs taught completely or partially in English, the website of the ComUE Université Paris-Saclay being especially impressive in this way.[31]

> *The websites of the various ComUE are an additional resource for finding academic programs of interest, especially for the international student.*

As examples of *établissements publics expérimentaux,* there are the new Université de Paris, recently created by the merger of Université Paris 5 René Descartes with Université Paris 7 Paris Diderot, and the Institut Polytechnique de Paris, which is under the joint tutelage of the ministries of the economy and of defense, and which includes both École Polytechnique and ENSTA ParisTech. An example of an *association* is the Université de Lorraine, described in more detail below.

It could be that with further consolidation, the ComUE and the other types of consortiums are destined to become the universities, and the current member institutions will be considered as different campuses. While some indications point in this direction, it is not clear today if this will happen, or if it does, how long that process will take.

About 30 public institutions of higher education and research in France have the status of *grand établissement*. This is a special status, created in 1984, awarded to a limited number of institutions, which allows them to negotiate their own particular rules of governance with the appropriate French ministry. As of this writing, two public universities in France are *grands établissements,* Université Paris-Dauphine and Université de Lorraine. As part of its special status, a French public university that is also a *grand établissement* is not obligated to accept students at entry level solely on the basis of having attained the *baccalauréat* degree. A *grand établissement,* even if not a *université*, could be accredited to award the three academic degrees, LMD. At least six *grandes écoles*, members of the CGE, are *grands établissements,* including Arts et Métiers ParisTech and CentraleSupélec, as well as Sciences Po. Interestingly, Université Paris-Dauphine is a member of the CGE. These institutions may offer the LMD degrees as well as the MS and MSc degrees accredited by the CGE. The École des hautes études en sciences sociales (EHESS) is an example of a well-known institution of higher education and research, neither a *université*, nor a member of the CGE, which is a *grand établissement*. It offers the *diplôme* de l'EHESS as well as the *master* and *doctorat* degrees, the MD part of LMD. About two-thirds of the *grands établissements* are under the aegis of the MESRI, perhaps jointly with another ministry. The École nationale supérieure des Beaux-Arts (Beaux-Arts Paris) is an example of a *grand établissement* under the authority of the Ministry of Culture.

Finally, we describe in more detail the Université de Lorraine[32] since it provides an example of the current landscape of higher education in France, and in particular the interconnectedness of the various networks of institutions. In its current form, it was established in 2012 as a merger of the various universities in the Lorraine region, notably the Université de Metz and the Universités de Nancy I and II, which administratively do not exist anymore as such. As mentioned above, the Université de Lorraine holds the status of *grand établissement*. It does not belong to a ComUE, but is the central establishment in the *Association d'établissements* called "Lorraine". The Université de Lorraine itself is huge, made up of nine separate colleges (*"collégiums"*). Among these nine colleges is the Lorraine INP (Institut National Polytechnique), which is itself a collection of 11 *grandes écoles* for engineers, and the associated *prépas*. In other words, these *grandes écoles* are part of Université de Lorraine, which also contains the merged universities from Nancy and Metz. This is an excellent example of how the mergers and consortiums of universities in France are reinforcing and reinvigorating higher education and research in the regions outside Paris. One very large establishment is serving an area including the major cities of Nancy and Metz, as well as many nearby smaller cities, such as Épinal.

(Many of the acronyms and French terms used or mentioned in this chapter can also be found in the "Glossary of Terms", page 123.)

Endnotes

1. The governing text about open admissions and selection for programs immediately following the baccalauréat is Article L612-3, paragraphs 1 and 6, of the code de l'éducation.
2. www.u-bordeaux.fr
3. www.univ-lorraine.fr
4. https://fr.wikipedia.org/wiki/Nouvelle_universit%C3%A9_de_Paris
5. www.sorbonne.fr/la-sorbonne/histoire-de-la-sorbonne;www.sorbonne.fr/la-sorbonne/histoire-de-la-sorbonne/la-sorbonne-au-xxe-siecle-de-lancienne-universite-de-paris-aux-13-universites-parisiennes
6. www.sorbonne-universite.fr/universite/histoire-et-patrimoine/histoire
7. www.cge.asso.fr
8. www.enseignementsup-recherche.gouv.fr/cid20256/liste-des-ecoles-d-ingenieurs.html
9. https://paristech.fr/en/node/210
10. www.ecoles2commerce.com/1044-les-differents-statuts-des-ecoles; www.ecoles2commerce.com; https://diplomeo.com/actualite-classement_grande_ecole_de_commerce
11. www.enseignementsup-recherche.gouv.fr/cid70660/les-ecoles-commerce-gestion.html
12. www.insead.edu
13. www.insead.edu/about/alliance-partnerships/sorbonne-universite
14. www.reseau-scpo.fr
15. www.sciencespo.fr/en
16. www.letudiant.fr/etudes/licence-professionnelle/poursuite-d-etudes-apres-une-licence-pro-11836.html

17. www.enseignementsup-recherche.gouv.fr/pid25366/acces-thematique.html?theme=112&subtheme=288
18. www.univ-catholille.fr
19. www.enseignementsup-recherche.gouv.fr/cid135727/enseignement-superieur-recherche-et-innovation-en-chiffres.html; www.enseignementsup-recherche.gouv.fr/cid134768/les-etudiants-inscrits-dans-les-universites-francaises-en-2017-2018.html
20. https://www.centralesupelec.fr/fr/droits-de-scolarite-et-bourses; www.letudiant.fr/educpros/actualite/institut-mines-telecom-droits-scolarite-geometrie-variable.html
21. www.campusfrance.org/en/tuition-fees-France
22. www.enseignementsup-recherche.gouv.fr/pid24670/etudiants-en-situation-de-handicap.html; www.univ-tours.fr/l-universite/nos-valeurs/mission-egalite; www.u-bordeaux.fr/Universite/Universite-ethique/Handicap; https://paristech.fr/fr/egalite-des-chances/la-diversite-dans-les-ecoles; www.lereseau.asso.fr/presentation
23. www.enseignementsup-recherche.gouv.fr/pid37384/parcoursup-la-plateforme-d-admission-dans-l-enseignement-superieur.html; (This author found the search tool on the website Parcoursup very cumbersome.)
24. www.campusfrance.org/en
25. www.onisep.fr/Choisir-mes-etudes/Apres-le-bac; https://etudiant.lefigaro.fr/etudes; www.letudiant.fr/etudes/annuaire-enseignement-superieur/formation.html
26. http://lorraine.gatech.edu
27. http://taughtie.campusfrance.org/tiesearch/#/catalog
28. www.enseignementsup-recherche.gouv.fr/cid94756/les-regroupements-universitaires-et-scientifiques-une-coordination-territoriale-pour-un-projet-partage.html
29. https://cache.media.enseignementsup-recherche.gouv.fr/file/Etablissements_et_organismes/68/2/Liste_regroupements_Associations_et_COMUE_et_associes_1er_fevrier_2018_890682.pdf
30. www.universite-paris-saclay.fr/en
31. www.universite-paris-saclay.fr/en/masters-degrees-in-english; www.universite-paris-saclay.fr/en/master-degrees-taught-in-french-and-english
32. www.univ-lorraine.fr

University Studies in France

Fred Weissler and Helen Shavit

One of the most striking features of French public universities is that the French *baccalauréat*, earned after successful completion of high school, confers guaranteed admission to the French public university system. This is true regardless of the type of French *baccalauréat*. The *baccalauréat général* specifically prepares the student for academically oriented university level studies. In addition, there are several other *baccalauréat* degrees, referred to as "professional" or "technological" *baccalauréats*, which also guarantee acceptance to a university. However, a student who obtains a *baccalauréat professionnel* or even a *baccalauréat technologique* will likely be inadequately prepared for academic studies at the university level.

Up until recently, the guaranteed admission policy at the university was valid only for the academic year immediately following the successful completion of the *baccalauréat* exam. However, as part of the effort to stem high dropout rates in the first year of university study, it is now possible to take a gap year *(année de césure)* without forfeiting admission. A year to explore one's interests or work can provide a useful perspective to the student who may be unsure of his/her objectives or may not be ready to commit to the discipline that university study requires. Once the student who wishes to take a gap year has accepted an offer of admission, he/she must contact the university to find out about the procedures and deadlines for obtaining approval. This usually entails submitting a letter of motivation indicating the objectives and nature of the gap year, such as civic service *(service civique)*, or another volunteer endeavor in France or abroad, a student job, or even taking a course in an unrelated area. During the *année de césure*, student status will still apply. (See the chapter, "The Gap Year", for further information.)

The university system in France is largely a commuter one. American-style dormitories are very limited and almost exclusively reserved for students with financial need or international students. In recent years, more and more privately-owned student residences that offer housing at affordable rates have opened near university campuses or public transportation hubs. However, these fill up quickly so students who reside far from their selected university should apply early. In France, it is customary for students to live with their parent(s) if their chosen university is the one in their geographic sector.

Having a commuter university system in a society like France, which values equal opportunity, implies that all the universities should be of equal or approximately equal quality, at least at the undergraduate *(licence)* level, and that universities should be equally accessible to all students having successfully completed *lycée*, i.e., earned the *baccalauréat*. While this was true historically, in recent years reforms have been instituted which both allow universities to distinguish themselves from each other, and modulate the admissions process for students, thus allowing selectivity. For example, while university degree programs must be approved and regularly re-evaluated and re-accredited by the MESRI (Ministère de l'Enseignement supérieur, de la Recherche et de l'Innovation), the government sets only the number of hours of class time required, allowing each university more freedom in determining the contents of its academic programs. While previously, a student having passed the *baccalauréat* could not in principle be refused admission to any standard (i.e., non-selective) university *licence* program, now such a student is only guaranteed admission into "a" *licence* program, not necessarily one of the student's initial choices. Furthermore, universities are free to create special programs, such as the *double licence*, which are academically more demanding, and for which admission is by special application. Finally, universities that are granted the status of *grand établissement* (currently Université Paris-Dauphine and Université de Lorraine) have much more freedom to select students based on academic record. Some of these reforms, and other reforms as well, will be discussed in more detail below.

The basic "undergraduate" degree is a three-year program leading to a *licence*. The three years of *licence* are referred to as L1, L2, and L3. It is followed by a two-year master's program, or "*master*" in French (the two years being called M1 and M2), followed by a doctoral program. The second year, M2, of a research-oriented master's program includes the coursework necessary to pursue a doctoral degree.

The academic year is comprised of two semesters of coursework and separate examination periods. Classes typically start in September and end in May or June. The subjects taught are organized as teaching units (*unité d'enseignement* or UE), which include lectures *(cours magistraux)*, typically held in large amphitheaters that seat upwards of several hundred students,[1] and smaller group tutorials (*travaux dirigés* or TD) or practicum (*travaux pratiques* or TP) that take place in classrooms or laboratories.

The grading system in France is based on a scale of 0 to 20, with 10/20 (50%) being a passing grade. Knowledge is evaluated through ongoing assessment *(contrôle continu)* over the course of the semester, as well as final exams. At the end of each academic year, an overall numerical grade average is calculated for each student. This is a weighted average of the grades from all the classes taken during the year. Separate semester averages are also computed. In order to pass from one year to the next, an overall minimum grade average of 10/20 for the year is required. This means that a student can pass the year without having passed each of the individual classes. This phenomenon is known as *compensation*, whereby a poor or failing grade in one subject can be compensated by a high grade in another subject.

Numerical grades in France correspond to what are called *mentions*, which resemble letter grades in the US. A grade of 16 or better is denoted by *mention très bien*; 14 or better, but less than 16, by *mention bien*; 12 or better, but less than 14, by *mention assez bien*; and 10 or better, but less than 12, by *passable*. There might be a tendency to consider these *mentions* as equivalent, respectively, to A, B, C, and D in the US system, but this would not be accurate. Few grades of 16 or better are given, and a grade of 12 (*mention assez bien*) is respectable. According to Scholaro Pro (www.scholaro.com/pro), a more accurate equivalence would be:

A+: 16 or better
A: 14 or better but less than 16
B: 12 or better, but less than 14
C: 10 or better, but less than 12

All final exams are given a second time, during what is called the second session (*deuxième session or session de rattrapage*) to give students who failed or who missed an exam (for any reason) another chance. The second session for both the fall and spring semester final exams is administered in June or July of the academic year concerned. Each university has a policy regarding absences from examinations, which can usually be found as part of either the *charte des examens* or the *règlement des modalités de contrôle des connaissances*. It behooves the student to know the rules about absence from examinations.

As mentioned above, a student needs an overall grade average of at least 10/20 for a given year to pass to the next year: L1 to L2, L2 to L3, and completion of L3. A student who has not passed L1 (first year *licence*) could be allowed to enroll in L2, if only one of the two semesters in L1 have been passed, i.e., if a final average of 10/20 has been obtained for one of the two semesters, but not for the whole year. The specific requirements to enroll in L2 in this case are set by the university, or even by the specific program. For example, the student must have successfully completed a certain percentage of the UE (*unités d'enseignement*) in the failed semester. In such a situation, this means that a student in L2, who has not successfully completed L1, must re-take the necessary L1 exams at the end of the year, in addition to all the L2 exams. Similarly, a student could be allowed to enroll in L3 if three of the four semesters in L1 and L2 have been passed, subject to additional conditions set by the university and/or the specific program. Before receiving the final degree of *licence*, the student must have attained a yearly average of 10/20 for each of the three years of study, L1, L2, and L3.

A student who fails the first year can repeat the whole year or enroll in the first year of a different *licence* program. The various courses of study being offered at the universities are now largely adapted so that a student can move from one *licence* to another at mid-year (after the first semester) of the first year of study.

It is important to note that to become a doctor or a lawyer in France, one must choose these areas of concentration at the first year of university study, unlike the US, where students enter law school or medical school only after earning an undergraduate degree. For example, a first-year student wishing to become a lawyer in France would choose a *Licence de Droit, Économie, Gestion: mention Droit*. Keep in mind that when there are more requests than spaces available for a first year medical or law program, admission will be selective. More information about the paths to becoming a lawyer or a doctor in France is provided in separate chapters of this guide.

Applying to Universities

Applications for post *baccalauréat* studies in France, to the university and *classes préparatoires* alike, are completed online during the last year of high school *(terminale)*, on one centralized website, called Parcoursup.[2] Students must register on this website and make their requests for programs during a limited time period, which runs from January to March; the exact dates are specified each year by the government.

The Parcoursup website can be accessed anytime to learn about the process and programs, however, the revised list of offerings, full program descriptions and admission criteria, and capacity for the coming academic year are available for consultation starting mid-December. This allows time for students to learn about the programs on offer even before registering on the site.

Keep in mind that one of the reasons that students drop out after the first year of university is that their experience did not meet their expectations. This is why it is important to start thinking about options and investigate schools before the year of *terminale*. Perusing the Parcoursup website in *première* is a good place to start the process. Attending one or two of the higher education fairs *(Salons de l'enseignement supérieur)* can spark an interest or motivate a student to improve his/her *lycée* performance. In *terminale*, students should also make sure to attend open houses *(journées portes ouvertes)* and participate in "immersion days" *(journées d'immersion)* in which *lycéens* may sit in on a lecture class or observe a lab class. Meeting professors and talking to students or just simply observing the action will provide valuable information and insight. A *lycéen(ne)* who is well informed is more likely to make the right choices.

In time, all first-year higher education programs accredited by the French government will be referenced and available for application on Parcoursup. Currently, there are more than 15,000 such programs from which to choose. Once an online dossier is created, the student has until mid-March to enter a maximum of 10 choices *(vœux)*. There is no need to rank them in order of preference, as all requests will be treated equally. Keep in mind that one applies to a specific program at a specific institution. The choices can include programs at universities, *prépas* (CPGE), and specialized schools, such as for nursing, social work, engineering, and business. While students may apply to a program at any university in France, if possible, they should also apply to the same or a similar program of interest offered at a university in their geographic sector, where they will have priority. In early April (the exact date may change from year to year), the student must finalize his/her choices, taking into account discussions with teachers and mentors and the outcome of the 2nd trimester *conseil de classe*.

> *Keep in mind that the student applies to a specific program at a specific institution.*

The prospective student should pay particular attention concerning applications to the various *licences sélectives*, which include *double licences, licences internationales*, or other special programs. Some of these programs are officially sanctioned by the government as selective, such as those in which some of the classes are given in a language other than French, or those requiring certain musical skills. These programs are also applied to via the Parcoursup website. Students wishing to apply to one or more of these should be sure to also apply on the Parcoursup website to a corresponding "normal" (non-selective) *licence* in the same area at the given university as a "safety". Students interested in a selective program should try a web search with the words *"double licence", "licence internationale"*, and either the geographic area or an academic area. For example, a web search of *"double licence Paris"* or *"double licence langues"* will give many relevant websites. Another good search item is *"licences à capacité limitée"*.

As mentioned above, a student who obtains the French *baccalauréat* is guaranteed a place in a university in the same geographic *secteur* for the year immediately following high school or if a gap year is requested, the year thereafter. These universities will be clearly indicated on the website, www.parcoursup.fr, once the student supplies his/her identifying information. Applications to universities outside the *secteur* are competitive, as are applications to *prépas*, and to the IUT. Thus, one should definitely include among his/her choices at least one non-selective program in a university in one's geographic *secteur*. It is important to note that as of 2019, *lycée* students who live in the Île-de-France region which includes the Academies of Paris, Versailles, and Créteil, have equal access to universities across the region. This rule gives *lycée* students who live in the close or distant Paris suburbs the same priority to universities located in Paris as those who reside in Paris itself.

Foreign (non-French) students who went to high school outside France and who did not take the French *baccalauréat* exam can find out how to apply to a French public university on the website, www.campusfrance.org. There is a strict window of time for making a preliminary application *(demande d'admission préalable* or DAP*)*, usually from November until mid-January for entry the following academic year. A DAP is not required for EU nationals. French universities accept the IB diploma (International Baccalaureate) as well as the British A-levels. However, an American high school diploma alone is generally not accepted without at least one year of US college study.

Undergraduate Studies *(Licence)*

The *licence* corresponds to the first level of studies in the LMD *(licence-master-doctorat)* framework. It provides the theoretical foundations for the student to further his/her studies either in a university master's program or a specialized school rather than to qualify him/her to enter the job market directly. The *licence* is earned after three years of study, corresponding to 180 credits *(crédits* or ECTS - European Credit Transfer and Accumulation System credits). The curriculum encompasses courses in a chosen subject area as well as other required courses set by each university, such as foreign language and computer courses. Thanks to reforms enacted in 2018, progressive specialization is possible. Sometimes, a student will be able to choose a major and minor path of study *(majeur et mineur)* in two different disciplines so as to facilitate an eventual reorientation. To help in the course selection process, orientation sessions are organized for entering first-year students and an *enseignant-référent*, available to each student, may be consulted for guidance.

In France, a *licence* may be pursued in major areas *(domaines)* of study: language, literature and the arts *(arts, lettres et langues)*; humanities and social sciences

(sciences humaines et sociales); law, economics and management *(droit, économie et gestion)*; and sciences, technology and health *(sciences, technologies et santé)*. Within a given domain, the student will select an area of concentration or discipline *(mention)*. There are nearly 50 disciplines[3] from which to choose, such as political science, philosophy, psychology, visual arts, computer science, mathematics, and civil engineering, to name but a few. A student applying to a French public university chooses a discipline *(mention)*. For example, a student could apply to a "*Licence de Sciences, Technologies, Santé: mention Physique-chimie*" or a "*Licence de Droit, Économie, Gestion: mention Administration économique et sociale*". Each *mention* may in turn offer further specialization in the third year. At the end of the first semester or the first year a successful student may reorient his/her studies to another area of concentration, another *licence* program or even another type of diploma such as a BTS or DUT delivered elsewhere. At the end of the second year of *licence* the student may opt to continue his/her training in an institution that awards a *licence professionnelle* if that proves to be more compatible with his/her career goals.

The first year then, provides foundation courses in the concentration/discipline chosen, as well as introduction courses in another discipline, affording the student an opportunity to discover another subject area. As a result, some students may choose to change their concentration or pursue a double major *(études bidisciplinaires)* within the same domain. By the end of the first year of *licence*, the student will have finalized his/her choice(s) of discipline and will follow the curriculum set by his/her university. In the third year the student completes the required coursework necessary for the mention.

In addition to classes, over the course of the *licence*, the student may be required to complete an internship *(stage)*. He or she may also opt to study abroad for a semester or even do his/her internship abroad through the Erasmus+ program. The student should inquire early on about which exchanges are possible and prepare well ahead, including acquiring or reinforcing necessary language skills.

By the end of the *licence* the student will have acquired a solid knowledge base in a chosen discipline(s), one or more foreign languages, and transversal skills (such as work methodology and utilization of documentary resources). He or she will be well prepared for entry into a master's level program. About two thirds of students who earn a *licence* enroll in a university *master* the following year.[4]

Students will attend, on average, 20-30 hours per week of classes and should allot a minimum of 20 additional hours per week for personal study and assignment preparation. The university student is expected to function autonomously; organization and discipline are essential! It is not uncommon for students to fail or perform poorly on first semester exams because of a lack of a consistent and effective work method. Attendance at lectures *(cours magistraux)* is not mandatory, however, it is required (and counted) for the tutorial classes *(travaux dirigés)* and practicum or lab classes *(travaux pratiques)*. As attending the *cours magistraux* is not obligatory it may be tempting to skip them; however, this would be highly imprudent. Important points and the professor's predilections will be missed. Furthermore, the notes taken in these lectures are essential for review purposes and helping to prepare for exams. It is emphasized that rigor, discipline, and organization are key to passing the first year (and subsequent years) of the *licence*.

> *The university student is expected to function autonomously; organization and discipline are essential.*

It should be noted that universities might also offer lectures via podcast and other internet-based learning tools. Some even offer an entire program online. At this writing, there are 90 three-year online *licence* programs available in France and an additional number of single-year curricula, usually for L3. To search these programs by diploma, domaine, and/or discipline, go to the website of the FIED (Fédération Interuniversitaire de l'Enseignement à Distance)[5], a government recognized network of French universities that offer distance-learning programs.

Reform of March 2018 - ORE

The law for the orientation and success of students or ORE *(la loi du 8 mars 2018 relative à l'orientation et à la réussite des étudiants)* was promulgated with the primary objective of increasing the success rate for all students embarking on a higher education path in France, regardless of their educational backgrounds. It is the outcome of Le Plan Étudiants initiated in 2017 to address the high failure rate for students at French universities, estimated to be as high as 60%. Among the measures, some of which have been previously mentioned, are:

1. The implementation of the application platform, Parcoursup, replacing the prior APB (Admission Post-Bac) system. The streamlined procedure for applying to first-year higher education programs also provides a mechanism by which universities can select students for certain programs, including those that are "non-selective" in conception but receive more requests than can be accommodated. In the past, when there was more demand than available spaces for a non-selective program the decision as to which students were admitted was based on a lottery system. Now, a commission *(la commission d'examen de vœux)* evaluates applicants based on the information provided by the student's Parcoursup *dossier (la fiche Avenir)*, which includes grades, class ranking, and comments of the principal teacher *(prof principal)*, subject teachers, and the school director *(chef d'établissement, proviseur)*.

   The Parcoursup platform is used by applicants in *terminale* as well as by students who are already in a first year of studies but wish to change direction. As described earlier, the candidate formulates a maximum of 10 primary requests without any order of preference. Students may also make secondary requests *(sous-vœux)*. An example of a *sous-vœu*, could be a request for the same discipline *(mention)* indicated in a primary choice *(vœu)*, but at a different university. A student may declare a maximum of 20 *sous-vœux* across all 10 *vœux*. See the Parcoursup website for a full explanation and timeline of the process, www.parcoursup.fr.

2. The formulation and signing of an individualized pedagogic plan for each student *(le contrat pédagogique pour la réussite étudiante –* CPRE) documenting the agreed upon study path and any measures deemed necessary to maximize success. Individualized support should be available to all students. Those who may not have the level necessary to succeed in their program of choice may be required to attend foundation or other supplementary classes that may prolong the duration of the *licence* to four years. Conversely, students who are very

highly qualified may be permitted to complete a *licence* in less than three years.

3. Progressive specialization and more options to change study paths. Universities may offer an initial multidisciplinary curriculum providing students the opportunity to learn about different subject areas before declaring their final choice of discipline *(mention)*. Orientation sessions are organized for all entering first year students and at major junctures in a program. Students are encouraged to consult the referent teacher *(enseignant – référent)* available to each student for guidance, if necessary. This is especially important during the first year of studies.

   Students who are enrolled in a BTS, DUT, DEUST, or *prépa* program may apply to continue their studies in a *licence* program at the appropriate level.

4. Automatic adhesion to the national social security health care system for all students. This reform overrides the prior separate social security plan for students. However, a fee to help cover access to preventive health care and the development of student cultural and sport programs must be paid before school registration can be finalized. This fee, *la Contribution vie étudiante et de campus* or CVEC (91 € for the 2019/20 academic year), does not apply to students in France on an international exchange program. Students receiving scholarships from the French government and refugees are exonerated, however, they must submit an exemption certificate *(attestation d'exonération)*.

5. The recognition of the gap year as a benefit that should be made available to all students regardless of level of study or university. As stated earlier, this also holds true for the student who has been admitted to a program but wishes to delay the start of studies in order to take a gap year.

6. A minimum enrollment of government funded students *(élèves boursiers)* is mandated for all *licence* programs, but the rules are different for selective and non-selective programs. In the case of non-selective programs for which there are more applicants than places available, disadvantaged students must be accepted in the same proportion that they applied.

   In the case of selective programs, the number of places reserved for *élèves boursiers* is established by the rector of each university.

7. At every *lycée*, the top performing students on the *baccalauréat* exams will have priority for admission into the higher education program of their choice, across all public institutions of higher learning, including those programs practicing selective admission. The percentage is set by decree and each academic authority will reserve a minimum number of spaces in each program for these students. Conditions may apply.

Students with Disabilities

Every university in France has a unit in place for students with disabilities and disabling health conditions that provides information and support, implements approved measures, and coordinates services. Modifications and adaptations provided may include changing a schedule to facilitate access to a class, provision of a personal assistant for note taking or pedagogical support and allocation of extra time *(tiers temps)* or a computer for exams. Most students with a disability will have been identified well before the beginning of the academic year and should have support measures in place by the time classes start.

Some students, however, manage to obtain their *bac* without drawing any special attention to or even recognizing a learning disability. The demands of university are such, however, that "getting by" will be unlikely without proper support. It is therefore imperative to seek help before difficulties become insurmountable. An internet search of the name of the institution followed by "*service handicap*" will yield relevant information and the contact details of the service coordinator *(référent handicap)*.

Fees

The current annual tuition for the *licence* is 170 €; for the *master*, 243 €; and for the *doctorat*, 380 €. The French government covers the rest of the real cost of university studies, amounting to an average of 10,000 € per student per year, for a total annual expense of more than 31 billion euros.[6] As mentioned in the introduction, it is possible that non-EU international students will soon be charged a more substantial tuition fee, the current proposal being 2,770 € at the *licence* level and 3,770 € at the level of *master*. International students should consult the Campus France website for current tuition fees prior to applying.[7]

IUT *(Institut Universitaire de Technologie)*, STS *(Section de Techniciens Supérieurs)*, and *Licence Professionnelle*

The IUT *(institut universitaire de technologie)* was conceived as a two-year program for students with a "technological" *baccalauréat* degree. A *baccalauréat technologique*, as opposed to a "general" *baccalauréat*, is not intended to prepare the student for academically oriented university studies *(formations générales)*. The idea is to teach these students practical skills, which would enable them to enter the job market after two years of post-*bac* study. The student-teacher ratio in an IUT is more favorable than in most academic programs in the first two years of university. Furthermore, students have more class hours at an IUT than in an academic *licence* program. They may also study abroad for a semester or complete an internship under Erasmus+. After successfully completing a two-year IUT, the student is awarded a DUT *(diplôme universitaire de technologie)*.

The DUT is a national diploma and technically gives credit for the first two years toward a *licence*. Instead of entering the workforce after completing the two-year DUT program at an IUT, students under some circumstances can move into third year university studies, at the level of L3 (third-year *licence*). Depending on the program, however, some students with a DUT need to start at the second year of an academic university program (L2). In both cases, entering a *licence* program at either the L2 or L3 level after obtaining a DUT is by selection, and not at all guaranteed.

While an IUT is part of a university (there are over 100 IUTs in France), it enjoys considerable independence within the structure of the university. In particular, an IUT is not required to admit just any student with a *baccalauréat*. Consequently, the best candidates are selected, including those with a "general" *baccalauréat (bac général)*. This situation is both ironic and regrettable: students with a "technological" *baccalauréat (bac technologique)*, who are among the less academically oriented students, may consequently be excluded from the very type of program created for them, and forced to enroll in the "non-selective", more academic university programs. To remedy this situation, the national reform of March 2018, mandated that a minimum percentage of students applying from a *bac technologique* be enrolled in an IUT.

It is also possible in some IUTs to earn a DUT in one year, either as a second DUT in another specialty or after having completed two years in a different institution of higher education (such as L2). This year is called *"l'année spéciale"*.

While not part of the university, the STS *(section de technicien supérieur)* is another two-year post *baccalauréat* program designed to prepare the student to enter the job market. This program, also selective, is offered principally (but not exclusively) in certain *lycées* and includes a significant portion of internships *(stages)* in related industries. Successful students are awarded a BTS *(brevet de technicien supérieur)*. The reform of March 2018 mandates that a minimum percentage of students who earned a professional baccalaureate *(bac pro)* be enrolled in an STS.

A *licence professionnelle* is a one-year program, offered at the university (most often by an IUT), for students who have obtained either the DUT or BTS, as well as students who have completed the first two years of a university *licence* program. It is designed to prepare the student to enter the job market directly, and is offered in such diverse areas as agriculture, technology, commerce, tourism and health services. At this writing, there are 173 *mentions* from which to choose.[8] As from 2017, almost 50 of the 113 IUTs in France are testing a new three-year program, called *parcours technologique de grade licence* (PTGL) that will allow students to proceed directly from a DUT to a *licence professionnelle* within three years. This would eliminate the need to pass the additional selection process that is normally required. The new three-year BUT (Bachelor Universitaire de Technologie) has just been announced and will be instituted in 2021.

The three *universités de technologie* located in Belfort-Montbéliard, Compiègne and Troyes as well as two of the four *instituts nationaux polytechniques* (INP), in Grenoble and Lorraine, also offer the *licence professionelle*.

Graduate Studies (Master and Doctoral Degrees)

After completing a *licence*, a student who wishes to continue his/her university studies may apply to a *master* program leading to the DNM *(le Diplôme National de Master)* called *master*, spelled as in English, but pronounced in French. The *master* is earned after two years of study and represents 120 ECTS – European Credit Transfer and Accumulation System credits. While admission to a *master* program is selective, there are sometimes a certain number of spots reserved for students who have completed a *licence* at the same university in the same area of study. The MESRI (Ministère de l'Enseignement supérieur, de la Recherche et de l'Innovation) has a dedicated website[9] listing all *master* programs in France, i.e., programs leading to the French national diploma of *master*, accredited by the MESRI, including programs offered by public or private institutions of higher education. On the other hand, this website does not include master's programs offered by some private *grandes écoles* that are not accredited by the MESRI. Prospective students who are considering pursuing a master's degree beyond a public university should check equivalencies. (See the chapter "Graduate Studies in France for the International Student" for further information about master's level programs in France.)

A given *master* program can serve primarily as preparation for doctoral level studies and research, or primarily for entry into the job market at a high level, or in some cases both. Different orientations within the same *master* are called *parcours*, and especially in the second year, the specific course of study followed depends on the *parcours* chosen by the student. Different *parcours* within the same *master* program may also indicate different areas of specialization. For example, a *master mathématiques et applications* could have one *parcours* on financial mathematics, preparing students for direct entry into a high-level career in finance, and another *parcours* preparing students to pursue a *doctorat* in probability and statistics. Successful completion of the first year (M1) guarantees acceptance into at least one of the *parcours* of the second year (M2) of the same program.

Doctoral studies are administered by the *écoles doctorales*, which are sometimes organized at the level of the ComUE *(communauté d'universités et établissements)* to which the university belongs, rather than the university. The doctoral degree itself could be awarded solely in the name of a ComUE, jointly by a university and the ComUE of which it is a member, or solely by the university.

The preliminary course work, which is usually part of the doctoral program in the US, takes place in the second year of the *master* program in France. Doctoral candidates must hold a master's degree or equivalent to apply. The doctorate (*doctorat*), often referred to as *"la thèse"* in French parlance because of the dominance of the research and dissertation aspects, generally takes from three to six years, depending on the discipline, to complete.

To be accepted into a doctoral program in France (i.e., accredited by the MESRI), one needs to have both a thesis project and a thesis advisor, as well as means of financial support, such as a *contrat doctoral.* Further information, as well as a comprehensive repertory of current research projects by area and region, can be found on the Campus France website, https://doctorat.campusfrance.org.

University-Based Engineering Schools

The public universities include a network of around 60 engineering schools,[10] which train about 20% of the engineering students in France. The diplomas issued by university-based engineering schools are recognized by the CTI (Commission des Titres d'Ingénieur). Entry to these programs is selective.

While generally not as well known as the long-established *grandes écoles,* university based engineering schools (the first of which opened in the 1970s), are growing in popularity. Classes are small so there is not the anonymity common in other university programs, and teachers are also researchers so students may benefit from access to partner laboratories, particularly for internships. Often, the programs are highly specialized, drawing the attention of employers in specific industries. An example is the marine engineering program offered by the SeaTech School of Engineering at the University of Toulon.

About half of the university engineering schools recruit students directly after the *bac*, either by *dossier* and an interview or through written and/or oral exams for admission into a five year program, beginning with two years of preparation courses *(cycle préparatoire)*. The majority of students have earned a *bac général* (with a science and math emphasis), though a large minority hold a *bac technologique*, specifically the STI 2D *(Sciences et technologies de l'industrie et du développement durable)* or the STL *(sciences et technologies de laboratoire)*. Of special interest, is the Polytech network (Réseau Polytech) that comprises 15 university based engineering schools, most of which are also *grandes écoles*, i.e., members of the CGE. Most of the Polytech network schools are also open to students who have completed the first year of medical studies allowing them to integrate directly into the second year of the preparatory cycle. For these students, the results of the first-year exams are considered as part of their application to the Polytech school.

The other university-based engineering schools, like the *grandes écoles*, recruit students for a three-year engineering program based on results of a competitive exam taken following two years of post-*bac* studies. Students here tend to be a more diverse group: about a third come from traditional *prépa* programs (see chapter "Classes Préparatoires aux Grandes Écoles: CPGE or *Prépas*"), about a third have earned a DUT or BTS, and about a third have earned a *licence* or a *master*. With certain exceptions, the tuition for university based engineering schools is 601 € per year (2019-20).[11] Students with documented financial need are exonerated from paying tuition.

In addition, there are three *universités de technologie:* Université de technologie de Belfort-Montbéliard (UTBM), Université de technologie de Compiègne (UTC) and Université de technologie de Troyes (UTT) and four *instituts nationaux polytechniques* (INP), located in Bordeaux, Grenoble, Lorraine and Toulouse, which also offer engineering degrees.

University Studies and Teacher Certification

In order to become certified as a teacher in France, both at the primary and secondary school levels, one must enroll in a special master's program, called *master* MEEF *(master métiers de l'enseignement, de l'éducation et de la formation)*.[12] In addition, the prospective teacher must take a competitive exam or *concours* resulting in a numerical ranking of all candidates. Only the top performers, the number of which is pre-determined by the government each year, succeed. Prospective elementary school teachers must take the CRPE, or *concours de recrutement de professeurs des écoles*. To become a secondary school teacher, one has to take the *concours* to obtain the CAPES *(certificat d'aptitude au professorat du second degré)*, with each academic discipline requiring a separate exam.[13] These competitive exams are taken at the end of the first year of the *master* MEEF; the first year of the program includes preparation for these. Application to a *master* MEEF is open to any student with a *licence*, however, admission is not automatic. Admission requirements vary from program to program, and depend on which *concours* the student wishes to take. Students who want to become school counselors, *conseiller principal d'éducation* (CPE), also must enroll in a *master* MEEF.

The program for a *master* MEEF includes 800 hours over two years, not counting classroom observation, practice teaching, etc. About half of the class hours are devoted to subject matter instruction, the other half to various aspects of pedagogy.

As for practical activities, during the first year, students spend six weeks in observation and supervised practice teaching.[14] In the second year, the students who have successfully passed the *concours*, become *fonctionnaires stagiaires*, take responsibility for a class for the year in a work-study context, and are paid a salary, starting around 1,600 € per month.[15]

The organization of the *master* MEEF program is the responsibility of specially created institutes, *instituts nationaux supérieurs du professorat et de l'éducation* or INSPE. These institutes, created in 2013, originally called *écoles supérieures du professorat et de l'éducation* (ESPE), are adopting the new designation of INSPE as of 2019, though the former designation of ESPE is still present on many websites, not yet replaced by INSPE. There are about 30 of these institutes in France, each one usually being part of a given university, but forming partnerships with other, nearby universities.[16] Every French public university may offer a *master* MEEF in partnership with some INSPE. A student who wishes to pursue a *master* MEEF will make the application to the appropriate INSPE,[17] and is of course strongly advised to look carefully at the website of the desired MEEF to be sure of the application procedure.

Starting in the academic year 2019-20, students who wish to become primary or secondary school teachers can begin pre-professional training, including classroom observation and some supervised contact with (primary and secondary) students starting at the level of L2. These activities take place in the framework of a *parcours de préprofessionnalisation*, as part of the normal *licence* program, and offer the student a modest financial remuneration.[18] These programs are not yet available at all universities, or in every discipline. Students may follow @enseignerdemain on Twitter in order to get up-to-date information about these programs.

Teachers who have already earned the CAPES qualification may later take a second competitive exam *(concours)*, called the *agrégation*. High school teachers who have successfully passed the *agrégation* exam are paid more, have fewer class hours, and teach more advanced classes. For example, the various *prépas* are taught by *lycée* teachers who have earned an *agrégation*. In recent years it has become a de facto requirement to have a *doctorat*, in addition to the *agrégation* in order to become a teacher in a *prépa*. It is also possible to take the *agrégation* exam without having first taken the CAPES exam.

Exchange Programs with Universities Outside France, Erasmus+

The Erasmus program, which since 2014 is incorporated under the rubric of Erasmus+, enables a student to spend one semester or one year at a university in another European country, normally at the L3, M1, or M2 level, sometimes at the L2 level, and rarely at L1. The academic program at the foreign university is organized to be as close as possible to the program the student would have followed in France, and full credit at the home university is granted. The European Credit Transfer and Accumulation System (ECTS) is designed for this purpose.

Each French university has its own specific network comprised of different European universities with which it has signed exchange agreements. These bilateral agreements determine the number of places in the foreign university reserved for students coming from the given French university, as well as the disciplines allowing an exchange. Moreover, each French university selects the students it will send to other European universities under this program. The tuition fees are determined by the university of origin in France. In other words, no fees are paid to the foreign university. A variety of scholarships are available to cover living expenses while attending the foreign (non-French) university.

If a student wishes to stay at the foreign university after the Erasmus year, the student can re-apply at his home university for a second Erasmus year. While being selected for a second year under the Erasmus+ program is not impossible, it is highly improbable. The student also has the option of applying directly to the foreign university, outside the Erasmus+ program.

Erasmus+ has established strong links with the labor market, enabling French university students to fulfill their internship requirement in a company or organization abroad. Furthermore, Erasmus+ facilitates access to study or internship opportunities abroad for those facing obstacles related to socio-economic conditions, disability, or health–related issues.

Another program that is part of the Erasmus+ initiative is the Erasmus Mundus Joint Master Degree (EMJMD),[19] which offers selected students the opportunity to study in two different European countries over the course of 12–24 months. It is an integrated international study program that awards 60, 90, or 120 ECTS credits. The successful completion of the program leads to either a joint degree issued on behalf of the two (or more) concerned higher education institutions of the EMJMD consortium or separate degree certificates issued by each institution. Full Erasmus Mundus scholarships, funded by the European Union, are awarded to the best candidates. Both EU and non-EU nationals who have completed an undergraduate degree or equivalent are eligible for the program and the scholarship. Applications are made between October and January for studies commencing the following academic year. Students may consult the EMJMD online catalog[20] to contact the schools of interest for more information about the programs and application procedures. It is interesting to note that Erasmus+ exchange programs exist for faculty as well, thus furthering the ideals of academic exchange.

In addition to Erasmus+, other exchange programs are available to French university students. For example, MICEFA (Mission Interuniversitaire de Coordination des Échanges Franco-Américains) is a consortium including most of the Paris area universities that promotes exchanges with over 60 partner universities in the United States and Canada.

Finally, many universities are acting individually to create international programs in conjunction with other universities. For example, the Université Paris-Est Créteil Val de Marne (UPEC) offers a series of double diploma programs called *Licence Administration Échange Internationaux* (AEI) in conjunction with universities in China, Europe, and the Americas.[21] Furthermore, UPEC has established other bilateral exchange programs outside the framework of Erasmus+ and MICEFA, enabling study at universities in Eastern and Central Europe, Africa, North America, and Asia.[22]

As another example, the Université Paris 1 Panthéon-Sorbonne offers 35 international double diploma programs in the domains of law, political science, economics, management, archeology, history, art history, philosophy, and tourism.[23]

Career Placement

Every university has a special office in charge of career development, called *le Bureau d'aide à l'insertion professionnelle* or BAIP, whose mission is to create more internship opportunities for students at all levels of the university, and to be a resource for students in planning their professional careers. This includes follow-up assistance once the student has entered the job market.

Extracurricular Activities

French universities offer a variety of extracurricular activities, including athletics. Sports instruction and intra- and inter-university competitions are available. The inter-university competitions are organized under the aegis of the FFSU (Fédération Française du Sport Universitaire). These competitions, however, do not command the same national attention as collegiate sports do in the US.

Cultural activities, including clubs and special one-time performances (theater, music, etc.) are often open to students, faculty, and administrative personnel alike. Detailed information for these programs can be found under the rubrics *"vie étudiante"* and *"culture"* on university websites.

Private Universities

The consortium, UDESCA (Union des Établissements d'Enseignement Supérieur Catholique), groups five large and reputed Catholic universities throughout France: in Paris, Lille, Lyon, Angers, and Toulouse. These multi-disciplinary schools offer undergraduate and graduate programs and confer state-sanctioned diplomas for certain of these.

There are a number of other private universities in France, such as FACO Paris (Faculté Libre de droit, d'économie et de gestion) and Pôle Universitaire Léonard de Vinci. These cannot grant French government sanctioned university degrees, unless they are in partnership with a French public university. They offer their own degrees, some of which are modeled on the French *licence* and *master*, others of which have a more international flavor. While the tuition fees are much higher than for the public universities, they are rather modest by US standards.

Finally, the American University of Paris is a non-profit liberal arts institution accredited by the Middle States Commission on Higher Education (MSCHE). It delivers American bachelor's and master's degrees exclusively. (For further information, see the chapter in this guide, "Undergraduate Study in English in France and the EU".)

Structural Reforms

Recent reforms of the French university system aim to improve the overall level of research in France and increase competition among the various universities and other research establishments. The restructuring of the system as exemplified by the creation of the ComUE and associations of institutions of higher learning in France has already reaped results in international recognition of French universities. As discussed in the introductory chapter, these consortiums of institutes of higher learning in France allow for the pooling and consolidation of resources as well as academic exchange among faculty and students. Research articles published by authors affiliated with a member university or research establishment, bear the name of the ComUE, usually in conjunction with the name of the specific institution. As the number of research publications credited to a university entity contributes to its standing in international rankings, the effect is clear. A recent example is the 2019 *Times Higher Education* World University Rankings[24] in which the ComUE, Paris Sciences et Lettres – PSL Research University Paris ranked among the top 50 universities in the world. Created in 2015 this ComUE includes 7 institutions of higher education and research, one of which is Université Paris-Dauphine.

Conclusion

The public universities constitute the main pillar of higher education in France. As in the United States, higher education in France is intended to be available to all qualified high school graduates, and the French public university system is structured with this precise ideal in mind. France is also mindful that in today's world, competition among universities takes place on an international scale, and is in the process of adapting its own system of higher education to this reality. The challenge is to create an educational environment which motivates students and faculty, can attract the best students and researchers internationally, while at the same time providing genuine opportunity and job training for less academically oriented students.

References and Resources

- List of post *baccalauréat* programs: www.parcoursup.fr/index.php?desc=formations
- French government website for higher education: www.enseignementsup-recherche.gouv.fr/pid20112/enseignement-superieur.html
- French government website on the various types of academic and professionally oriented university programs: www.enseignementsup-recherche.gouv.fr/pid20122/formations-et-diplomes.html
- French government listing of public establishments of higher education: www.enseignementsup-recherche.gouv.fr/cid49705/liste-des-etablissements-d-enseignement-superieur-et-de-recherche.html
- List of licences professionnelles: www.legifrance.gouv.fr/affichTexte.do?cidTexte=JORFTEXT000029039732
- Procedures for applying to a *master* and list of programs: www.trouvermonmaster.gouv.fr
- Instituts Universitaires de Technologie: www.iut-fr.net
- Information on the *master*: www.enseignementsup-recherche.gouv.fr/cid20193/le-master.html
- UDESCA (Union des Etablissement d'Enseignement Supérieur Catholique): www.udesca.fr
- Erasmus+: https://ec.europa.eu/programmes/erasmus-plus/node_en
- MICEFA, Mission Interuniversitaire de Coordination des Echanges Franco-Américains: www.micefa.org
- LMD *(licence-master-doctorat)*: www.enseignementsup-recherche.gouv.fr/cid20190/organisation-licence-masterdoctorat-l.m.d.html
- International programs at the Université Paris 1 Panthéon-Sorbonne: www.univ-paris1.fr/international
- Information on student grants, housing and student dinning: www.cnous.fr
- Campus France: www.campusfrance.org and www.usa.campusfrance.org
- Information for students with disabilities: www.enseignementsup-recherche.gouv.fr/pid24670/etudiants-en-situation-de-handicap.html; and www.etudiant.gouv.fr/

- pid38441/etudiants-en-situation-de-handicap.html
- Practical Information for Students in France: www.etudiant.gouv.fr
- Registration procedures for universities: www.etudiant.gouv.fr/cid130435/vous-occuper-de-la-cvec-une-demarche-obligatoire-pour-vous-inscrire-dans-l-enseignement-superieur.html
- Guide to doctoral studies in France: www.findaphd.com/study-abroad/europe/phd-study-in-france.aspx
- Guide to engineering schools: www.onisep.fr/Choisir-mes-etudes/Apres-le-bac/Principaux-domaines-d-etudes/Les-ecoles-d-ingenieurs/Les-ecoles-d-ingenieurs-internes-aux-universites
- *Grandes écoles* engineering schools: https://diplomeo.com/etablissements-grandes_ecoles_d_ingenieurs
- www.gouvernement.fr/conseil-des-ministres/2018-09-12/la-mise-en-uvre-de-parcoursup-
- http://lepetitjournaldedroitpublic.com/2018/03/la-loi-du-8-mars-2018-relative-a-l-orientation-et-a-la-reussite-des-etudiants.html
- www.scholaro.com/pro/Countries/France/Grading-System
- www.enseignementsup-recherche.gouv.fr/cid137863/parcoursup-2019-une-procedure-raccourcie-et-acceleree-pour-que-chacun-trouve-sa-place-dans-l-enseignement-superieur.html
- www.enseignementsup-recherche.gouv.fr/cid141206/parcoursup-les-voeux-2019-d-orientation-vers-l-enseignement-superieur.html
- www.service-public.fr/particuliers/vosdroits/F2326
- www.vie-publique.fr/actualite/panorama/texte-discussion/projet-loi-relatif-orientation-reussite-etudiants.html
- https://ec.europa.eu/programmes/erasmus-plus/opportunities/students_en
- www.enseignementsup-recherche.gouv.fr/cid143234/les-effectifs-universitaires-en-2018-2019.html
- www.enseignementsup-recherche.gouv.fr/cid134446/l-universite-p.s.l.-premier-etablissement-francais-a-entrer-dans-le-top-50-du-classement-world-university-ranking.html

Endnotes

1. www.campusfrance.org/en/French-higher-education
2. www.parcoursup.fr
3. www.legifrance.gouv.fr/affichTexteArticle.do;jsessionid=408D442636A3B1B070788B3DEC360E99.tplgfr21s_2?cidTexte=JORFTEXT000028543633&idArticle=LEGIARTI000038743997&dateTexte=20190827&categorieLien=id#LEGIARTI000038743997
4. www.enseignementsup-recherche.gouv.fr/cid139337/parcours-et-reussite-en-master-a-l-universite-les-resultats-de-la-session-2017.html
5. www.fied.fr
6. www.enseignementsup-recherche.gouv.fr/cid144277/rentree-2019-l-etat-s-engage-en-faveur-des-etudiants.html
7. www.campusfrance.org/en/tuition-fees-France
8. www.enseignementsup-recherche.gouv.fr/pid25330-cid20181/la-licence-professionnelle.html
9. www.trouvermonmaster.gouv.fr
10. www.onisep.fr/Choisir-mes-etudes/Apres-le-bac/Principaux-domaines-d-etudes/Les-ecoles-d-ingenieurs/Les-ecoles-d-ingenieurs-internes-aux-universites; www.service-public.fr/particuliers/actualites/A13379
11. www.service-public.fr/particuliers/actualites/A13379; https://mines-nancy.univ-lorraine.fr/admission/inscription-ingenieur-civil-des-mines
12. www.devenirenseignant.gouv.fr/cid98901/de-licence-master-meef.html
13. www.devenirenseignant.gouv.fr/pid33985/

enseigner-au-college-ou-au-lycee-general-le-capes.html; www.devenirenseignant.gouv.fr/pid33983/enseigner-de-la-maternelle-a-l-elementaire-le-crpe.html
14. www.devenirenseignant.gouv.fr/cid98894/la-annee-master-meef.html
15. www.devenirenseignant.gouv.fr/cid98897/la-2e-annee-de-master-meef.html
16. www.devenirenseignant.gouv.fr/pid33962/les-espe-pour-former-les-futurs-enseignants.html; www.devenirenseignant.gouv.fr/cid142150/former-aux-metiers-du-professorat-et-de-l-education-au-21e-siecle.html; www.vousnousils.fr/2019/02/04/les-espe-font-place-aux-inspe-620648
17. www.reseau-espe.fr/integrer-une-espe/s-inscrire]
18. www.devenirenseignant.gouv.fr/cid137417/preprofessionnalisation-une-entree-progressive-et-remuneree-dans-le-metier-de-professeur.html
19. https://ec.europa.eu/programmes/erasmus-plus/opportunities/individuals/students/erasmus-mundus-joint-master-degrees_en
20. https://eacea.ec.europa.eu/erasmus-plus/library/scholarships-catalogue_en
21. http://www.u-pec.fr/formation/niveau-l/licences-droit-economie-gestion-645296.kjsp?RH=FOR_TTE
22. http://aei.u-pec.fr/international/les-partenaires-de-la-faculte/
23. www.pantheonsorbonne.fr/international/etudiants-etrangers/doubles-diplomes/#c611478
24. www.timeshighereducation.com/world-university-rankings/2019/world-ranking#!/page/0/length/25/sort_by/rank/sort_order/asc/cols/stats

Student anecdotes

I chose this university because it was one of the only ones that offered the program I wanted and it was not in Paris. It's a very good university and a perfect fit for me. There are many resources. The student body is socially very diverse and there are a fair amount of international students. Although there is always a big difference between high school and college, the program is made to help you adapt quickly. Do not hesitate to ask for help or advice; the administration and teachers will not go out of their way to ask you if there is a problem, but they are helpful if you go to them as soon as there is one.   – *Caroline*

I chose my Catholic university in Lille for its Foreign Applied Languages program. Since I wasn't sure of what I wanted to study at that point, specializing in a language program allowed me to continue to study more general subjects as well: history, law, and international relations. I was also able to learn a completely new language, Arabic, in addition to English and Spanish. I am quite satisfied with my choice, since it led me to where I am today: extensive travel and a great job. The academic environment involved learning a scope of different subjects rather than specializing right away, which gave me an openness and a general culture. The university was a good continuation of *lycée*; you had more freedom but professors still kept an eye on you. The classes were small (about 30 students most of the time) and Lille is a great city for young students. I also spent a year abroad in Madrid. Since I moved many times in my youth, I adjusted fine to my new environment. My advice would be to do a gap year. Take your time and choose a program that excites you, something that you think is really interesting. Your future career will design itself only after having tried many different jobs/internships and meeting different people.   – *Heloise*

I chose my Catholic university because it is small and I wanted to attend a school with a limited student/teacher ratio. The teachers here are hands-on and attentive to their students' needs. There are several associations that help new students integrate into the school with ease. Also, the friends I made helped me to adjust and stay on track by studying together. The light workload of my public *lycée* is worlds apart from the work I have at my current program.   – Caroline T

University in France: a British Student's Experience – Mariamne Everett

Though I am a British citizen, I came over to Paris from Cork, Ireland four years ago (August 2015). I had finished my BMus (Bachelor of Music) Honours Degree at the CIT Cork School of Music and like many recent graduates was, to put it mildly, freaking out about my future. It just so happened that I saw an ad on Facebook for an agency that recruits English babysitters in France on a part time basis. I applied, did a Skype interview and was accepted. I had visited Paris with my mother upon completing my Leaving Certificate (equivalent to the *bac*) for my 18th birthday and was determined I would go back. So I did; I found a place to live thanks to a friend's recommendation and found a language school where I could take French classes to line up with my babysitting schedule (after school hours). Anyway, fast track two years later and I decided that I wanted to study in France. Why? It's cheap, I know the language, and, as I had decided at the time that I wanted to do a master's in cultural management, had heard of the reputation of the Sorbonne (Paris 1 and Paris 4 in particular) for its liberal arts programmes. I had a friend who was completing a *licence 3* in art history at Paris 4. Paris 4, according to her and many of my other friends, is known for being conservative and traditional: both in its mind-set and courses on offer. Paris 1 also offers a cultural management master's programme. They are known for being more open minded and contemporary in their tastes. I decided that I would also apply to Sciences Po's cultural management programme. I was a bit concerned about being able to pay for my degree at this *grande école* but was reassured when I found out on their website that fees for European citizens are on a sliding scale; they calculate them based on the student's parents' income.

Applying

Universities in France have different application procedures for their degree programmes *(licence, master,* and *doctorat)* depending on the applicant's nationality and previous educational background (whether you've already completed a course of study or not). As a European passport holder (British, well at least for the moment!) and someone who had already completed a bachelor's degree, I applied via the online platform, eCandidat (today, EU candidates apply through the website, Parcoursup). The application deadlines and submission requirements via this procedure differed between schools and even departments. For Paris 1, I had to submit my applications by post to the relevant department(s). For Paris 4, I uploaded the documents directly to the website. The list of required documents varied between the departments, and Sorbonne schools, but the basic ones were as follows:
- The completed online application form, dated and signed.
- CV and cover letter.
- Copy of ID (Passport).
- Copy of high school/secondary school diploma (equivalent to the *baccalauréat*), university diploma (equivalent to *licence/master*) where relevant, and

transcripts of grades obtained at university. If these documents are not in French, they must be accompanied by an official translation.
- DELF/DALF or TCF level B 2 for those applying to the 1st and 2nd year of a bachelor's degree *(licence 1* and *2)*. The C1 level was required for those applying to the 3rd year of a bachelor's programme *(licence 3)* or *master 1* and 2. These certifications were required from applicants who came from countries where French is not the official language.
- Letter of recommendation written by a professor (optional).

Another note to add: my French friend Emilie, knowing the master's programme I wished to apply to (in cultural management) and my previous course of study (BMus degree), recommended I apply to both the *master 1* and the corresponding *licence 3* (history of art), and *licence 2* programmes. (Even Paris 1, known for being a bit more flexible than the average French institution still maintains a fairly rigid outlook, far more than American institutions for example).

The deadline for hearing back on acceptance was different for every department and university. Upon being accepted into a course, I had a week to confirm my place.

Once I had applied to my programmes, I applied to CROUS for financial aid by filling in a DSE *(dossier social étudiant)*. This must be sent in even before you've been accepted into a programme to ensure smoother and faster processing of your application. Your grant allowance can either take the form of being allocated a place in CROUS run student housing or receiving a monthly allowance. Among the documents I needed to provide were my parents' tax notification from the previous year and proof of the activity of any siblings I may have. I had been receiving a monthly allowance towards my rent from the CAF *(Caisse d'allocations familiales)* as a part-time worker. I needed to update my status to continue receiving it.

*My friend Lina, a non-EU national from Saudi Arabia, applied via an office of Campus France. Campus France is part of the culture section of French embassies that aims to promote French higher education and helps with the application procedure. Lina met with an agent from Campus France in her local city who asked for her basic information including her education background, a written statement of two/three paragraphs indicating why she wanted to study in France and a list of her three choices of university in France. Lina knew she wanted to study in Paris, so she listed three Paris based universities. Once she had completed her French language courses and obtained her B2 certificate, she sent that in to form part of her application. She heard back from the agent within two months and was called in for another appointment to help her choose universities based on her profile. Once she was accepted into her program, her next step was to apply for her student visa (also through Campus France). She was required to provide the following documents:
- An official acceptance letter into an accredited program at a French institution.
- Proof of sufficient funds for living in the country.
- Proof of return ticket home.
- Proof of medical insurance.
- Proof of accommodation.
- Proof of proficiency in French, if you are studying a French-language course.

Upon arrival in France, Lina had to present herself at the *préfecture* for a final yes/no. Every subsequent year, she needed to return to the *préfecture* to renew her visa (passing her final exams, while not mandatory, was an easy assurance that her visa would be renewed yearly).

Please note, applying through Campus France might vary between countries. (Today, the internet platform called Études en France enables students from 44 non-EU countries, including the US, China, and Russia, to apply online to schools in France. See www.campusfrance.org for the complete list of qualifying countries. Nationals from other non-EU countries should contact the nearest Campus France office or French consulate.)

Studying

I was delighted the day I received an email from admissions informing me that I had been accepted to study in a *licence 3* in History of Art at Paris 1. I am glad I decided to study at Paris 1 over Paris 4 (aside from the obvious reason that I would have had to practically restart my studies in a *licence 2*). The course at Paris 1 allowed me to take classes covering a wide range of disciplines (not only visual arts, but also cinema: the birth of French cinema and Hollywood) and across centuries (history of photography and the Italian Renaissance focusing on the works of Michelangelo).

A few things I noticed during my time there (which contrasted with my time at an Irish university): I noticed consistently a lack of participation from students in tutorial classes (until we had teachers who gave us participation grades). Additionally, a much more formal relationship was established between teachers and students. In fact, I remember being chastised in an email for addressing a professor by his first name and had to spend my next email explaining that in Ireland, students and professors are seen as equals at university level and so we go by first names!

A word of advice, if you are going to study at a French university, you need to be serious and work smart and hard. There is much more of a sink or swim attitude here. When I failed a test, I needed to go directly to the teacher to receive help as well as ask advice from a friend of mine who was studying at the Sorbonne and so knew the French system well. The French language requirement of B2/C1 to study should be seen as a bare minimum. I remember my first few weeks being utterly overwhelmed at the speed at which the lecturers spoke. Not only that, but some professors didn't care that I wasn't a native French speaker and docked marks for my grammar in my assignments and exams. However, I was feeling much more at ease by the second semester despite having harder classes. Coming from a non-academic course in English, I was overwhelmed by the idea of having to research and write up a 20-minute presentation (in French no less!) within one to two weeks. By the second semester, I was getting to the point where I was enjoying the researching and writing of this and other assignments.

My year at the Sorbonne not only introduced me to a whole new subject, one which I have great passion for and which I learnt a lot about. It also taught me a lot about myself … how much I can achieve when I persevere, but also how much better I do when I take pressure off myself to be perfect.

Classes Préparatoires aux Grandes Écoles: CPGE or Prépas

Elaine Rothman

In France, unlike the United States or the United Kingdom, entry into an "elite" university level school (called a *grande école*) does not occur immediately after *lycée* (US high school or UK Year 13). Instead, entrance into one of these top-notch schools comes after successfully passing a series of competitive exams *(concours)*. A two-year preparatory program called *Classes Préparatoires aux Grandes Écoles* (CPGE or, simply, "*prépa*") prepares the student for those *concours*. The *"voie royale"* is how the French have traditionally referred to the CPGE/*grande école* education path as it virtually guarantees high-level employment opportunities upon graduation. While this path retains its prestige and value, other schools are gaining popularity, offering a high quality and innovative education to the outstanding student.

There are over 5,000 CPGE programs offered in some 400 establishments across France, the number having increased significantly in the last several years. Three major types of *prépas* correspond to the focus of studies undertaken by the student for the *baccalauréat général*, be it math or science, the social sciences, or literary subjects. Students in a technological *baccalauréat* program may apply to corresponding technological *prépas* as well as to business and literary *prépas*. However, students who have not studied math or science subjects cannot apply to a *prépa technologique* without additional studies. While the implementation of the current *lycée* reforms are eliminating these tracks per se, students will still need the necessary coursework to apply to each type of *prépa*.

A *prépa* is not for everyone. For example, in 2017, 643,000 students obtained the *bac*, and of those, 337,500 earned a *bac général*. Only about 7% of the total or 13% of those with a *bac général* went on to study in a CPGE. Of interest is the fact that about 60% who take this route pursue a scientific *prépa*, 24% follow an economic/business track, and 16% choose a literary track.[1]

Students in a *prépa* are expected to study very hard for two years to be adequately prepared for the *concours*. Sometimes a third year is necessary to improve chances of gaining admission to the student's preferred school. *Prépa* programs are often located in *lycées*, both public and private, although some private *prépas* are not connected with any *lycée* and offer classes on their own premises.

It is important to note that candidates are selected for admission to *prépa* based on their *lycée* grades from *première* (equivalent to US grade 11) and the first two trimesters of *terminale* (US grade 12). Some *prépas* also request grades from *seconde* (US grade 10). This means that the selection of students is made before the *baccalauréat* exam. Students should prepare early if they wish to pursue this path of study, ideally collecting information about the CPGE system while one is still in *seconde*.

The Different Types of *Prépas*

Prépa Scientifique

The scientific *prépas* cover a selected range of scientific subjects, and often target the *concours* for specific *grandes écoles*. The first year in a *prépa scientifique* is referred to as Maths Sup (*Mathématiques supérieures*) and the second year is called Maths Spé (*Mathématiques spéciales*), regardless of the science curriculum path chosen.

Students in a *prépa scientifique* must select among one of four curriculum paths (*voies*) to follow, chosen in accordance with their subject preferences, affinities, and future career goals. These paths are summarized below. It should be mentioned that access to the *concours* for a particular *grande école* may be open to students applying from different *voies* and even different *filières* (*scientifique, économique-commerciale*, etc.). Thus, if the student is determined to attend a specific *grande école*, it would be advisable to look at the number of students previously accepted to that school from each *voie* or curriculum path (and *filière*, if applicable) and consequently, consider the program which offers the highest probability of acceptance.

The four *voies* offered in a *prépa scientifique* are:

- **MPSI** (Mathematics, Physics, and Engineering Science) the first year, followed by either MP (Math and Physics) or PSI (Physics and Engineering Science) the second year. Computer Science *(Informatique)* has now been added to MPSI as an option. Generally students can expect to spend 34+ hours in class per week.

- **PCSI** (Physics, Chemistry, and Engineering Science) the first year, followed by PC (Physics and Chemistry) or PSI (Physics and Engineering Science). Two hours per week of Computer Science has recently been added bringing total class time to 36+ hours weekly.

- **PTSI** (Physics, Technology, and Engineering Science) followed by PT (Physics and Technology) or PSI (Physics and Engineering Science). This requires some 35+ hours per week including two hours of Computer Science.

- **BCPST** (Biology, Chemistry, Physics, and Earth Sciences) followed by BCPST2. This *voie* also prepares for the *concours* to veterinary school. Students have one and a half hours of Computer Science in their weekly total of 33 hours of coursework.

Based on grades obtained during the first year of *prépa*, the best students are selected to take the "star" *(étoile)* courses (e.g., PC* or MP*) in the second year. These are advanced classes, which better prepare students for the *concours*, thereby increasing chances of admission to the very highly selective schools such as École Polytechnique, (often referred to as "X"), and CentraleSupélec. Even if a student is not admitted into a star class he/she may be motivated to try even harder and might nonetheless perform well in the *concours* for these schools.

Lycée students in a technological *bac* program *(bac* STL - *sciences et technologies de laboratoire* ; *bac* STAV - *sciences et technologies de l'agronomie et du vivant;* or *bac* STI2D - *sciences et technologies de l'industrie et du développement durable)* who envision studying in a *grande école* must apply to a *prépa* corresponding to their specific coursework. These *prépas* provide more practical and technical training than the more theoretical *prépas scientifiques,* however, these programs do prepare students for the *concours* for admission to numerous prestigious *grandes écoles* including École Polytechnique, Institut Mines-Télécom, and CentraleSupélec. These more technological *prépas* are:

- **TSI** (Technology and Industrial Sciences) for students with a *bac* STI2D or STL; preparation for engineering *concours*
- **TPC** (Technology, Physics, and Chemistry) for students with a *bac* STL; preparation for chemistry *concours*
- **TB** (Technology and Biology) for students with either a *bac* STL or STAV; preparation for agronomy, biology, applied science, and veterinary *concours*.

Nonetheless, only about 1.5% of those who have earned a technological *bac* pursue studies in a CPGE.

Prépa ATS *(adaptation technicien supérieur):* Graduates of the DUT or BTS post-*bac* technical programs who wish to integrate into an engineering school must first complete a year of a special *prépa* called ATS to prepare for the *concours* reserved for these candidates.

Prépa Economique et Commerciale

The programs preparing students for the *concours* for elite business and management schools are sometimes also referred to as Prépa HEC (after the well-known *grande école,* HEC).

A student will study in one of the following curriculum paths *(voies):*

- **ECS** (Scientific option): This curriculum puts an emphasis on mathematics (algebra, statistics, probability, and algorithms) as well as social sciences. Economics, cultural studies, as well as two modern languages, complete the curriculum. A student must have taken math and science courses to be eligible for a *prépa* ECS. Expect 31 hours of class per week with one hour dedicated to Computer Science.
- **ECE** (Economics option): This path focuses on statistics and economics (macro and micro), cultural studies, philosophy, literature and history with an emphasis on current events, plus two modern languages (English is mandatory). Some

prépas do not accept students from *bac* S into a *voie* ECE (since students with a *bac* S would have an unfair advantage due to their advanced level in math). These classes are for *bac* ES students. There are 30 class hours a week including one hour of Computer Science. It remains to be seen how this option will change with the latest *bac* reform.

- **ECT** (Technology option): Economics, mathematics (statistics and probability), history of technology, modern languages (English is mandatory), cultural studies, management, corporate/organizational strategies and law compose the curriculum. This option is generally open to graduates of the *bac* STMG *(sciences et technologie du management et de la gestion* — one of the technology *bac* diplomas). Generally, 33 hours per week of class, with Computer Science included within the required six hours of mathematics.

- **ENS D1:** This path covers studies in law, economics, and management and prepares students primarily for the competitive exams *(concours)* necessary for applying to the École normale supérieure Rennes, but also certain business schools, IEPs *(Instituts d'études politiques)* and CELSA. With an emphasis on law, students are also enrolled at a university and follow a law curriculum three days a week. The two years of *prépa* ENS D1 count towards a *licence droit*.

- **ENS D2:** Students spend 12 hours per week studying six subject areas: mathematics and statistics, monetary analysis and/or political economics, economy, methodology, and foreign languages. At the same time, ENS D2 students are enrolled in a *licence* program for economics and management, attending classes at a university three days a week. The *prépa* ENS D2 prepares students for the concours ENS Paris-Saclay (formerly ENS Cachan), certain business schools, ENSAI (École nationale de la statistique et d'analyse de l'information), IEPs *(Instituts d'études politiques)*, and CELSA.

Prépa ATS *(adaptation technician supérieur)* Economics and Management: For students with a BTS or DUT, this one-year program offers preparation for business school *concours*, while at the same time permits completion of the third year *licence* program.

Prépa Littéraire

These programs prepare students who have a strong interest in the humanities and social sciences, as well as good critical analysis skills, for the *concours* to the École normale supérieure (ENS). This course of study can also lead to admission, via a special *concours* or equivalency procedure, to further studies in schools of business, communications and journalism, as well as master's level programs in universities, political science institutions and even military schools.

Over half of the students enrolled in a *prépa littéraire* hold a *bac* L *(littéraire)*, but the program is also open to students with a *bac* S *(scientifique)* or ES *(économique et social)*, each accounting for some 20% of class enrollment. **Keep in mind, the *bac* reforms eliminate the S, ES, and L nomenclature as of 2021.** Hence, *lycée* coursework should be a guiding factor in choosing an appropriate *prépa*. The first year of study, Prépa ENS Lettres, is popularly referred to as "*hypokhâgne*" or "*Lettres supérieures*", and the second as "*khâgne*". Students generally have 28 to 32 hours per week of course work, with an optional five to seven additional hours.

The first year courses are identical. Second year courses, however, are more tailored to the *concours* for certain *grandes écoles,* and therefore the curriculum is more specialized. Among the following *prépas,* the first two emphasize literature and social sciences.

- **Prépa Lettres Ulm** is geared to the student who enjoys classical literature, Latin and Greek, and the study of ancient civilizations. It is called "Ulm" because the corresponding ENS is located on this street in Paris. Students in this *prépa* may also take the *concours* for admission to École nationale des Chartes.

- **Prépa Lettres Lyon** is the second year of the *prépa lettres* and teaches many of the same subjects as above but emphasizes modern languages and literature, philosophy, history and geography. This track also prepares for admission by concours to the ENS Paris-Saclay.

- **Prépa Lettres et Sciences Sociales** (LSS, also known as *prépa* B/L) is geared to students with a science or social sciences background. The curriculum covers the humanities, contemporary civilizations, social sciences, and economics and includes a strong component of mathematics. In addition to the ENS Lyon, Paris-Ulm, and Paris-Saclay, a student in this *prépa* may aim for admission to to the national schools of statistics, (ENSAI or ENSAE ParisTech - École nationale de la statistique et de l'administration économique). Also of interest the *prépa* LSS prepares students for the *concours lettres et sciences économiques et sociales* (LSES) permitting entry to business schools, engineering schools and ENSG (Écoles nationale des sciences géographique), CELSA, Université Paris-Dauphine, ESIT (École supérieure d'interprète et de traducteur), and ISMaPP (Institut supérieur du management public et politique).

- **Prépa Chartes** places a strong emphasis on history as it prepares students for the extremely selective concours for admission to the École nationale des Chartes. Because this institution, which trains future museum curators and archivists admits such a small number of students, those who do not gain entrance after *prépas* often continue their studies in universities or specialized schools.

- **Prépa Arts et Design** is for applied arts students planning on a teaching career in the arts or a career in design. Students in a *bac STD2A (sciences et technologies du design et des arts appliqués)* or a *bac général* program with an emphasis on arts study may apply for this *prépa.* This *prépa* prepares students for the design *concours* to enter ENS Paris-Saclay (formerly ENS Cachan). Only seven students are accepted per year. In addition, this *prépa* program prepares students for the Écoles nationales supérieures d'art and for the Écoles supérieures d'arts appliqués.

- **Prépa Saint-Cyr Lettres** is offered through three military *lycées,* and prepares students for the entry exam for the ESM (École spéciale militaire) Saint-Cyr.

The *Concours*

The two years of intensive *prépa* classes lead to the *concours*, a very competitive series of exams that will determine one's acceptance to one or more *grandes écoles*. The *concours* are not ordinary exams where one earns a score or a pass/fail grade, but rather a competition to obtain the best possible ranking. The objective is to do better than other students taking the exam, as acceptance into a *grande école* is determined by one's ranking. Hence, a *grande école* with 50 openings will accept the 50 top performers.

The *concours* comprise several individual exams called *épreuves*. These include written exams *(épreuves écrites)*, followed a few weeks later by oral exams *(épreuves orales)* for those who qualify to take them by virtue of their ranking on the written exams.

The student must sign up for the *concours* for admission to his/her targeted school(s) in late autumn/early winter of the second year of *prépa*. It is crucial to be aware of and remember the deadlines for registration. Certain *grandes écoles* organize common exams *(banque commune d'épreuves)* for their group of schools. This allows students to test for several schools without taking a separate *concours* for each one. The registration fees can vary greatly (for engineering schools anywhere from 50-300 €).

The *concours* begin in late April with the *épreuves écrites*. This two-week period is quite stressful. Although the student may do very well, his/her final result will depend on how well he or she ranks compared to the other candidates.

If the ranking obtained on the written exams is high enough, the student is deemed "*admissible*", meaning he/she has qualified to take the *épreuves orales*. (The student may be *admissible* to several schools.) Taking the oral exams is one step closer to being accepted. Upon completion of the *épreuves orales* the student is attributed a new ranking taking into account the ranking already attained on the written exams. Should the final ranking *(classement)* qualify the student for admission to one or a number of schools he/she is accepted *(admis)*.

Once final rankings are assigned there will be a short shuffling period as the higher-ranked students make their choice among the schools to which they have been accepted, thus opening spaces on the waiting lists. Students monitor the progress of their rankings on the internet.

If a student is disappointed with the outcome of his/her ranking (i.e., the school(s) to which he/she was accepted) and hopes to attain a better ranking on another try, it is possible to make a request to repeat the second year of *prépa*. This option is subject to approval by the *conseil de classe* (a council of teachers and program administrators). A student can repeat the second year only once and he or she may wish to change institutions for that final year. (Repeating the first year of *prépa* is not permitted.) The potential benefits of repeating the second year should not be underestimated. It often happens that this third year brings both personal and intellectual maturity and the reward is a higher *classement* in the *concours*. However, depending on the *concours*, a student repeating the second year (i.e., "*cuber*" or to be a "*5/2*") may be somewhat at a disadvantage compared to a student who has not repeated, because the latter may be given a certain number of bonus points *(bonification)*; this is more often the case in the engineering *concours*. An extra year of studying might yield a ranking that is no better, or perhaps worse. One should think through the pros and cons of repeating another year, perhaps changing *lycées*, or even accepting admission to a *grande école* with a lesser reputation than the one targeted. Much personal questioning will be necessary at this point to determine whether the professional path envisaged would truly require a further year's dedication to *prépa* studies.

Another option is to continue at a university, providing that the student has previously registered through the concurrent enrollment procedure *(inscription cumulative)*. This procedure is now mandatory to avoid losing one or more academic years in the event that the student does not enter a *grande école* or wishes to leave the *prépa* program at any point. The *inscription cumulative* allows the student to obtain credit for studies completed in *prépa*, depending on the curriculum followed, existing agreements between the *prépa* and the university, grades obtained and the assiduousness of the student. *Prépa* students are exempted from attending university classes but may have to take final exams, allowing automatic validation of coursework by the university and the possibility of transfer to another university if desired.

The *Prépa* Experience

The two years of *prépa* are said to be the toughest stage of the "*voie royale*" and among the most challenging years in French higher education. Students should choose a path in which they have a demonstrated talent, strong interest for the subject matter, and a willingness to work very hard. They must also have the physical stamina to withstand the highly demanding schedule. Class schedules are challenging. With homework, it is possible that a student will be studying 60 or 70 hours a week. In addition to the long hours devoted to regular classes and studying, students take individual or group oral quizzes known as *colles* (or *khôlles*) at regular intervals, outside of normal school hours. Grades on the *colles*, as well as on quarterly written evaluations, are usually much lower than *lycée* grades, and students are ranked. Morale takes a blow, but it is most helpful to be aware—and constantly reminded—of this aspect. A certain bonding among the students takes place as they go through this school of "tough love and hard knocks".

Furthermore, it should be noted that almost any French employer acknowledges that a two-year stint in a *prépa* is testimony to a student's—and future employee's—ability to persevere, withstand pressure, and think logically and precisely. Not only has a *prépa* student had to absorb a huge amount of information but he/she has acquired new methods of reasoning and perfected his/her time-management skills. *Prépa* is often considered a "sacrifice" of two years, but the richness of the experience and the knowledge gained can make it an excellent educational choice in its own right.

> *Students should choose a path in which they have a demonstrated talent, strong interest for the subject matter, and a willingness to work very hard.*

In the beginning of *prépa*, students should expect to feel overwhelmed. A certain amount of attrition is not uncommon but after the first semester, students settle into the routine and have learned to better organize their time. Parents should be advised to provide as much support as possible throughout the entire program—especially the period leading up to and following the *concours*.

A good piece of news is that once a student is out of *prépa* and in a *grande école*, the situation improves. Courses are more aligned with one's field of interest, competition is less intense and bonding continues among the students in an even more permanent way. Professional networking for the future often begins here.

Making the Decision to Apply to a CPGE *(Prépa)*

Visit Education Fairs *(Salons d'Éducation)*
There are education fairs organized by *l'Étudiant* and *Studyrama* throughout France that are specific to the *grandes écoles* and include areas devoted to the *prépas*. Students and parents can talk to representatives of schools, attend conferences, and purchase publications. Students in *terminale* can come with photocopies of their grades and show them to the counselors or the representatives of certain CPGEs to obtain an opinion of their chances of being accepted into a program.

Another fair, held annually in Paris, is the Salon de Concours et Prépas. The dates of all these salons are easily found on the internet or from *lycée* teachers or counselors.

Another important education fair is the Salon Postbac, usually held at the beginning of January in Paris. This fair is similar to the others and in addition offers information sessions on the internet-based application system (www.parcoursup.fr) used by most of the *prépas* and universities. Parcoursup supplies questionnaires to help students determine their priorities. Students will learn about Parcoursup from their *lycées* where they will be provided with instructions for the application procedure.

For students in the Paris area, le Salon européen de l'éducation held in the fall incorporates three school fairs: Salon de l'Étudiant, Salon l'Aventure des métiers, and le Salon de l'Orientation – Onisep. This is a good starting point for all students, even as early as the class of *troisième*, and can be particularly helpful for those who are weighing multiple post-*bac* paths.

Before attending an education fair, students should check the website of the fair to find out which *prépas* will be represented. They should also look at the individual school websites so that they can prepare a list of any questions they might have. The fairs are usually crowded and the students who have prepared for their visits will be able to seek out more quickly the representatives of the schools that best correspond to their interests.

Visit the CIO *(Centre d'Information et Orientation)*
In addition to consulting the library resources or talking to the counselors in one's own *lycée*, the student can go to the CIO closest to home and consult Onisep handbooks (www.onisep.fr) and directories. One can also meet individually with a counselor and take career aptitude tests which can help determine which type of studies are most suitable for one's talents and interests.

Consider Your Academic Profile
While *prépas* seek the best students from a *lycée*, they particularly look for students who work hard, are invested in their studies, and have the ability to progress. Admissions committees will look at grades and will appreciate a student whose performance has improved with time. They will also consider teachers' evaluations as well

as the school director's assessment of the student's potential to do well in *prépa*. The student's age may also be considered. It is always helpful to talk with the teachers and/or the Principal *(directeur* or *proviseur)* of one's *lycée* to get feedback. The *prépa* admissions committees are aware of the ranking and reputation of *lycées*, so a 14/20 in an academically challenging *lycée* would be deemed a better grade than a 16/20 in a less demanding *lycée*. The admissions committee, however, is most concerned with the student's grades in the core subjects related to the desired *prépa*. For example, in a *prépa scientifique*, one's grades in math and physics will be very important; however, at least adequate grades in French and foreign languages are also expected.

Reflect on Possible Career Choices
To make the search for the right school a smoother process, the student must be able to answer the following questions, especially the first one. This will demand some careful thought and reflection. A visit to the CIO and a battery of career aptitude tests will help answer some of these questions:

- What type of a job and career do you want?
- Which *grandes écoles* will lead you to a job in that sector?
- Which *concours* must you take for those schools?
- What *prépa* program must you enter to prepare for these *concours*?
- Are there certain *voies* (such as MPSI or PCSI) that you should follow in order to access the *concours* for your target school(s)?

Evaluate the Schools and Their Programs
One important criterion in choosing a *prépa* is to consider the number of its students who have successfully passed the *concours* and gained admission to a *grande école*. (This information is available from Onisep and various online sources, including the websites of the CPGEs.) Nevertheless, there is another significant factor that is equally important: assessing the probability of being accepted by the targeted *prépa*. Since the national application procedure, Parcoursup, limits students to 10 CPGE choices, it is now required to choose at least one "safety" school even while aiming for the more prestigious *prépas*. Students should establish their list of preferences with advice from their teachers or counselors. In any case, it is best to apply to *prépas* that correspond to the student's interests, academic strengths, and intended career path.

A school's reputation for "nice" teachers and treatment of students should be investigated ahead of time. A reliable means is getting in touch with past and present students to find out about the general atmosphere of the *prépa*. In addition, many *prépas* hold an "Open House" *(Portes Ouvertes)* mid-winter, providing an excellent opportunity for first-hand verification. Prospective students should make every effort to attend even if they had previous contact with representatives of the different schools at education fairs. In fact, the *prépa* teachers are often present and can counsel students regarding the compatibility of their academic profile with the *prépa* program.

Students planning to attend *prépas scientifiques* should verify that all of their desired classes are offered during the second year—some of the smaller *prépa* programs do not offer all second-year classes, such as a PC or PC* class. In that case, students studying PCSI, for example, in their first year and who are interested in taking either PC or PC* in the second year may have to transfer in order to take the courses that they need.

Consider location and travel time. It is important not to waste time in traveling to and from the school. A good rule of thumb would be no more than a 30-minute trip each way. For those attending a CPGE away from home, housing is an important issue: Are there dormitory rooms *(internat)*? How much would local housing cost? Does the *prépa* offer a meal program *(internat-externé)* or have a student cafeteria? This is a particularly important point since it would enable a student to remain "on campus" in the evenings and allow more time for studying. It is a well-known fact that *prépa* students do not have time to shop for groceries or prepare meals!

Application Procedure for CPGE

Students applying to CPGE use the same internet-based system as applicants for university programs, Parcoursup (www.parcoursup.fr). As from December of *terminale*, students can access the Parcoursup website for an explanation of the application process. Students can make their applications via the site from mid-January to mid-March. The exact dates may change from year-to-year. In 2020, March 12th is the last day to declare choices *(vœux)* and April 2nd is the last day to finalize choices. Remember that the Parcoursup system is extremely precise. Deadline dates must be respected scrupulously and incomplete applications will be rejected. A parent or someone else experienced with the process should oversee the student's application to ensure that ALL requirements are met several days before deadlines.

Some schools require different application procedures to be followed. Institutions such as Université Paris-Dauphine as well as some engineering schools with *prépas intégrées* are not included on the Parcoursup website and must be applied to directly.

A word of warning: do not wait until the last day during any of the application stages. Some students have been unable to access the Parcoursup website due to the great number of students trying to connect close to the deadline dates. Despite protests in preceding years from parents and students, no exceptions were allowed to these latecomers. If a student does not sign up by the specified date, he/she must wait until the end of June and hope to get into a *prépa* that still has openings.

> *Consider location and travel time. It is important not to waste time in traveling to and from the school. A good rule of thumb would be no more than a 30-minute trip each way.*

In mid-January, students receive a registration number and a confidential code so that they can sign up on the website. In this first stage of the application process, students list their individual school and program choices *(vœux or demandes)*; students can list up to ten. Secondary requests are possible for some programs (such as dormitory accommodations). A change from the previous system is that students no longer need to prioritize their selection. In 2020, March 12th was the last day to declare choices *(vœux)* and April 2nd was the last day to finalize choices. Documents required to support an application may include photocopies of grades, letters of motivation, etc., depending on the program or school chosen.

Some CPGE also provide housing *(internat)*. The request for *internat* is counted as a *sous-vœu* on the Parcoursup site. Most schools with dormitories do not have enough space for all the students they accept. Therefore, it is advisable to make two requests for each *prépa* that offers housing: one with *internat* and one without *(sans internat)*. Together, these would count as a single *sous-vœu*.

Note that, if a student is accepted into a school that cannot provide a room in the *internat*, the school will provide addresses of other student lodging *(foyers)*. *Internats* and *foyers* offer separate spaces for boys and for girls, so your choice may be limited by space available for your gender. Also, some *foyers* accept only students aged 18 or older, so it is best to apply early, well before Parcoursup results are given.

Students need to verify that their applications are complete and have been received by the schools by mid-May. This is done via the website, which students should check regularly.

By the end of May the admissions committees of the individual schools will have examined the *dossiers* and uploaded the lists of their preferred candidates to the Parcoursup site. The committees select the students based on their grades and letters of motivation. Students must confirm their choice of school and program of study by mid-July.

The previous process of selecting a program and school has been greatly simplified. The student now makes just ten *vœux* and once they receive their acceptances, it's the student's turn to decide. There is a fallback procedure for students who fail to receive any offer. Students at that point may still connect to the Parcoursup website from the end of June to mid-September to apply for admittance to a CPGE that has still not filled all its places. These students may ask for individual or group help finding a school or program to continue their studies.

Prépas Intégrées

An alternative to the CPGE system for future engineers or business school students is to apply to a *grande école* offering a *prépa intégrée*, a preparatory program integrated within a five-year program of study. Students are admitted to this type of school based on their high school grades and/or a *concours* taken during their last trimester of high school. In these schools, a system of regular exams administered throughout the five-year program enables students to earn an engineering or business degree without some of the stress associated with the CPGE system. It is important to note, however, that just because a student is accepted by a school offering a *prépa intégrée*, he/she will not necessarily be allowed to stay in the school for all five years. The student will still have to earn acceptable grades in order to continue to the next year.

Schools offering a *prépa intégrée* have varying degrees of prestige and recognition with future employers. Some of them are very specialized, so students should look carefully at the curricula to make sure that the schools correspond to their career plans. A number of these schools allow select students to study abroad for one year or more, which could be a good opportunity for students interested in international careers. A well-chosen school delivers a first-rate education and excellent job opportunities without the stress of a *concours* at the end of two years of study.

One way of evaluating a *prépa intégrée* is to check its rankings on the annual listings published by the magazines *Le Point* or *L'Express* entitled *"Palmarès des Écoles d'Ingénieurs"* or *"Palmarès des Écoles de Commerce"*. One can compare criteria such as statistics on how long it takes to get a job upon graduation and the average salary of graduates.

References and Resources

- Ministry of Higher Education, Research and Innovation website on CPGE: www.enseignementsup-recherche.gouv.fr/pid25333/classes-preparatoires-aux-grandes-ecoles-c.p.g.e.html
- Onisep, a very useful comprehensive site with many publications: www.onisep.fr
- Onisep website for CPGE: www.onisep.fr/Choisir-mes-etudes/Apres-le-bac/Organisation-des-etudes-superieures/Les-classes-preparatoires-aux-grandes-ecoles-CPGE
- Onisep website for *Prépas Scientifiques:* www.onisep.fr/Choisir-mes-etudes/Apres-le-bac/Organisation-des-etudes-superieures/Les-classes-preparatoires-aux-grandes-ecoles-CPGE/Les-prepas-scientifiques
- Onisep website for *Prépa Economiques et Commerciales:* www.onisep.fr/Choisir-mes-etudes/Apres-le-bac/Organisation-des-etudes-superieures/Les-classes-preparatoires-aux-grandes-ecoles-CPGE/Les-prepas-economiques-et-commerciales
- Onisep website for *Prépas Littéraires:* www.onisep.fr/Choisir-mes-etudes/Apres-le-bac/Organisation-des-etudes-superieures/CPGE-FILIERES/Les-prepas-litteraires
- List of CPGEs: www.parcoursup.fr and http://prepas.org
- List of *grandes écoles* included in the Conférence des Grandes Écoles: www.cge.asso.fr
- List of the *concours* for engineering/scientific schools: www.scei-concours.org
- List of *concours* for business schools: www.concours-bce.com
- Information on *prépas* and *concours* for business schools: www.prepa-hec.org
- Information on Sciences Po Paris: www.sciencespo.fr
- Magazines for *lycéens:* www.phosphore.fr and www.letudiant.fr
- Information centers for orientation: www.education.gouv.fr/cid160/les-lieux-d-information-de-l-orientation.html&xtmc=cio&xtnp=1&xtcr=1#les-centres-d-information-et-d-orientation-c-i-o-
- Centre d'Information et de Documentation Jeunesse: www.cidj.com
- Open Houses *(Portes Ouvertes):* www.onisep.fr/Pres-de-chez-vous/Ile-de-France/Creteil-Paris-Versailles/Agenda-de-l-orientation/Portes-ouvertes/Portes-ouvertes-dans-l-enseignement-superieur-en-Ile-de-France3
- Salon Postbac: www.reussirpostbac.fr/salon/presentation-du-salon
- Salon de l'Étudiant: www.letudiant.fr/etudes/salons/salon-letudiant-paris
- Salon Studyrama: www.studyrama.com/salons
- Individual websites of the CPGEs.
- *"Réforme du bac, continuum: comment évoluent les classes préparatoires?"*, Olivier Rollot, 27 Nov 2018: https://blog.headway-advisory.com/ou-vont-les-classes-preparatoires
- Additional information on scientific *prépas:* https://forum.prepas.org
- Additional information on literary *prépas:* www.etudes-litteraires.com/forum

Endnotes

1. www.education.gouv.fr/cid118789/resultats-de-la-session-de-juin-du-baccalaureat-2017.html; www.sup-admission.com/2017/12/cpge-nombre-etudiants

Student Anecdotes

I chose my *prépa* as it was close to home, offered an interesting course of study, is renowned, and cheap (around 200 € with parallel registration at the neighboring university). Also, I would be going with friends. My track (MPSI-MP) was very demanding and the level of my class was high, but it prepared me for the *concours* to the *grandes écoles* very well. The work environment was motivating and very helpful and the social setting was very good. The classes were small (about 130 students), you got to know everyone, and share fun times in the neighboring dorms. My *bac* S at a public *lycée* prepared me well for the *prépa*, but nonetheless I was at the bottom of my class for most of the time. Nonetheless, I was motivated to keep working because the class level was high, the students and teachers were helpful, and the social setting was very good. The objective was to beat the other schools, not to compete with your classmates. I would advise not to take *prépa* grades too seriously, but to get into a school that can push you as high as you can go.   – *Nathalie*

I chose my *prépa intégrée* because it provided a full business curriculum with official certifications, is renowned, and has an extensive alumni network. The student body is mainly French, however, we did have a mandatory semester abroad. The only regret I have is not having joined an association, which is always beneficial in the eyes of future employers.   – *Jennifer*

I chose this *prépa* to keep my options open: I'd like to work in France but am unsure about whether research or engineering is more interesting to me. I enjoy getting to know everyone in my class as we are together for every subject. The high number of class hours helps me stay active and focused. I find almost every subject fascinating and the atmosphere among the students is great. The academics are structured and fast-paced, and largely focus on preparing us for the *concours* to the *grandes écoles*. One great part of *prépa* that is particularly helpful for preparing for the *concours* is the *colles* (two hours per week of oral exercise, three students per teacher). These give students the opportunity to ask questions about something they didn't understand in class. The class atmosphere is great and I joined the orchestra, even though the selection of extracurricular activities is quite limited. Other club activities are more closely related to the subjects studied in class, such as "Physics Olympics" or "Galois theory in LLG". My *lycée* definitely prepared me well for *prépa* in terms of the subject matter but the rhythm is a serious "step up"! I decided to live in a *foyer* (residence) next to the school so I don't have to worry about shopping or cleaning, which simplified things for me. I go back home every weekend so I get to see my family often. If you enjoy sciences, math and physics, *prépa* is the place for you.   – *Jack*

Grandes Écoles

Elaine Rothman

Traditionally, the *grandes écoles* have been considered the elite of French institutions of higher education. These very selective schools, founded independently of the university system, are unique to France. Candidates for these schools typically gain admission after completing at least two years of special preparatory programs called *classes préparatoires aux grandes écoles* or *prépas*, and successfully passing written and oral exams. In recent years, efforts have been made to open the *grandes écoles* to students applying from other educational backgrounds. Students considering these particular schools should be academically inclined and have the stamina and motivation to withstand the pressure of this highly demanding path of study. (See chapter "*Classes Préparatoires aux Grandes Écoles:* CPGE or *Prépas*".)

A recent development is the establishment of consortiums and associations of *grandes écoles* and other eminent institutions of higher learning in France. Currently there are 19 consortiums, known as *Communautés d'universités et d'établissements* (ComUE), and seven *associations*, located throughout the country.[1] These groupings of by and large public institutions of higher learning, allow for the coordination of program offerings and research within a given geographic region, facilitate exchange among faculty and students, and promote the visibility and recognition of French institutions on the national and international stage.

A History of the *Grandes Écoles*

The origin of the *grande école* system dates back to the 17th century when an oral entrance exam in mathematics, created for the military engineering corps, led to the establishment of a military engineering school with selective entry. Other engineering schools were established soon thereafter, including the École royale des ponts et chaussées (1747), École royale des mines (1783), and École centrale des travaux publics (1794), the future École Polytechnique.

The first business school, École supérieure de commerce de Paris was founded in 1819 by a group of economists and merchants. HEC Paris (École des hautes études commerciales de Paris) was founded by the Chamber of Commerce of Paris in 1881. Regional *chambres de commerce* and private entities established other *grandes écoles* for the study of business throughout France.

The École normale supérieure, the first national teacher training institution, was founded in 1794 in Paris. Today this institution is considered to be among the top university-level schools in the world.

These *grandes écoles* benefit from immediate name recognition throughout France and often abroad. Their long-standing reputation as the "gold standard" continues today, however, numerous other institutions of higher learning offer an equally excellent education and are gaining renown.

Admissions

The admissions procedure to the *grandes écoles* is complex and linked to a student's performance, ability, and a little bit of luck. It most often requires two (and sometimes three) years of *prépa* and a high ranking on competitive exams known as *concours*, consisting of both written and oral exams *(épreuves)*. The student's ranking on the written exams will determine if he/she may go on to take the oral exams. These exams are exceptionally challenging, as the jury looks for knowledge as well as leadership skills, maturity, and the quality of clear, concise, and well-presented responses. Many schools use a common exam *(concours commun)*, saving the student who is applying to several institutions both time and money.

> *Many grandes écoles benefit from immediate name recognition throughout France and often abroad.*

Some *grandes écoles* offer five-year programs with an integrated preparatory program *(prépa intégrée)* in which the first two years of study replace the more general and traditional *prépa*, dispensing a curriculum more specifically related to the later program of study. Students opting for an institution with a *prépa intégrée* enter the program directly after the *baccalauréat*, thus avoiding the stress and unknowns of the *concours* that follow the two years of the traditional *prépa*. These schools, while not as prestigious as the *grandes écoles* entered following a traditional *prépa* path, do offer good employment opportunities, albeit often with a lower level of responsibility and pay scale. Their curricula need to be considered carefully as some of these schools produce excellent generalists while others specialize in more narrow disciplines.

Efforts have been made in recent years to accept students coming from the university system, thus allowing those who did not enter a *prépa* immediately after high school the opportunity to attend a *grande école* later. These students may have studied medicine, law, or other subjects, and earned a university degree *(DUT, licence, or master)* or a BTS *(brevet de technicien supérieur* – advanced technician's certificate). Holders of the DUT or BTS must first complete a year of a special *prépa* called ATS *(adaptation technicien supérieur)* to prepare for the *concours* reserved for these candidates. Students are usually accepted based on their application file *(dossier)* and the results of the *concours*. There are some *grandes écoles* that select students based solely on their *dossiers*.

The admissions procedure for foreign students is different, but equally competitive. (See chapter "Graduate Study in France for the International Student".) Foreign students need to present an excellent *dossier* and must demonstrate proficiency in French for programs not taught in English. In recent years, there has been a burgeoning of programs dispensed entirely in English; admission is still highly selective. Again, a *concours* may be part of the admissions process.

Some Features of the *Grandes Écoles*

Most *grandes écoles* have a small student body compared to the universities, with enrollment ranging from 1,500 to 4,000 students. Class format typically ranges from large lectures to small seminars. Students are often encouraged to work in teams, using the latest technology for their projects and case studies.

The teaching staff is usually composed of a small core of permanent professors as well as many other teachers including visiting professors, businessmen, consultants, experts, researchers, lecturers, and language teachers.

> *Programs that alternate periods of coursework with apprenticeships may be offered, enabling students to gain valuable work skills and earn salaries. Some companies will hire a student who has performed well.*

Schools establish partnerships with corporations to enable students to complete one or more internships. This allows students to benefit from participating in the working world and to experience what will be expected of them in their future careers. Furthermore, these partnerships permit the *grandes écoles* to adapt their programs to the demands of business and industry. An increasing number of *grandes écoles* require their students to complete internships abroad in a foreign language.

Some *grandes écoles* (as well as some universities) offer degree programs that alternate periods of coursework with paid apprenticeships in the working world *(formation en alternance)*. For example, a student will alternate between working for three months and attending classes for three months during a two-year period. *Formation en alternance* is an option to take into consideration when making the choice of a *grande école,* as it enables students to not only gain valuable work skills in internationally known companies but also to earn salaries with advantages such as retirement points, health benefits, and eligibility for unemployment compensation. This prolonged professional experience which can help pay for tuition and living expenses also gives the student an advantage when entering the job market. Sometimes the participating company will then hire the student who has performed well while working in *alternance*.

Student Life

Some *grandes écoles* have a campus with student centers, dormitories, and cafeterias although these are not quite comparable to what is customary in the United States. After two years of the pressure of *prépa*, the *grande école* experience often seems "easier" and "freer" for many students. Indeed, some of the students have a bit of trouble settling down and getting back to their studies after they have reached their objective of getting into a *grande école*. In contrast, those entering a *grande école* from an alternate route of studies may require a greater period of adjustment as they get used to a heavy workload.

Extracurricular life is very rich, with most *grandes écoles* offering abundant artistic, cultural, and social activities as well as student clubs and sports. The BDE *(bureau des élèves)* is a student-run office that organizes activities and events and serves as a student information hub. Participation in such activities is usually considered an essential part of the *grande école* experience and prospective employers may evaluate job candidates on their participation for qualities such as leadership, team spirit, entrepreneurship, values, and persistence. It is also during these activities that lifetime friendships and future networking contacts are often made.

Diplomas

The *grandes écoles* award master's level diplomas, certified by the French government *(diplôme visé par le ministre chargé de l'enseignement supérieure)*. Until recently, the *grandes écoles* awarded their own diplomas, but since the Bologna Process, which aimed to harmonize the higher education systems within Europe, most of them now award master's degrees conforming to the *licence-master-doctorat* (LMD) structure. (See "Glossary of Terms", page 123.)

The CTI *(Commission des titres d'ingénieur)* is the official accrediting agency for engineering schools and diplomas in France. The *grandes écoles de commerce et de management* are certified by the French governmental agency, CEFDG *(Commission d'évaluation des formations et diplômes de gestion)*. Many of them are also accredited by one or more professional associations: AACSB International, AMBA (Association of MBAs) and EQUIS (European Quality Improvement System).

It is advisable to choose a school that is certified since its diploma will be recognized internationally and will likely have more value on the job market. In addition, certification simplifies the process of obtaining a school loan or scholarship.

Tuition fees for *grandes écoles* range from several hundred euros for public schools to several thousand euros for private schools. For French nationals, business schools such as HEC and ESSEC charge around 15,000 € per year plus room and board. *Bourses* (scholarships) are available to reduce the costs of attendance.

The Schools

Detailed information about the *grandes écoles* is available through several sources: Onisep website and publications, school websites, libraries in the *lycées*, national information centers (CIO and CIDJ), specialized magazines, and education fairs. (See chapter "*Classes Préparatoires aux Grandes Écoles:* CPGE or *Prépas*".)

Engineering Schools

There are over 154 public or private engineering schools in France considered *grandes écoles*. The domains studied can be general (engineering science and technology) or more specialized, such as engineering for agronomy, biology, chemistry, aeronautics, electricity, telecommunications, transportation, and computer science. In addition to scientific subjects, students can take courses in finance and management. All now have computer science classes and some specialize in this discipline. (See chapter "Graduate Study in France for the International Student" for additional information.) Some examples of renowned engineering schools are École Polytechnique, Institut Mines-Télécom, CentraleSupélec, and École nationale des ponts et chaussées (ENPC).

Business and Management Schools

Although there are over 150 business and/or management schools in France, only 42 are members of the Conférence des Grandes Écoles. These *grandes écoles*, which award master's level degrees, are usually entered following a *prépa* and *concours*, and are considered the most prestigious business schools in France. The government recognizes many of the other management schools but there are different levels of certification, which the student should verify. These schools prepare students for careers in diverse domains such as auditing, marketing, human resources, finance, logistics, and purchasing, to name just a few. Business and Management schools all charge tuition. While fees have increased significantly in the last few years, they are still considerably less than the cost of a US education. (See chapter "Graduate Study in France for the International Student" for additional information.) Examples of highly reputed business schools are HEC Paris, EM Lyon Business School, and EDHEC Business School in Lille.

Political Science and Journalism

Sciences Po (Institut d'Études Politiques - IEP)
The preeminent French institute for the study of political science is Sciences Po Paris (*Institut d'études politiques* or IEP). Founded in 1872, it has a long tradition of educating leaders of the public sector. Even though Sciences Po remains faithful to this emphasis (it is still the gateway to the prestigious ENA, the National School of Administration), it has undergone tremendous changes in the past several years and now offers programs in various fields such as communications, law, journalism, urban planning, human resources, management, finance and strategy, economics, marketing, and international affairs. Sciences Po is particularly well known for its multidisciplinary teaching and emphasis on skilled oral and written communication. Of special note, Sciences Po Paris is a member of the prestigious ComUE, Université Sorbonne Paris Cité.

Sciences Po Paris has its own admissions procedure, which is separate from the other IEP programs in the provinces. In addition to the standard procedures, there are two alternative undergraduate admissions processes for Sciences Po Paris: one for exemplary students with outstanding high school (*lycée*) records and a *mention très bien* on their *bac* for whom an exemption from the written entrance exams (*concours*) may apply; and one "affirmative action" process for students applying from specific high schools in underprivileged areas with which Sciences Po has established an agreement. Many candidates enroll in *prépa* Sciences Po programs while still in *lycée* to prepare for the *concours*. As of 2021, the written *concours* will be replaced by a selection by *dossier* (including grades obtained in *lycée*, *baccalauréat* results, and a personal essay). Oral evaluations will ensue for those who pass the pre-selection process. The purpose of these changes is to equalize the playing field for admissions and thereby allow for greater diversity and opportunity for students from less privileged backgrounds.

Sciences Po Paris also has campuses in several cities around France and each one has its own specialty. The Sciences Po Paris campus is the founding location and is an historic institution with one of the best libraries in France. The other campuses and their specialties are Dijon (Eastern and Central Europe); Le Havre (Asia); Menton (the Middle East and the Mediterranean); Nancy (German-speaking countries); Poitiers (Spain, Portugal and Latin American countries), and Reims (North America). Sciences Po Paris is also known for its many research institutes.

There are eight other *instituts d'études politiques* independent of Sciences Po Paris and seven of them have created a common entrance exam. These IEP are located in Aix-en-Provence, Lille, Lyon, Rennes, Saint-Germain-en-Laye, Strasbourg, and Toulouse. The other two are located in Bordeaux and Grenoble.

Two highly regarded *grandes écoles* that focus on journalism and related subjects are CELSA Sorbonne Université and CFJ (Centre de formation des journalistes), both in Paris. Other reputable schools of journalism, while not members of the Conference des Grandes Écoles, may confer certain degrees in journalism in conjunction with a *grande école*. Examples, are EJDG (École de journalism de Grenoble) and ESJ (École supérieure de journalisme de Lille).

École National d'Administration (ENA)
One of the most prestigious schools in France is the École nationale d'administration or ENA. Created by governmental decree at the end of World War II, ENA trains its students for senior-level civil service careers. Admission is highly selective and there are only about 100 graduates per year. ENA is a member of the ComUE, Paris Sciences et Lettres - PSL.

Prospective students must possess at least a *licence*-level degree, or have a certain number of years of professional experience in either the public or private sector. Many successful candidates are graduates of Sciences Po Paris. Those who pass the written exam must then take an oral exam. Foreign students may also study at ENA. French students are paid throughout their studies as civil servants and must commit to working at least 10 years for the French government after graduation. Graduates of this school are commonly called "*Énarques*". Many high government officials in France are *Énarques*.

Humanities, Mathematics, and Sciences

École Normale Supérieure (ENS)
There are actually three different campuses of the École normale supérieure that are located in Paris, Cachan (a suburb of Paris), and Lyon. The campus in Paris is called simply ENS (formerly known as ENS Ulm), the school in Cachan has been renamed ENS Paris-Saclay (formerly ENS Cachan); and the campus in Lyon is ENS de Lyon. The ENS provides a world-renowned education in the humanities, mathematics, and various fields of science. (A detailed description of each school's curriculum can be consulted on the corresponding school's website.) Admission is highly selective. The procedure for entering after the *baccalauréat* is to complete two to three years of *prépa* and successfully pass the written and oral competitive exams *(concours)*. An interesting feature of the ENS is that both French and European students are paid while studying at these institutions. The ENS students also acquire the status of intern/civil servant. Non-European students are awarded scholarships but are not civil servants.

Admission to a three-year program is possible for students coming from the university (master's or doctoral level), graduates of engineering schools, and foreign students. A well-documented application with references is required and an admissions committee makes the final selection after an interview with the candidates.

ENS offers exchange programs of one to three years with many foreign universities; the selection of the hundred or so participating students is carried out by the universities. The École normale supérieure awards LMD degrees *(licence-master-doctorat)* as well as an ENS diploma. Graduates are committed to working for ten years after graduation in some field of French civil service, such as teaching or research. Should the graduate wish to make a career in the private sector, it is possible to reimburse the government and thus be freed from this commitment.

Veterinary Schools
France has four national veterinary schools, all of which are *grandes écoles*. These schools are located in Maisons-Alfort (near Paris), Lyon, Nantes, and Toulouse. After completing a *prépa* and successfully passing the *concours*, a veterinary student will follow a five-year curriculum, including four years of core courses and one year of specialization.

Foreign students must already have a diploma that would allow them to enter a higher education program in their home country; they would then be accepted to the two-year *prépa* depending on their *dossier*. To be admitted directly to veterinary school, the candidate must have studied for several years in a relevant field in his/her home country with satisfactory results.

Design, Art and other literary specialties

There are 31 specialized *grandes écoles,* or other schools with programs recognized by the Conférences des Grandes Écoles. Some are described below. These schools are public, private, and a mix of public and private; the subjects vary widely.

Schools:

- ENSAD (École nationale supérieure des Arts Décoratifs)
- ENSCI - Les Ateliers (École nationale supérieure de Création Industrielle)
- IFM - Institut Français de la Mode

Programs:

- Gobelins, *l'école de l'image*, has a well-known program for video games that is recognized by the CGE.
- FERRANDI *(l'école française de gastronomie et de management hôtelier)* offers a *mastère spécialisé* in food technology recognized by the CGE.
- Itescia *(l'école de i-Management)* offers a CGE-recognized program for computer coding.

Other Selective Institutions of Higher Education

Grands Établissements
Other highly reputed education institutions that practice selective admissions, but are not *grandes écoles,* have been granted the French status of *grand établissement*. These schools teach a wide variety of subjects from art history and oriental

languages to library science, politics, or biology. While most, but not all, *grands établissements* do not require a *prépa*, there is a rigorous admission process, which may include oral and written exams, a *dossier*/portfolio, a letter of motivation, and an interview. Some of the *grands établissements* are also *grandes écoles*. (See chapter "Introduction to the French Higher Education System".)

One particularly renowned *grand établissement* is the Institut National des Langues et Civilisations Orientales (Inalco). Inalco (formerly known as *Langues O'*) is the direct descendent of the École des Jeunes de Langues founded by Colbert in the 17th century and the École des Langues Orientales Vivantes. About 100 languages along with their cultures and civilizations are taught at Inalco, specifically, those of Central and Eastern Europe, Asia, Oceania, and Africa as well as the languages of the indigenous populations of the Americas. In addition to languages and civilizations, other specialties such as international commerce, communications and intercultural training, and international studies are taught at this school. Inalco is a member institution of the ComUE, Université Sorbonne Paris Cité.

École 42

Recent innovative higher education alternatives have been established in France, such as the École 42, which is not recognized by the state, but has earned a reputation for training students to become software engineers and coders, and provides know-how to the start-ups the French government is encouraging. Although not a *grande école* nor a *grand établissement*, admission is selective.

Conclusion

Although the *grandes écoles* have always been considered the elite schools of the French educational system, there has been a real effort in recent years to move away from the stereotype of the "royal path" *(voie royale)* for a certain category of privileged students who have been groomed to enter a *prépa*. The ambition of the Conférence des Grandes Écoles is to open these schools to diverse talents. Recruitment practices have evolved, providing students from different social, cultural, and educational horizons the opportunity to enter a *grande école*. Excellent students have been recruited from universities and technical schools, resulting in a significant increase of recent *grande école* graduates who did not enter these schools via the traditional *prépa* path. More than 300 institutes of higher education including many *grandes écoles* participate with universities and *lycées* in a government program called *"Cordées de la réussite"* with the objective of encouraging motivated, socio-economically disadvantaged students to expand their horizons and choose schools that correspond to their interests and talents. Another long running program, *"Une grande école, pourquoi pas moi? (PQPM)"* created by ESSEC Business School, organizes tutoring and counseling for *lycée* students who might not otherwise consider pursuing this educational path.

Most graduates of a *grande école* appreciate both the quality of education and the subsequent career opportunities made available to them. They often have an advantage in the job market because employers can expect to hire professionals who possess a solid foundation in their fields as well as strong analytical and problem solving skills. The friends and contacts made during the student years provide the beginnings of a network that will continue to expand beyond graduation. Alumni associations often help graduates find jobs and provide career support throughout their professional lives.

References and Resources

- Conférence des Grandes Écoles: www.cge.asso.fr
- Cordées à la Réussite: www.cordeesdelareussite.fr
- Website of the ESSEC tutoring program PQPM ("*Une grande école, pourquoi pas moi?*"): https://sites.google.com/a/essec.edu/thesee/nos-programmes/pqpm
- École normale supérieure of Paris: www.ens.fr
- Sciences Po Paris: www.sciencespo.fr
- École nationale d'administration: www.ena.fr
- Liste des établissements d'enseignement supérieur et de recherche: www.enseignementsup-recherche.gouv.fr/cid49705/liste-des-etablissements-d-enseigne-ment-superieur-et-de-recherche.html
- Centre d'Information et de Documentation Jeunesse (CIDJ): www.cidj.com
- Ministry of Education website offering information on higher education and vocational training for students: www.onisep.fr
- Website of the magazine *l'Étudiant*: www.letudiant.fr

Endnote

1. www.enseignementsup-recherche.gouv.fr/cid94756/les-regroupements-universitaires-et-scientifiques-une-coordination-territoriale-pour-un-projet-partage.html

Student Anecdote

I chose my *grande école* for its campus life, diploma value, and networking possibilities. I would describe the academic environment as elitist, generalist, not too demanding, and with very flexible choices in the curriculum. My *prépa* prepared me very well for this school; the rigorous work methods and learning strategies paid off! There is a very strong focus on student and campus life, through over 200 associations and clubs. I have adjusted very well and am a member of as many associations as I can fit into my schedule. My social life is the most fun I've ever had. My advice to someone contemplating studying at a *grande école* would be to aim high in *prépa*: prepare the exam for your dream school above all others. Do not stop studying after the written tests! A general engineering school is a great place for anyone with a well-defined professional project because of all the partnerships and networks. It's also a great place to rediscover life after *prépa*, and find a field of work you like if you still have no idea (like me).   – *Nathalie*

Becoming a Doctor in the French System

Dr. Marine Halbron

Medical studies in France begin in the first year of university right after high school. This first year is open to all students who have earned any of the French *baccalauréat* diplomas. The program is divided into three cycles *(cycles)* of studies and training. These last respectively, three years *(premier cycle)*, three years *(deuxième cycle)*, and three to six years *(troisième cycle)*. Roughly speaking, the first cycle of studies corresponds to a pre-med program in the US. The three-year second cycle corresponds to medical school in the US and the third cycle corresponds to internship and residency.

One distinguishing and very positive feature of medical school in France, compared to medical programs elsewhere in Europe and in the US, is that the medical student gains clinical experience with patients in a hospital setting much earlier. Short hospital rotations begin in the second year of the first cycle, (i.e., the second year of studies after the high school *baccalauréat* exam), and remain an integral part of all three years of the second cycle of medical studies.

The First Year

Through 2019, students registered for their 1st year of medical studies in a program called PACES *(première année commune aux études de santé)*. At the end of the 1st year, they took a very competitive exam *(concours)* which led to a ranking. Depending on the rank obtained, students could continue on to the 2nd year of study in one of four medical domains: medicine, dentistry, pharmacology, or midwifery, however, only a very small number of spots for each discipline was available. If a student's ranking was not high enough, he or she could repeat the 1st year of medical studies. If after two years of PACES, a student had not made the rank necessary to access one of the four medical disciplines, he or she had to switch to another field, starting over as a first-year student.

As from 2020, PACES will no longer exist as such. It will be replaced by two alternative first-year paths as preparation for possible entry into a second-year medical program. This reform has been enacted as a measure to broaden access to medical studies and to promote student success.

Students will have the option to choose from two different paths or "*accès santé*" to initiate their medical studies, as described below.

Parcours spécifique santé (PASS)

The student registers for his or her 1st year of university in a medical faculty for *études de santé* (*Médecine, Maïeutique, Odontologie, Pharmacie* – MMOP) i.e., medicine, midwifery, dentistry, and pharmacy. In addition, the student chooses a "minor" *(mineur)* in another discipline of interest, such as law, biology, or math. Each university determines the number of second-year places available *(numerus apertus)*, based on the needs of the different medical disciplines in its geographic region. This has the goal of ultimately improving accessibility to medical care throughout France. Candidates for entry into one of the four medical disciplines will be evaluated on the grades earned during the first year, and the results of complementary oral and written exams required of some students. The option to repeat the 1st year of medical studies will no longer be available. A student who does not obtain a rank allowing him or her to access one of the four medical disciplines, but who has nonetheless successfully completed the first year of studies (earned 60 ECTS credits), can continue directly to the second year of a *licence* program (L2) in the chosen minor and will still have the possibility to reapply to the medical faculty at the end of L2 or at the end of L3. If successful at that point, he or she may join the class of 2nd year medical studies in one of the four disciplines noted above. Students, on the other hand, who failed their first year (PASS – *parcours spécifique santé*) will need to reorient their subsequent studies via the website, Parcoursup.

Licence avec une option accès santé (L.AS)

Here, the student would enroll in a traditional university undergraduate *(licence)* program, in any number of disciplines, such as chemistry, information technology or even history or English, and "minor" in the option *accès santé*. The L.AS is a good choice for students undecided about a future career in a medical field, or for those who live far from a university with a medical faculty. An option L.AS will be offered at all universities. Check that the L.AS chosen leads to the medical specialty desired (medicine, denstistry, midwifery, or pharmacy). At the end of this 1st year, the student may apply for admission into the 2nd year of studies in the targeted medical discipline *(filière)*. If the initial admission criteria are met (such as a minimum grade point average), the student may be required to take complementary oral and written exams, the results of which will be added to his/her application file *(dossier)*. Students who are not admitted into the desired 2nd year of medical studies can still continue in the 2nd year of their "major" *licence* curriculum. They can reapply to a medical program at the end of L2 or L3, and if successful, may integrate into the 2nd year of studies. If the student fails L1 (L.AS), he or she may repeat the year but cannot reapply to medical studies. Alternatively, the student may reorient his or her studies via the Parcoursup website.

Thanks to these modifications, access to second year medical studies will be broadened to include a range of student profiles. Furthermore, those students who have passed their first year, but have not achieved a high enough ranking to permit them to continue medical studies, will not have lost a year. Of the available places in each medical discipline, 60% will be reserved for students applying from PASS and 40% will be reserved for those applying from L.AS, though this ratio may vary.

The Second and Third Years of the First Cycle

The 2nd and 3rd years of medical studies (known as DFGSM2 and DFGSM3 or *diplôme de formation générale en sciences médicales*), are two very academically challenging years, which build upon the foundation sciences studied in the first year and are supplemented by practical seminars. The student should be prepared for an intense and competitive learning environment.

The Second Three-Year Cycle of Medical Studies

The following three-year period (referred to as DFASM1 - DFASM2 - DFASM3 or *1ère, 2e, 3e année du diplôme de formation approfondie en sciences médicales*) roughly corresponds to the four years of medical school in the US. During this period, the medical student in France is called an *externe*. An *externe* does hospital rotations every morning, starting in DFGSM3, seeing patients as part of a team along with an *interne* (third-cycle medical student) and a senior physician, learning the basics such as taking medical histories, examining patients, and technical procedures. Afternoons are devoted to classwork. The hospital rotations, which last three or four months, often correspond to the subjects being studied in class. The integration of classwork with hospital rotations starting in the first year of the second cycle is a very positive feature of medical school in France. As the *externe* works five half days in a hospital he/she is remunerated with a small salary.

During these three years, the student is regularly evaluated on his/her practical work and through written exams, always on a scale of 0 to 20. As in other university programs, a student needs an overall average of 10/20 to be promoted to the next year. *Externes* are required to have also worked 25 night shifts over the three-year cycle and at least once in each of a number of specialty units in order to validate their degree. At the end of these three years, one is not yet officially a "doctor" in France, but he/she is authorized to write medical prescriptions in a hospital setting.

International Exchanges During Medical Studies

International exchanges in a medical program are possible during the second cycle of medical studies. The Erasmus+ program allows such exchanges within Europe. In some medical schools, only full year exchanges are permitted, while in other schools shorter periods, corresponding to one or more three-month rotations, are possible. Due to the fact that French medical schools include patient contact earlier than in other countries, France attracts many students from throughout Europe via the Erasmus+ program. Many French medical schools welcome foreign students and provide information in English on their websites.

It is also possible to arrange for a summer hospital rotation elsewhere in the world, including the US. It is up to the student to take the initiative in finding the foreign medical school or hospital where the rotation takes place, and to ensure that all appropriate administrative procedures are followed. In particular, an internship agreement *(convention de stage)* needs to be signed by the concerned parties. In addition, certain medical schools in France offer specific exchange programs for their students.

In keeping with the principles of the LMD reform, French medical degrees are recognized throughout Europe, however, it is not necessarily a simple matter to obtain medical training in one country, and practice in another.

The Third Cycle of Medical Studies: TCEM

The next stage in medical studies is the *internat*, also called TCEM *(troisième cycle des études médicales)*, which lasts from three to five years, depending on the specialization. This corresponds in the US system to internship and residency combined. For every medical specialization, each region in France has a specific number of internat positions to offer.

Until 2020, the results of a competitive written exam, ECN *(Épreuves Classantes Nationales)*, taken at the end of the 6th year of medical studies determined the medical specialties that a student could choose from and the region in which he or she could complete their *internat*.

The new reform will considerably modify this stage of medical studies. The ECN exam will be replaced by a broader evaluation consisting of theoretical tests centered on the fundamental knowledge students need to have acquired by the end of the 5th year, as well as an evaluation of students' clinical and relational skills at the end of the 6th year. A student's individual university career will also be considered, such as international experience, other scientific master's degrees earned, or tutoring other students. For example, a student who hopes to enter a surgical specialty and has worked as an operating room assistant, will have this experience taken into account under the reform.

Based on the results of this broader evaluation completed at the end of the 5th and 6th years, students will be directed towards the specialties to which they have applied and been accepted (general medicine, surgery, psychiatry, or another medical specialization).

For every medical specialization, each region in France has a specific number of *internat* positions to offer. The highest-ranking students will have the widest choice, while those students who received a lower ranking will far less likely be placed in their first or second choice *internat*. Actually, this ranking determines the order in which students choose the *internat* (both the specialty and the region) they wish to follow.

During the 3rd cycle, the medical student is called an *interne*. While the *internat* is administered by a specific university, each six-month rotation takes place in a different hospital within a given region.

Depending on the specialization, there is still a certain amount of required classwork. At the end of the *internat*, the student is awarded the degree of DES, *Diplôme d'études spécialisées de médecine générale*, for a *généraliste* (general practitioner). The DES diploma can also be obtained for a range of specialties such as dermatology, oncology, neurology, etc., which would require an additional one to two years of study. Further to completing the *internat*, every medical student must write a thesis before becoming a doctor. The DESC (*Diplôme d'études spécialisées complémentaires*) may be earned following an additional two or more years of training within a specialty domain. An example from the Université de Bordeaux is a training program leading to the DESC – *Pathologie infectieuse tropicale clinique et biologique*.

During the period between completion of the *internat* and completion of the thesis, one can work as a *médecin remplaçant* (substitute doctor). A *médecin remplaçant* can fill in for a practicing physician who is ill, on leave (e.g., maternity leave), or on vacation, but cannot practice as a doctor in his/her own right. The license to be a *médecin remplaçant* can be obtained after completion of specific rotations determined by one's specialization.

A student who wishes to pursue a career in medical research must complete an additional year of research training during the *internat*, at the level of a second-year master's program, M2.

Costs

Tuition and fees for medical school in France are about 500 € a year throughout the entire program. It should be kept in mind that books, personal medical equipment, and private exam preparation courses can add significantly to the cost.

Starting at the level of TCEM1, the *interne* is paid approximately 1500 € a month, with modest increases in subsequent years. The *interne* may also choose to work night shifts and earn 100 € per shift.

References and Resources

- Health Studies in France, official government websites: www.enseignementsup-recherche.gouv.fr/cid146432/suppression-de-la-paces-les-nouvelles-modalites-d-etudes-de-sante-publiees.html
- www.enseignementsup-recherche.gouv.fr/pid25335/etudes-de-sante.html
- http://paces.remede.org/documents/paces-tout-sur-la-reforme-des-etudes-de-sante-2020.html
- https://librairie.onisep.fr/Collections/Grand-public/Parcours/Les-metiers-du-medical

We would like to acknowledge the work of Fred Weissler and Nicole Dardel who wrote "Becoming a Doctor in the French System" for the first edition of this publication. Our thanks to Corinne Ott for translation assistance with this chapter.

Student Anecdotes

I have wanted to be a doctor since I was a kid. Paris Sud University was the closest one to my parents' house. I was prepared for these studies as I went to a private lycée so I got to study very hard for many years before going into med school. We had a few events to meet the other students at the beginning of my first year. We don't have a social or cultural environment at my school; it's all about medicine. If you are passionate and are not afraid of hard work med school is possible. These are the best studies ever (but the hardest as well).   – *Ines*

As I wanted to be a psychiatrist, I moved from a medical school in Nice to one in Paris due to its reputation in this specialty. The adjustment to the new environment was hard as most students were already in social groups formed in the first year, but I made friends outside of medical school. I'm satisfied with my choice as I met great professionals who helped me build a strong clinical knowledge, and who taught me the importance of good leadership as a psychiatrist working with a team of professionals from different backgrounds and training. I got a good job offer before the end of my residency. There are opportunities to take on new challenges and move projects forward if you are motivated. Medical schools are pretty competitive, but I managed to meet great people who have become wonderful and trusted friends. While my prior academics helped to prepare me for medical school, discipline is really important; you have to be able to work on your own, know your rhythm, your qualities and flaws, and move forward. Be prepared to work hard, not only the first year, but also until the ECN — and even after. If you want to be a doctor, start preparing before your first year in order to avoid a lack of knowledge in major subjects in medical school; it will make your life easier after. If you want to do it, go for it! It is worth it!   – *Lee*

Becoming a Lawyer in France

Laura Paget and Anne-Laure Moya-Plana

In the French system, the study of law *(droit)* begins at the undergraduate level, unlike the United States where a bachelor's degree is a prerequisite for entry into law school. In France, there is no entrance exam; students simply apply to first year law – usually at the university located in their geographic sector, where they will have priority. One can also apply to a university in a different sector; however, in this case, admission is selective and can be quite competitive depending on the reputation of the particular program. For students who are unsure about committing solely to a law program or those who wish to obtain an undergraduate degree *(licence)* in two disciplines, there is an alternative: pursuing a dual curriculum program, called a *bi-licence, double-licence,* or *licence double cursus,* depending on the institution. Admission is by *dossier* and is highly selective. Examples are law and economics, law and history, and law and a foreign language.

Even though law is studied at the undergraduate level in France, it does not mean that the path to becoming a lawyer is any shorter than in the US. Law studies in France entail three years of undergraduate work and an additional three to five years of advanced study and exam preparation. Success on the bar exam is required in order to receive full credentials as a lawyer.

A degree in law may theoretically lead to diverse professions but early specialization in France makes it difficult to step out of a chosen track. Whereas in the US, lawyers can redirect their careers into other fields or diverse business ventures, it is more difficult and much less common for lawyers to do so in France.

Keep in mind that there are no equivalencies between the French and Anglo-Saxon legal systems, as they are so fundamentally different. However, there are a number of dual degree *(double-diplôme)* programs in law offered by some French universities in conjunction with schools in the UK and the US. These may lead to dual qualifications in the two countries. English language skills must be strong and admission is selective.

Law Degrees

Licence
The first year of the *licence* curriculum is comprised of foundation courses in law. The second year continues to focus on foundation subjects but in addition, students can choose elective courses in specific law domains. In the third year, while students still follow a common core curriculum, they may begin to specialize in the direction of either public or private law, by virtue of their elective courses.

The more well-known law programs in France are located in the larger cities. These generally have larger faculties with the advantage of research centers, professors with greater notoriety, and usually a wider range of courses. On the other hand, the lectures *(cours magistraux)* may be attended by upwards of several hundred students in huge amphitheaters, and the overall atmosphere may feel anonymous and competitive. In contrast, smaller programs have fewer students per class and professors who, while perhaps less well known and younger, may be more motivated and eager to try innovative teaching methods.

An undergraduate degree in law *(licence)* theoretically qualifies an individual to work as a *juriste*, which in France refers to a legal advisor who works exclusively as counsel within a company *(juriste d'entreprise)*. However, this field is extremely competitive and companies usually hire people with more advanced degrees, most often, a *Master 2*.

Master 1 (M1) and Master 2 (M2)
The first year of the master program is referred to as *Master 1*. While previously, a student who completed a *licence* in law was assured of entering a *Master 1* program in law, a recent reform is modifying the conditions of this policy such that admission may be determined by *dossier*. Those who do not gain entry to the program of their choice will be proposed an alternative that takes into account their professional objectives and the university in which the licence was obtained. It is expected that in the future, the M1 and the M2 years will be fused into a single master's program that will assure continuity between the two years and still provide for further specialization in the second year.

The *Master 1* curriculum is usually completed at the same institution in which the *licence* was obtained, although one can apply to another. A *Master 1* corresponds to the first year of graduate studies in France and serves to expand a law student's knowledge of a specific domain in law such as tax and/or business law, intellectual property law, private or public law, etc.

The *Master 2* in law is the second year graduate program, that enables the law student to acquire in-depth knowledge of the field or fields chosen during the *Master 1*. Admission is selective. Law studies may also be pursued at the graduate degree level (both *Master 1* and *Master 2*) at an IEP *(Institut d'études politiques)* such as Sciences Po Paris; admission is also selective.

In order to become a lawyer or *avocat*, one must pursue a further program of study at a Centre Régional de Formation Professionnelle des Avocats, commonly referred to by its acronym, CRFPA, and then, as in the United States, pass the qualifying bar exam. To prepare for the entry examinations into the CRFPA, the graduate of a *Master 1*, or both *Master 1* and *Master 2* programs must attend an institute for legal studies, called Institut d'Études Judiciaires (IEJ), which is usually affiliated with the university in which the student is enrolled. The IEJ attended will determine the CRFPA he or she may test for, which in turn may determine which bar *(barreau)* a lawyer will be registered with, once qualified. The preparation classes at the IEJ are not meant to fill all of a law student's time, so it is possible, and even advisable, to study at an IEJ while enrolled in a *Master 2* program or while interning at a law firm. Although the entrance exam for the CRFPA is open to graduates of a *Master 1* program, law firms seldom employ lawyers who have not completed a *Master 2*, as the subjects studied in a *Master 2* may determine a lawyer's field of expertise in the future. It is also possible to pursue a *Master 2* as part of the CRFPA program, within the scope of what is called the PPI *(Projet pédagogique individuel)*.

> *There are no equivalencies between the French and Anglo-Saxon legal systems, as they are so fundamentally different. However, dual degrees in law may be obtained which would lead to dual qualifications.*

The CRFPA prepares the student for the actual bar exam, which if passed, certifies the individual to practice law as a full-fledged *avocat* (CAPA / *Certificat d'Aptitude à la Profession d'Avocat*). The CAPA qualifies a lawyer to work anywhere in France, even though one is required to register with the "Order" *(Avocat inscrit au tableau de l'ordre)* in the circumscription where he or she works.

In summary, the IEJ a law student attends will determine which CRFPA the student may test for, which in turn may determine which bar *(barreau)* the student will be registered with once qualified. For instance, an IEJ in Paris will enable a law student to take the entrance exam for the Paris CRFPA and, after having obtained the CAPA, register with the Paris Bar (Barreau de Paris), provided that he or she finds employment in a Parisian law firm or decides to open his or her own practice in Paris.

In regard to the exam for entry into a CRFPA, it is important to note that this exam tests students' knowledge of law rather than intellectual aptitude. Sometimes the most talented law students miss the point of questions due to an overly analytical approach. A private preparation course, which can be taken during the summer months before the CRFPA entrance exam in the fall, is advisable to help candidates prepare for both the written and oral components. The entrance exam is the same for candidates all over France and consists of a written eligibility examination, which if passed, will be followed by an oral examination. Overall, each year only 20% to just under half of the students taking the exam in any given region will gain entry into a CRFPA. One can sit the entrance exam for a CRFPA three times; after a third failed attempt, it is no longer possible to obtain the CAPA via the IEJ / CRFPA route.

CRFPA candidates who have obtained a doctorate in law may enter a CRFPA directly. Students who have failed to gain entry to a CRFPA following the IEJ may choose to follow a doctoral program as a way to obtain admission. This path, however, is also difficult as a doctorate involves years of research (between three to five years after a *Master 2*), the writing of a thesis, and its defense before a jury. A doctorate will more often lead to a position as a law professor in a university. However, many lawyers or in-house counsels also hold a doctoral degree.

The CRFPA program is divided into three six-month periods. The students must complete a six-month internship in a law firm; spend another six months in the legal department of a company and/or in a jurisdiction; or pursue a *Master 2* (via a *projet pédagogique individuel*); and follow six months of classes given by lawyers or former lawyers about proceedings (including the preparation of mock trials) and ethics.

Candidates to the bar must take a written exam; they will be asked to draft either a summons, or submissions (documents which are drafted by a claimant and a defendant to a court case), or an opinion (written advice given to a client in a given situation). In addition, the candidate must take the oral ethics examination, often considered to be the most difficult of the three. As difficult as the bar exam might appear initially, it may seem easy in comparison to the entrance exam for the CRFPA.

In the event of failure to pass the bar exam, or alternatively, a lack of interest in becoming a lawyer, a *Master 2* degree will enable a young candidate to obtain an interesting career as an in-house counsel, or legal advisor in a company. This position is similar to that of a lawyer, with the main difference being that in-house counsels cannot in most instances plead cases for the company before most law courts. Another major difference is that in-house counsels are employees of the company that hires them, whereas lawyers are usually self-employed.

Indeed, although some lawyers are employees of large law firms, most in France are self-employed *(profession libérale)*. A lawyer who is employed as an associate *(collaborateur)* in a law firm, invoices the firm he or she works for at the end of each month. At the same time, he or she may be permitted to build a private client base while using the resources of the law firm in question, however in practice, the workload may be such that this could prove difficult.

Although it is probably something that may be said of any occupation, these authors wish to stress that practicing law is hard work and the competition is fierce. Lawyers must be confident in the advice they give and be proactive in finding clients and building a long-term relationship with them. Both lawyers and in-house counsels must be willing to work very long hours to meet short deadlines. At the same time, law is a career that brings a sense of freedom, usefulness, exhilaration, and much satisfaction.

Specialized Schools/
Écoles Spécialisées

Kathleen Choiset and Noémie Choiset

The title of this chapter is deceptively simple. In fact, the term *école spécialisée* represents a concept that is extremely difficult to present in a clear and concise manner. There are over 3,000 such institutions of higher learning in France, and they do not share any particular common denominator, other than they offer curricula principally pertaining to one specific field of study. Certain specialized schools may also be designated as *grandes écoles* and others may be connected in some way with a university or a *lycée*. This categorization covers both public and private institutions. Admission may be based on the results of a selective exam and interviews or according to another process specific to the particular school. The length of study usually varies from two to five years following the French *baccalauréat*. Tuition fees can differ widely from one school to another and the resulting diploma may or may not be recognized by the French Ministry of Higher Education, Research, and Innovation.

It should be pointed out, however, that such schools attract students who already have some propensity for the program, and that the school's objective is to develop particular talents and skills nascent in its students. These schools teach an in-depth curriculum within a highly structured framework, in contrast to universities which offer a wider variety of programs in a less supervised context, and to the CPGE *(prépa)* with its intense and demanding academic environment.

The list of opportunities concerning specialized studies is long, varied and impressive. Fields of study are indeed far-reaching, ranging from artistic creation (i.e., music, art, textile design, fashion, cinema, architecture, photography, etc.) to technical expertise (gemology, data processing, telecommunications), and others such as journalism, allied health professions, real estate, culinary arts, banking, landscaping, and hotel and tourism management, just to name a few.

Some schools offer admission immediately following the French *baccalauréat*, while others require several years of preparatory study. In order to narrow down the vast number of possibilities, the future student should have a clear idea of his/her interests and goals. Documentation regarding the targeted field of study and a compilation of corresponding schools – as well as academic counseling – can be of aid in determining which leads to follow. While many of these institutions handle their admissions process through Parcoursup for the basic application, it should be noted that the *dossier*/portfolio required when applying to certain schools may include not only academic transcripts and a letter of motivation, but also an indication of a future professional project and a list of previous internships *(stages)*. Personal interviews are usually part of the admission process.

Due to the diversity of standards and objectives of specialized schools, careful attention must be paid to certain points. This means determining the value of the school's diploma, its renown in the professional world, and how this justifies the annual cost of the program. Courses are very often taught by professionals in the field, classes are small, and upon graduation students are qualified to seek employment.

The sheer number of such schools, plus the lack of a concordance or national ranking, can render the selection process quite daunting. However, narrowing down the field of interest and taking into consideration variables such as specific skills acquired, tuition, location, and diploma—the task becomes easier. The creation of the ComUEs *(Communautés d'universités et établissements)*[1] and other associations or alliances of institutions of higher education in France has fostered interdisciplinary exchange. It has also raised the national and international recognition of the constituent institutions, including those of the specialized schools. For example, Beaux-Arts de Paris is a member of the ComUE, Paris Sciences et Lettres or PSL. PSL comprises 25 prestigious schools, which share resources and facilitate exchanges among their students. Thus, when searching for a program, the student should also find out about the school's affiliations and partnerships.

Length of studies, admission requirements, and the level of expertise taught are important points to consider when choosing a specialized study path. The BTS and DUT post-*bac* diplomas are a mirror at an entry level of the more academically oriented specialized schools. For example, the BTS diploma *(brevet de technicien supérieur)* is conferred after two years of specialized post-*bac* study. The BTS programs are usually dispensed in *lycée* settings and are geared to training students for skilled positions in any one of over 150 different domains (sales, accounting, graphic arts, interior design, electrician, real estate, optician, etc.). Class instruction, coupled with "hands-on" experience, is a key characteristic of this course of study, leading to almost certain job prospects following graduation. A BTS diploma also grants 120 ECTS (European Credit Transfer System) credits towards an undergraduate degree at a French university, allowing the student to enter into the third year of a professional *licence* program in his/her field or into the second year of a general *licence* program.

Another two-year specialized post-*bac* diploma is the DUT *(diplôme universitaire de technologie)*, which is earned in over 110 university-based institutes of technology known as IUT (as opposed to the BTS, which is *lycée*-based). The DUT provides training in 24 different manufacturing and service specialties. DUT holders generally aim to pursue further studies after they graduate, which may be less the case with BTS students. DUT graduates may opt to enroll in a *licence professionnelle* or take a business school entrance examination. Holders of an industrial DUT also have the option of transferring into a school of engineering. The DUT has been harmonized with the European higher education degree schema and carries 120 transferable credits or

ECTS (European Transfer Credits).

If English is of major importance for a particular field or school, it is definitely worthwhile looking into the program's English language entrance requirement, the amount of English used in the curriculum, and any exit proficiency exams. Some programs require a minimum score on a standardized test, such as the TOEFL, TOIEC, or IELTS, for graduation.

Concerning recognition of French diplomas and accreditation for coursework completed in France to pursue graduate work in US institutions or elsewhere, one must consult each school individually. Candidates should inquire about this point early if interested in certain US/international exchange or graduate programs. For information specific to the United States, see the chapter "Graduate School in the US for International Graduates". Many specialized schools are aligning their programs of study with the LMD structure *(licence-master-doctorat)*.

It is sound advice to explore all leads and not limit one's choice of schools to a single possibility. The admissions process is often quite complicated—and the selection competitive. Candidates should investigate the strong points and attractiveness of each school and compare with alternatives. It is advisable to submit applications to several institutions. In addition, students may consider specialized francophone schools in Belgium and Switzerland offering similar opportunities.

Practical and comprehensive information about the French higher education system, including specialized schools, can be found on the Onisep website (Office national sur les enseignements et les professions – www.onisep.fr). Onisep produces both printed and downloadable catalogs, which list schools and programs (in French), complete with explanations and charts which are of help in viewing the complexity of the subject from within.

In addition, Campus France (www.campusfrance.org) offers a wealth of information in English for the international student considering higher education in France. Although it does not provide a complete list of specialized schools, it does give an excellent outline of the subject and answers a number of essential questions.

In summary, France offers a multitude of choices for specialized higher education. The following section will introduce the student to a number of renowned specialized schools in France as a starting point for more in-depth investigation.

Most, if not all, of the specialized schools mentioned below are extremely selective; they also tend to be small. Admission is therefore very difficult. Only those with talent and proven achievement (through practical experience, a portfolio, etc.) need apply. They should expect to work hard and be "pushed" hard by their teachers. As not all schools can possibly be cited here, priority has been given to public and private institutions granting diplomas recognized by the French state. For many fields, numerous private schools offer diplomas and certificates not recognized by the state, but nonetheless highly regarded. Some, on the other hand, can be very costly and potentially of doubtful value. It is therefore imperative to research extensively before enrolling. A school with a very easy admissions policy and high fees should raise concerns.

Most but not all specialized schools require a good command of the French language;

some will test for language proficiency. More and more specialized schools are offering specific programs in English in an effort to attract international students. For further information on programs offered with English as the language of instruction, please refer to the chapters "Undergraduate Study in English in France and the EU" and "Graduate Study in France for the International Student".

Arts

A. Fine and Applied Arts

The Écoles Nationales Supérieures d'Art, have a prestigious reputation, small incoming classes and admission by *concours* (a highly selective, competitive exam):

- École Nationale Supérieure des Beaux-Arts, or ENSBA in Paris, (Beaux-Arts de Paris): www.beauxartsparis.fr
- École Nationale Supérieure des Arts Décoratifs or ENSAD in Paris, (Les Arts Déco): www.ensad.fr
- École Nationale Supérieure de Création Industrielle or ENSCI in Paris (Les Ateliers): www.ensci.com
- École Nationale Supérieure de la Photographie (ENSP), Arles: www.ensp-arles.fr
- Le Fresnoy-Studio national des arts contemporains, Tourcoing: www.lefresnoy.net
- Écoles Nationales, Régionales or Municipales des Beaux-Arts are located in various cities around the country, and issue nationally recognized diplomas.

A complete list of public schools and their specialties is available on the website of ANdÉA (the national association of postsecondary schools of art): www.andea.fr.

Applied Arts schools lead to careers in various fields of design such as fashion, advertising, publishing, interior design, arts and crafts, furniture etc. Some overlap is possible with the Fine Arts category above. The school's reputation among practitioners in the respective fields is of primary importance. Admission is extremely selective. Procedure as follows — Parcoursup, plus *concours*, interview, portfolio.

Public schools of applied arts
- École Duperré – École Supérieure des Arts Appliqués (ESAA) in Paris; fashion, textile, etc.: www.duperre.org
- École Estienne Paris (École Supérieure Estienne des Arts et Industries Graphiques or ESAIG); graphic design, book design, publishing, etching, engraving, bookbinding, gilding, visual communication: www.ecole-estienne.fr
- École Nationale Supérieure des Arts Appliqués et des Métiers d'Art -Olivier de Serres (ENSAAMA) in Paris; design, especially in fresco painting, lacquer painting, mosaics, metals, sculpture, jewelry, stained glass, interior, environmental and industrial design: www.ensaama.net
- École Boulle in Paris; an institution of higher learning which includes both post and pre-*baccalauréat* curriculums (cabinetry, furniture design, interior design,

jewelry, sculpture, etc.): www.ecole-boulle.org
- École Supérieure des Arts Appliqués et du Textile (ESAAT) in Roubaix: www.esaat-roubaix.com
- Haute école des arts du Rhin (HEAR) combines the former École Supérieure des Arts Décoratifs de Strasbourg (ESADS), and the École Supérieure d'art de Mulhouse, with courses in art, communication, design, stage design, animated film, etc., and the former Académie Supérieure de Musique de Strasbourg for music: www.hear.fr

Private schools of applied arts
- Penninghen, formerly known as École Supérieure de Design, d'Art Graphique et d'Architecture Intérieure - ESAG Penninghen Paris; design, graphic arts, visual communication, interior architecture/design: www.penninghen.fr
- ECV–Creative Schools & Community, formerly École de Communication Visuelle (ECV) in Paris, Bordeaux, Aix-en-Provence, Nantes, and Lille; publishing, graphic design, advertising, visual identity, package design, multimedia: www.ecv.fr
- EFET Photographie and EFET Architecture Intérieure, formerly the École Supérieure de Photographie et d'Audiovisuel – EFET in Paris; photography, audiovisual and interior design: www.efet.com
- École Camondo; decorative arts, design, interior design in Paris and as of September 2019, Camondo Mediterránée in Toulon: http://ecolecamondo.fr/en
- Institute Français de la Mode is the merger of the former École de la Chambre Syndicale de la Couture Parisienne and IFM. Currently in two campuses, they will relocate in 2020 to one location at the Docks–Cité de la Mode et du Design; fashion design and technique: www.ifmparis.fr/en
- Studio Berçot in Paris; fashion design and technique: www.studio-bercot.com

B. Art History, Archeology, Museum Studies

The École du Louvre is a unique and very well-known institution of higher learning (and under the Ministry of Culture) whose premises are actually in the Louvre Museum. It was originally created to educate curators, relic excavators, and missionaries about archeology, but then branched out to cover art history and anthropology. Many varied subjects are taught and the scope of the subject matter ranges from ancient and modern languages to numismatics. It offers three cycles of studies (three years of undergraduate studies, two years of graduate studies, and three years of post-graduate studies) and a preparatory class for the *conservateur du patrimoine* competitive exam.

In addition to providing courses leading towards a diploma, courses may be attended by auditors (fees are charged). Evening classes and summer school sessions are also offered as well as the possibility of attending classes within the framework of *formation continue* (continuing education).

Admission requires a secondary school diploma, a special test and completing an application form, all of which is explained on its website: www.ecoledulouvre.fr.

The Institut National du Patrimoine (INP) in Paris, an institute of higher education under the auspices of the French Ministry of Culture, recruits through a competitive entrance examination and provides training to heritage curators for state and local government civil service authorities. The INP set up an integrated preparatory class to prepare students for external competitive curator examinations. This program is intended for French and European students, irrespective of age, for degree holders or those in the course of obtaining one. The program is organized in partnership with the École du Louvre and the École Nationale des Chartes. The INP also offers a wide range of continuing education programs: www.inp.fr

The Paris-based École Nationale des Chartes, (member of the Paris Sciences et Lettres consortium) is a prestigious *grande école* providing university instruction to students in the humanities and social sciences, and particularly history. The school offers three initial training programs: i) a three-year and nine months *archiviste-paléographe* program for future conservators (competitive entrance exam open to students with an undergraduate diploma or two-year CPGE); ii) master's programs *(Technologies numériques appliquées à l'histoire, Humanités numériques, Histoire transnationale, Études médiévales,* and *Concepteur audiovisuel)*; and iii) PhD *(histoire, lettres, histoire de l'art)*: www.chartes.psl.eu

C. Performing Arts (Dance, Drama, Music, Film)

Dance and Music: Public Schools

- Conservatoire National Supérieur de Musique et de Danse de Paris (CNSMDP): Ancient, classical, contemporary music, jazz and improvised music, musicology, composition, instruments, voice, direction, acoustics, dance, choreography, teaching, etc. Candidates must follow application procedures as well as an audition: www.conservatoiredeparis.fr

- Conservatoire National Supérieur Musique et Danse de Lyon (CNSMDL), same subjects as the Paris conservatory: www.cnsmd-lyon.fr

- Conservatoires à Rayonnement – régional (CRR), départemental (CRD), communal (CRC), and intercommunal (CRI), throughout France offer music, dance, drama classes: www.crr-paris.fr (Paris)

Dance and Music: Private Schools

- Conservatoire Russe de Paris Serge Rachmaninoff in Paris: www.conservatoire-rachmaninoff.com

- La Schola Cantorum in Paris: www.schola-cantorum.com

- École Normale de Musique de Paris Alfred Cortot: www.ecolenormalecortot.com

There are many other schools of dance and music in France. Please note, however, that it is important to thoroughly investigate each school that you consider in France as there are no restrictions for opening music or dance schools, other than those related to tax and employment.

Drama: Public Schools
- Conservatoire National Supérieur d'Art Dramatique (CNSAD), member of the Paris Sciences et Lettres consortium; considered by many to be **the** public drama school. Admission after *baccalauréat* plus *concours*, in addition to one year of intensive theatrical training or professional theatrical experience: www.cnsad.fr
- École Supérieure d'Art Dramatique du Théâtre National de Strasbourg (ESAD/TNS): www.tns.fr
- École Nationale Supérieure des Arts et Techniques du Théâtre de Lyon (ENSATT-Lyon); classes in production management, drama, arts and humanities, costume design and creation, technical direction, writing for the stage, direction, lighting, sound, set design. Admission after the *baccalauréat*, plus *concours*: www.ensatt.fr

There are also many regional or municipal *conservatoires* offering excellent drama classes. The following schools are also renowned, and supervised by the French Ministry of Culture: Conservatoire de Bordeaux; Conservatoire à Rayonnement Régional de Montpellier Méditerranée Métropole; École du Théâtre National de Bretagne; École de la Comédie de Saint-Etienne – Centre Dramatique National (CDN); École Régionale d'Acteurs de Cannes & Marseille; École du Nord in Lille.

Drama: Private Schools
- Cours Florent in Paris, Bordeaux, Montpellier, and Brussels: www.coursflorent.fr
- Le Cours Simon in Paris: www.cours-simon.com

Film
Two national schools train students in all fields related to cinema and classes are taught by film industry professionals. Admission is very selective; *baccalauréat*, two or three years of preparatory studies, plus *concours*.
- École Nationale Supérieure des Métiers de l'Image et du Son, known as *La Fémis*: www.femis.fr
- École Nationale Supérieure Louis Lumière (ENSLL) in Paris has three sections, cinema, sound, and photography. Diploma at the Master level: www.ens-louis-lumiere.fr

These schools of visual arts are administered by their local Chambers of Commerce and charge tuition:
- Gobelins, l'École de l'Image, in Paris and Noisy-le-Grand: www.gobelins.fr
- École des Métiers du Cinéma d'Animation (EMCA) in Angoulême, which takes students after the *baccalauréat*, plus *concours*: www.angouleme-emca.fr

Tuition varies among private cinema and audiovisual schools. When choosing a school, one should make sure the diploma is recognized by the Répertoire National des Certifications Professionnelles (RNCP) or by the State: www.rncp.cncp.gouv.fr

A reputable private film and television school in Paris is EICAR the International Film & Television School: www.eicar.fr

Architecture

There are twenty-two schools recognized by the State and the Ordre des Architectes: the public ENSA network of schools (Écoles nationales supérieures d' architecture) supervised by the French Ministry of Culture, one private school, ESA / Paris (École spéciale d'architecture), and one public engineering school, INSA / Strasbourg (Institut national des sciences appliquées).

The twenty ENSA schools (among which six are in the Paris region), train 90 percent of the future architects in France. Admission: *baccalauréat* (most often students with science-related coursework on their *bac*) plus portfolio/*dossier*, and interview:

- École nationale supérieure d'architecture Paris-Malaquais: www.paris-malaquais.archi.fr
- École nationale supérieure d'architecture Paris-La Villette: www.paris-lavillette.archi.fr
- École nationale supérieure d'architecture Paris-Belleville: www.paris-belleville.archi.fr
- École nationale supérieure d'architecture Paris-Val de Seine: www.paris-valdeseine.archi.fr
- École nationale supérieure d'architecture de Versailles (ENSA-V): www.versailles.archi.fr
- École d'architecture de de la ville & des territoires Paris-Est: http://paris-est.archi.fr

The two other schools are:

- Institut National des Sciences Appliquées de Strasbourg (a *grande école* of engineering and architecture): www.insa-strasbourg.fr
- École spéciale d'architecture (ESA) in Paris (a private school): www.esa-paris.fr

Landscape Architecture

There are a few schools that train landscape architects *(paysagistes)* - three years of post-*bac* studies are a minimum:

- École nationale supérieure de paysage in Versailles, close to the Château, is in charge of restoring and maintaining the Potager du roi (the King's Vegetable Garden). A second campus is in Marseille. Admission: *baccalauréat*, plus two years of post-*lycée* studies, plus *concours*: www.ecole-paysage.fr
- École nationale supérieure d'architecture et de paysage in Lille. www.lille.archi.fr or Bordeaux: www.bordeaux.archi.fr
- École supérieure d'architecture des Jardins (ESAJ) , is a private school in Paris. Admission: *baccalauréat* plus interview: www.esaj.asso.fr

It is also possible to earn an engineering degree with landscape specialization (at the Institut national supérieur des sciences agronomiques, agroalimentaires, horticoles et du paysage de Rennes - www.agrocampus-ouest.fr, or at the Institut supérieur d'agriculture Lille - www.isa-lille.com).

Journalism

Numerous specialized schools exist for journalism studies and students should investigate the possibilities according to their desired career, such as print versus television journalism. Admission is highly selective and may occur immediately after the *baccalauréat* or only after several years of university-level studies. Degrees vary from school to school (for example, *licence-master-doctorat* or a *diplôme universitaire de technologie*). Fourteen schools, both public and private, are officially recognized by the profession. These are listed below.

Public Schools

- CELSA Sorbonne Université, l'école des hautes études en sciences de l'information et communication, a reputed journalism school housed within the Université Paris-Sorbonne (Paris 4). Admission: competitive entrance exam (30 places)[2] with studies leading to a *Master*. www.celsa.fr
- Centre universitaire d'enseignement du journalisme (CUEJ) in Strasbourg offers a varied curriculum with the possibility of a dual diploma with the University of Fribourg in Germany: www.cuej.unistra.fr
- École de journalisme de Grenoble: www.ejdg.fr
- École de Journalisme et de Communication d'Aix-Marseille: ejcam.univ-amu.fr
- École supérieure de journalisme de Lille (ESJ) offers various programs including a dual degree diploma with Sciences Po Lille: www.esj-lille.fr
- École publique de journalisme de Tours offers a *Master* in journalism: epjt.fr
- Institut Français de Presse (IFP), which is part of the Université Paris 2 Panthéon-Assas, offers a *Master* in journalism and numerous opportunities for study abroad: https://ifp.u-paris2.fr/fr
- Institut de journalisme de Bordeaux Aquitaine (IJBA): www.ijba.u-bordeaux-montaigne.fr
- Institut Pratique du Journalisme (IPJ Paris-Dauphine) offers numerous journalism programs. Admission: applicants need to have *licence* or *grade de licence*, and take a competitive entrance exam: www.ipj.eu
- Institut universitaire de technologie (IUT–Lannion) offers journalism programs leading to a *diplôme universitaire de technologie* (DUT) and *licence professionnelle* (LP): www.iut-lannion.fr
- Institut universitaire de technologie (IUT–Nice Côte d'Azur) offers a DUT and LP in journalism at their Cannes campus: http://unice.fr

Private schools

- Centre de formation des journalistes (CFJ) in Paris is a *grande école* of journalism and communication with higher technical and vocational education. It is an extremely selective school (1000 applicants for 35 places).[3] *Bac+3* required, master's-level diplomas: www.cfjparis.com.
- École de journalisme de Sciences Po. This prestigious school offers various

journalism master's degrees, including a French/English bilingual program in economic journalism, and a dual degree in journalism, with Columbia University in New York: www.journalisme.sciences-po.fr

Outside of Paris, there are also the EjT (École de journalisme de Toulouse), and the ESJ Lille (École supérieure de journalisme de Lille). Tuition fees for the two and three-year programs are considerably more than the public schools listed above.

Communications

Studies in communications encompass a variety of subjects such as advertising, marketing, public relations, internal communications, and human resources work for corporations and institutions.

CELSA Sorbonne Université, École des hautes études en sciences de l'information et communication, is a reputed journalism school housed within Université Paris-Sorbonne (Paris 4). In addition to journalism, this prestigious school offers curriculum in communication studies: www.celsa.fr

Also, a BTS or DUT in communications can lead to a *licence* or *licence professionnelle*.

Private Schools

- ISCOM (formerly the Institut supérieur de communication et publicité) is a private institution offering programs from a BTS *(brevet de technicien supérieur)* to a *grande école* program with schools in Paris, Lyon, Lille, Rouen, Strasbourg, Toulouse, Bordeaux, and Montpellier. It also offers continuing education: www.iscom.fr

- EFAP (formerly the École française des attachés de presse and known today as École des nouveaux métiers de la communication), is a private specialized school with campuses in Paris, Bordeaux, Lille and Lyon (as well as New York and Shanghai). Strong emphasis is put on work experience gained through internships: www.efap.com

- Audencia SciencesCom in Nantes (a *grande école* and part of the Audencia Business School) has a well-known communications department, offering bachelor's and master's degrees with various specializations: https://sciencescom.audencia.com

There are many private schools and when considering a school, as suggested earlier, it is good to check that the diploma offered is listed in the Répertoire National de la Certification Professionnelle (RNCP): www.rncp.cncp.gouv.fr, or recognized by the French state.

Library and Information Science

The Conservatoire National des Arts et Métiers (CNAM) whose motto is "We teach everyone, everywhere" offers several diplomas in library and information science. A range of degree programs from certificates to a licence professionnelle to a data analysis *Master* are offered through the Institut national des sciences et techniques de la documentation: http://intd.cnam.fr

It should be mentioned that the CNAM, which is a public scientific, cultural and professional institute and also a *grand établissement*, offers nearly 600 diplomas and certifications: www.cnam.fr

Conclusion

It is obvious that with so many schools providing instruction in such vast and varied fields of learning, the above information is more or less a beginner's guide. Much more extensive investigation is possible — and advisable. In fact, one should not wait until the last year of *lycée* to start examining all the options that are available. A great deal of information can be gleaned through an internet search. School fairs *(salons d'étudiants)* provide an excellent introduction to programs and schools, enabling one to narrow down the choices. Actual visits to schools all contribute to making the right choice, leading to the right diploma and in the end, the right occupation — making all the time spent in research worthwhile!

Endnotes

1. http://cache.media.enseignementsup-recherche.gouv.fr/file/Etablissements_et_organismes/68/2/Liste_regroupements_Associations_et_COMUE_et_associes_1er_fevrier_2018_890682.pdf
2. www.cnmj.fr/basedocumentaire/ecoles-journalisme-reconnues
3. https://ressources.campusfrance.org/guides_etab/etablissements/fr/univ_cfj_fr.pdf

Student Anecdotes

I chose my specialized school for fashion design as it was my dream school. The adaptation to my new academic environment was quite easy, indeed I felt it was the continuation of the education I received in high school, with the difference being I studied what I loved. Nowadays, the most difficult thing isn't to find a school, but to find out who we are; it takes time to know, but we have to take this time and not be anxious about it. And my last advice, but not least, it's ok to do several things at the same time. In a sense it's ok not to choose just one thing or subject. In my mind it's crucial. Eat up all you can, life is short. *– Lucia*

My cooking school was a great choice for me as it combined two aspects key to the culinary world today – cooking and entrepreneurship. The school is multicultural with about 40 nationalities represented. I adjusted well to the program by focusing on how I can improve. My advice for future students is to believe, stay in, and keep moving. *– Andreas*

Undergraduate Study in English in France and the EU

Lisa Fleury and Sallie Chaballier

Higher education has gone global. Institutions of higher education are competing for students not just from within their own country but from the world over. As a result, students now have more options than ever before to receive their education in a country other than their own. The ubiquity of English as the international lingua franca has given rise to a proliferation of university programs taught in English in non-Anglophone countries. While graduate programs in English have been multiplying in recent years, many European countries now offer undergraduate programs in English as well.

This is good news for Anglophone international students, as they have more and more options for undergraduate study outside Anglophone countries. The growth of degree programs taught in English in Europe has resulted in greater international student mobility, as well as increased international visibility for those institutions to attract foreign talent. An international student body enriches all concerned: students pursue their degree in a diverse multicultural environment, while the university expands its horizons with an influx of students from different cultural and linguistic backgrounds.

Beyond Erasmus

The possibilities for undergraduate study abroad in Europe have moved beyond the semester or year abroad in exchanges offered by the Erasmus program (now Erasmus+) to enrollment in higher education degree programs directly after secondary education. The advantages of studying in a second or third language country are many: exposure to an additional language and culture, an enriching intellectual and personal experience, learning in English at a university level, and increased options for graduate study. The fluent English/French speaker will have many postgraduate opportunities thanks to his or her bilingualism. Students studying internationally can return to their home country with a third language, lifelong adaptability to different cultures, a global network of classmates, and enhanced employment possibilities.

International student mobility throughout the European Union has been made easier by the Bologna Process, a series of European-wide reforms designed to achieve the mutual recognition and reciprocity among European university programs. Among the reforms was the creation of the European Higher Education Area (EHEA). The EHEA's goal is "to increase staff and students' mobility and to facilitate employability."[1] It has led to the standardization and recognition of coursework and diplomas throughout its 48 member states, principally through the European Credit Transfer and Accumulation System (ECTS). Student mobility is further encouraged by the proliferation of degree programs offered in English.

University degrees are organized in a three-cycle structure (i.e., *licence-master-doctorat*) throughout the EHEA. The member countries have agreed upon and defined the learning outcomes for each of these three cycles. The ECTS determines credit hours for undergraduate and graduate coursework. Furthermore, thanks to common nomenclature and standards, non-European countries can now more easily evaluate a graduate's European degree.

Undergraduate Study in France in English

France has joined the race to internationalize its study programs and undergraduate admissions in order to attract top students and to remain competitive among the world's institutions of higher education. It is endeavoring to almost double the number of international students enrolled in its higher education programs by the year 2027. This goal is part of the strategy, *Bienvenue en France*,[2] developed by the current government to attract foreign students. As part of this plan, the process of obtaining a student visa is being simplified and streamlined. At the same time, tuition fees for foreign students are increasing significantly; however, it should be noted that the cost of a higher education in France (2,770 € annual tuition in 2019[3] for undergraduate study at a public institution) remains much more affordable than in most Anglophone countries. Furthermore, scholarships or exoneration from tuition fees will be available to highly qualified students with demonstrated financial need. The availability of French as a foreign language classes (FLE – *français comme langue étrangère*) for non-Francophone students will also be increased.

As part of the effort to attract international students, the number of programs taught either partially or exclusively in English has increased dramatically and this trend will likely continue to develop over the coming years. In addition, most study at the graduate level in France now requires a high level of English proficiency, so that French as well as international students benefit from the preparation afforded by undergraduate study in English.

> *Higher education has gone global. Universities increasingly are competing for students not just from within their own country but from the world over.*

It is important to note that there are some differences between the undergraduate degrees in France known as the *licence* and the *bachelor*. The *licence* is granted after the first three years of study after the *baccalauréat*, usually within the public university system, and represents a national degree recognized by the Ministère de l'Enseignement supérieur, de la Recherche et de l'Innovation (MESRI). A student must complete 180 ECTS credits to obtain a *licence*.

The *bachelor* is usually a three-year (sometimes four-year) undergraduate program and is in some ways an international equivalent of the *licence*; successful completion is marked by the accrual of 180 ECTS credits as well. Recently, year-long *bachelor* programs have opened to students who have already obtained 120 ECTS credits and who wish to complete a third year of study in a professional area; some of these are offered in English in professional areas that have an international emphasis, such as global business. A *bachelor* at a business or management school is usually granted as a first degree within a five-year business program; a majority of students who obtain a *bachelor* in a business school go on to a master's program. Though the *bachelor* is not a degree officially recognized by the ministry of higher education (MESRI) in the LMD schema, a French accrediting committee, the France compétences,[4] under the auspices of the *Ministère en charge de la formation professionnelle*, evaluates, certifies and accredits these study and training programs. Institutions that have submitted their programs and have been accredited by France compétences can be certified as *enregistré au* RNCP (*Répertoire national des certifications professionnelles*).[5] An accredited undergraduate bachelor would add the qualifier, "*titre certifié Niveau II*" or the same level as a *licence* or *maîtrise* (bac+3, bac+4). There are also international accrediting bodies that audit and confer quality labels to business schools and their study programs, such as EQUIS[6] (European Quality Improvement System). Students must be aware that there is no single accrediting entity for the *bachelor*, so they should enquire about a school's quality of teaching, reputation, ties, and placement in the industry, and the strength of the school's alumni network before enrolling in a *bachelor* program.

A plethora of *bachelors* are now offered in France, many taught in English, and mostly offering a degree within three (or four) years. An emphasis is usually placed on developing an international profile through professional skills and field experience including international study and internships. These tend to be in business and management related areas, tourism, fashion, computer and digital studies, culinary arts or hospitality, and international relations – fields where international opportunities abound and English is absolutely essential, rather than the type of liberal arts programs that are offered in English in some other European countries.

More and more French institutions have opened exclusively English track curriculums alongside their French tracks to expand their offerings to international students. At the time of this writing, there are 84 *bachelor* programs taught entirely in English at institutions of higher learning throughout France. Examples include: a Bachelor of Science program at École Polytechnique, near Paris, offering double majors in math and physics, math and computer science, or math and economics; a Bachelor in International Culinary Arts Management at the Institut Paul Bocuse near Lyon; a Bachelor in International Hotel Management at the Vatel Hotel and Business School, in Nîmes; a Bachelor in Fashion Design at Esmod in Paris; and a new program, an International Bachelor Ygrec in Modelling and Data Science offered by the University Paris Seine at EISTI (École Internationale des Sciences du Traitement de l'Information).

Not to be overlooked are accredited American universities such as the American University of Paris and The New School / Parsons Paris, both of which offer a variety of full degree programs.

Many institutions of higher learning in France also have developed exchange agreements with foreign universities, increasing the opportunities for students to study abroad for a semester or a year. Numerous institutions offer joint degrees with non-French institutions where study in English is essential, leading to joint bachelors and Bachelor of Arts or Bachelor of Business Administration degrees. These partner institutions can be found throughout North America, the UK, Australia, Asia, and elsewhere.

Special mention should be made of the *Instituts d'études politiques* (Sciences Po) regional programs located in various cities, which offer Sciences Po bachelor degree programs specializing in Europe-Asia,[7] Europe-North America,[8] and the Middle East and Mediterranean.[9] These programs are offered in English and French and do not require students to speak French to enroll; however, there is mandatory French language instruction for non-Francophone students. Students also have the opportunity to take additional language classes in relation to their program's regional focus. Sciences Po also offers dual bachelor's degree programs in English, with no prior study of French required, in conjunction with prestigious North American, British, Asian, and Australian universities.[10]

It is important to note that students applying to a program in English will need to demonstrate proficiency in English. Also, even though a French institution's curriculum may be offered in English, its admissions policy may require students to take a language proficiency test for French. Schools often require that non-Francophone students take French language classes even if all subjects are taught in English. Institutions may also require the prospective student take an additional entrance exam.

The annual autumn higher education fairs, *Studyrama* Salon des Formations Internationales and the *l'Étudiant* Salon Partir étudier à l'étranger, provide useful resources, and offer opportunities to meet with staff and students to learn about the burgeoning offers in programs with English as the language of instruction in France and throughout Europe.

Students living in France can also find out about the programs offered in English on the French or English language pages of the Campus France[11] website. For students living in the United States wishing to investigate study programs in France, they may consult the website of Campus France USA,[12] administered by the French embassy. Campus France USA provides information and assistance to students who are American citizens or resident aliens of the US who wish to pursue a program of study in France for a period of more than 90 days. Additional Campus France websites are tailored to address the needs of prospective students in numerous other countries around the world.

Undergraduate Study in English in the European Union

Software engineering in Germany, international relations in Estonia – the possibilities for English university programs in Europe are myriad. The European Higher Education Area (EHEA) actually extends beyond the geographic boundaries of Europe, including Turkey and the countries of the former Soviet Union, so there exists a broad variety of university programs offered in English. A student can now consider enrolling in an English international section of a university in a large number of countries. These sections most often offer programs leading to international careers in business administration, finance, or political science. One such program is the Bachelor of International Economics, Management and Finance at the Università Bocconi in Milan. The number of these programs has increased significantly in the last few years alone.

At the same time, undergraduate liberal arts programs are now offered in countries as diverse as Slovakia and Greece. Swedish universities offer undergraduate programs in English not only in business, science and technology, but also in the humanities.[13] In Spain, the Universidad de Navarra offers bilingual undergraduate degrees not only in management, economics and law, but also in philosophy and the humanities, as well as a dual-degree in history and archeology. In Germany, students can choose from over 100 bachelor-level programs in English, ranging from architecture at the Berlin International University of Applied Sciences to international relations, politics and history at Jacobs University Bremen to molecular ecosystem sciences at the University of Göttingen. The Netherlands boasts public universities that offer many of their undergraduate programs in English (see chapter "Higher Education in the Netherlands"). These are but a few examples to convey the growing options for the English-speaking or bilingual student.

As in France, many institutions offer a curriculum in English in order to attract foreign students. International sections may have a large, if not exclusive, component of courses taught by native and/or non-native English speakers specialized in a given field. As mentioned above, studying in English in continental Europe can be good preparation for later studies in Anglophone countries. The possibilities have burgeoned in recent years and are changing each year as well, to the point where it is impossible to compile a comprehensive listing. However, an internet search will readily yield up-to-date sources of information on the range of European undergraduate degree programs partially or entirely taught in English. See websites in the section, References and Resources, found at the end of this chapter. One caveat: it is essential to check the accreditation of any such program.

American University Campuses Abroad

In addition to degree programs within the framework of European universities, students with a good level of English can also follow an entire American undergraduate degree program on foreign campuses in Europe and beyond. These programs are distinct from spending a year or semester of study abroad, and they offer a wide range of options to international students. Moreover, a student can begin his or her undergraduate studies in Europe and then transfer to an institution in the US. While many universities in the US have developed joint degree programs with foreign universities, some now have their own foreign campuses in Europe and worldwide (for example, Saint Louis University in Madrid, Temple University in Tokyo, Bard College in Berlin or New York University in Abu Dhabi or Shanghai and a future expanded campus in Paris of the University of Chicago).

Students with a good level of English can follow an entire American undergraduate degree program on foreign campuses in Europe and beyond at a lower cost than comparable undergraduate institutions in the US.

The American universities and colleges in Europe, too numerous for an exhaustive list, attract many international as well as American or bi-national students. They share the common goal of preparing global citizens who can live and work in many cultures. Although most have relatively small student bodies, they nonetheless boast students from 40 or more countries, making for a balance of American and international education. Some, like the American University of Paris, the American University of Rome, or John Cabot University in Rome, offer a fairly broad liberal arts curriculum while others, such as the International University of Monaco or Vesalius College in Brussels, concentrate on business, communications, or international relations. Webster University is unusual in that it has campuses in Geneva, Leiden, Vienna, and Athens, plus other locations in Africa and Asia in addition to its home campus in Saint Louis, Missouri. Its academic offerings overseas do not cover the entire liberal arts spectrum, but students may transfer from one international site to another without ever studying in the US.

Many of these programs have the added benefit of being relatively less expensive than a comparable undergraduate institution in the US. For students whose home is in Europe, travel and health insurance costs are also less onerous.

A helpful resource to start investigating American universities in Europe is the group of American Universities Abroad (www.americanuniabroad.com).

References and Resources

- Website for foreign students wishing to study in France: www.campusfrance.org/en
- European Higher Education Area website with links to university programs in all the member countries of the EHEA: www.ehea.info/page-members
- Directory of university programs in Europe at all levels, with links to programs in English: www.euroeducation.net
- European Liberal Arts Initiative database listing liberal arts (B.A./B.Sc.) programs in Europe: https://liberal-arts.eu
- Websites for foreign students wishing to study in the Netherlands: www.eurogates.nl and www.studyinholland.nl
- Website for students wishing to study in Germany, DAAD - German Academic Exchange Service: www.daad.de/en/
- Listing of degree programs taught in English in Italy: www.ceebd.co.uk/study-in-italy
- Network of resources for education, jobs, and travel aimed at students abroad; has listing of colleges, universities, and career training programs in many countries: www.learn-4good.com
- Website of the group of American Universities Abroad: www.americanuniabroad.com

Endnotes

1. www.ehea.info
2. http://www.enseignementsup-recherche.gouv.fr/cid140055/appel-a-projets-bienvenue-en-france.html
3. http://www.enseignementsup-recherche.gouv.fr/cid140055/appel-a-projets-bienvenue-en-france.html
4. www.francecompetences.fr
5. www.rncp.cncp.gouv.fr/
6. https://efmdglobal.org/accreditations/business-schools/equis
7. www.sciencespo.fr/college/en/campus/le-havre
8. www.sciencespo.fr/college/en/campus/reims

9. www.sciencespo.fr/college/en/campus/menton
10. www.sciencespo.fr/admissions/en/content/undergraduate-international-admissions.html
11. www.campusfrance.org/en; Campus France is the French governmental agency that promotes higher education in France and international mobility of students.
12. www.usa.campusfrance.org
13. www.studyinsweden.se

Graduate Study in France for the International Student

Elyse Michaels-Berger and Helen Shavit

France is a leader of innovation and renowned for academic excellence, attracting some of the best students from around the world. If you are an international student planning to study in France for your postgraduate education, you will follow in the footsteps of many brilliant minds. France is appreciated on the world stage as a global technology giant supportive of young innovators and start-up businesses. With over 60 Nobel Prize recipients, France's tradition of academic excellence speaks for itself, boasting among the best postgraduate study programs worldwide in domains as varied as art and architecture, business studies, engineering, biotechnology, nuclear energy, space and aviation, history, and political science, among others.

French universities, schools of art and architecture, as well as the highly prestigious *grandes écoles,* have become increasingly attractive to international students. While state-funded French universities have historically opened their doors to students holding the French *baccalauréat, grandes écoles* have traditionally been more selective; these offer specializations in science and engineering, humanities, business, as well as administration and political science. Institutions such as HEC Paris, École Polytechnique, and Sciences Po, among others, are of international renown. Although not all higher education institutions in France are featured in global rankings, French academic institutions consistently offer quality, specialized education across disciplines, and are considered among the best cost/quality offerings in Europe, if not the world. Moreover, thanks both to global rankings and alumni who are increasingly international, the palette of offerings has become more well known and appreciated worldwide.

As international graduates attest, educational opportunities in France are readily accessible for non-French students, whether you hail from within or outside of the European Union. While the majority of programs are taught in French, graduate courses at leading higher education institutions are increasingly taught in English for both French and international students alike, rendering them popular destinations for a non-French student body.

So, you want to study in France, where to start?

First, be clear about your personal and professional reasons to study in France. Making a few decisions up-front will help you determine your path and identify the resources available to you.

Why France?

Determine your end goal. Be as specific as possible about your objective and the learning environment you're seeking. Are you looking for an experience with an international student body and teaching staff? Are you focused on the academic experience or are you hoping for a mix of student club life and academic coursework? Do you intend to immerse yourself in French, or remain in an environment where English is prevalent? Today, there are a significant number of leading degree-awarding programs as well as certificate options in both languages.

Some graduate students choose a specific path based primarily on a school's ranking and learning environment. Others are Francophiles motivated more by the opportunity to spend time in France and immerse themselves in the French culture and language. Others are eager to benefit from the French Tech[1] ecosystem for start-ups. For a sampling of varied students' experiences in France, see the "Student Anecdotes" section at the end of this chapter. You may also consult the "e-ambassadors" rubric on the Campus France website.[2]

What opportunities exist?

As you explore the options available to you, consider how long you plan on staying in France. Academic options range from short-term summer programs, to long-term degree-awarding experiences ranging from one to five years (in the case of specialized master's or even doctoral programs).

Short-term stays

If you are interested in a short-term option, a wide offering of short-term summer programs is available. Summer programs attract a global student body, many of whom may later opt to return to France to pursue a Master's. Courses are proposed in both English and French and can last anywhere from one to eight weeks. Offered in diverse domains, a short-term experience offers a chance to test out both the academic and cultural experience. Others consider short-term programs as an opportunity to tack on an accredited academic experience onto an international holiday in France. Offerings vary from light in workload to intense summer experiences for academic credit. Finally, these programs are usually open to all applicants, whether you are a current student or recent graduate and whatever your specialization. To explore short-term summer school opportunities, consult websites of your target educational institutions and/or the Campus France directory.[3]

International exchanges

Thanks to the proliferation of academic cooperation across higher education, current graduate students seeking to study abroad in France can also choose to benefit from an international academic exchange. In these cases, admission to a partner academic institution in France is granted for a pre-determined period of time, usually a term, through a cooperation agreement with the student's home institution. Exchange students apply directly through their home institution, which in turn makes the student placement abroad and facilitates many elements of the international transition.

Long-term, degree-awarding options

French higher education follows the European standardized degree system: *licence-master-doctorat* (bachelor's-master's-doctorate), known as the LMD system. *Le master* is often referred to as its subsets: M1 (the first year) and M2 (the second year). Degrees are earned in ECTS (European Credit Transfer and Accumulation System) credits, which facilitates international mobility across Europe. French degrees are recognized by the French state, certified by the French Ministry of Higher Education, Research, and Innovation or registered in the French Directory of Professional Certifications (*Répertoire national des certifications professionnelles* – RNCP).[4] In the case of business and engineering schools, certain independent organizations also issue accreditations.

There are different types of Master's degrees in France. The most common is the "*master*", leading to the state recognized diploma, the DNM *(le Diplôme National de Master)*. It is granted by institutions of higher learning accredited by the MESRI, such as universities, Sciences Po (IEP), and the École normale supérieure (a member school of Université PSL). The student may choose a professionally oriented or a research-oriented path *(parcours)*, usually in the second year of the master's curriculum. The *master* is a two-year program that confers 120 ECTS credits. Subjects studied range from comparative literature, history, and economics to mathematics, physics, urban planning, and environmental studies. Go to the government website, *"trouver mon master"*[5] to find a comprehensive listing of all master's programs conferring the DNM. An increasing number of master programs are delivered entirely in English. For further information about studying at a public university see the chapter, "University Studies in France".

If you are looking to specialize in a particular professional field, you may also consider the MSc degree conferred by a *grande école* or other higher learning institution that is a member of the Conference des Grandes Écoles (CGE). The MSc degree program requires one to two years of study and confers 90 ECTS credits. It is offered in business and engineering schools in fields as varied as finance, environment, cultural management, communication, public law, health, tourism, biotechnology, etc. It is open to students who have completed a Bachelor's degree (or *bac* + 4 in France). It offers the opportunity to focus on a very specific field, and has a strong international orientation with at least fifty percent of the curriculum taught in a language other than French. The MSc can include an internship in France or internationally, and certain schools can require a semester abroad. Examples are the MSc in Aerospace Systems – Navigation and Telecommunications (MSc AS-NAT), offered by ENAC in Toulouse, the MSc in Finance at HEC Paris and the MSc in Creative Business and Social Innovation offered by EDHEC in Lille.

Students considering general management studies in France can choose between the MIM or the MBA, depending on their age and professional experience. (The MIM has been widely adopted internationally as the nomenclature for the Master in Management.) MIM students usually begin the program with little professional experience, while most MBA programs require participants to have several years of work experience. The MIM can span up to three years (including one year of professional internship) whereas MBA programs can last between 10 months and two years. The MBA and other master's in management programs can be pursued at *grandes écoles* and public universities and many are taught exclusively in English. Leading offerings can be found among institutions such as HEC Paris, EMLYON, ESSEC, INSEAD, and Audencia, among others. These degree opportunities are highly focused on preparing students for the workplace and can lead the student to a rich network of professional opportunities worldwide. When investigating any professional school one should ascertain its accreditation, reputation, and post-graduate networks.

If you already have a Master's degree and are seeking more advanced, specialized studies, you can consider the MS *(Mastère Spécialisé)* or "advanced master's", which is a one-year diploma program. (Certain schools will open a few spots for exceptionally talented Bachelor graduates, however, such seats are limited.) The MS is offered by *grandes écoles* and other higher learning institutions that are members of the CGE. The objective is to prepare students for employment in a specialized field such as airport management, digital business strategy, spatial planning and urban development, among many others. An example of a program taught entirely in English is the Advanced Master in Biotechnology and Pharmaceutical Management offered by the Grenoble École de Management. There are more than 400 specialized master's programs across 40 disciplines offered by engineering schools, business schools, and other specialized schools throughout France.[6]

Dual degrees at the Master level

For those who are seeking to broaden their academic network, educational institutions offering Master level programs have progressively developed their international portfolio so that students can earn two degrees, known as a dual or double degree, which can span regions and at times disciplines. This can be an ideal opportunity for students who are seeking a degree and network in different regions of the world. Consult individual university or Master program websites for these offerings. Admissions requirements often necessitate application to each institution separately. In other cases, a student can only apply once enrolled in a partner institution.

One of the most recent offerings is the M2M, launched by HEC Paris with three other leading business schools, including the Yale School of Management (SOM), the Hong Kong University of Science and Technology (HKUST), and Fundação Getúlio Vargas (FGV) in Brazil, which are part of the Global Network for Advanced Management. Participants have the opportunity to complete two Master's degrees. For example, as part of the HEC Paris – Yale School of Management M2M, students attend HEC Paris in year 1 and the Yale SOM Master of Management Studies in Global Business and Society during the second year of the dual degree. For additional examples of dual degree opportunities, see the section "A Sampling of Graduate Schools and Programs" found later in this chapter.

Doctoral studies in France

Many French universities and higher institutions of academic learning, including *grandes écoles,* offer individuals the opportunity to earn a doctorate degree, the highest academic degree attainable. The doctorate degree significantly differs from other academic degrees in that it emphasizes original and independent research and qualifies individuals to teach at the university level. Therefore, while doctoral programs are usually part of a university or a *grande école,* they are generally affiliated with research laboratories, as well. Depending upon the field of study, a doctoral student can anticipate their program requiring three to six years to complete in a public institution under the supervision of a thesis advisor. Doctoral offerings in management at private institutions, such as HEC Paris or INSEAD, last five years.

Students ultimately present their research in the form of a written dissertation and oral defense. The doctoral degree is conferred upon orally defending the dissertation during a public defense. The need for French language proficiency will vary between programs and institutions, however, for the hard sciences interactions between the student and his/her thesis advisor are in English.[7] The dissertation may be written and defended in English, however the thesis summary must be submitted in French. In the humanities and social sciences, a good level of French (B1 – B2) is generally necessary. In business and management studies, English can be the sole language. Please verify language requirements before applying. (For further information on doctoral studies at universities, see the chapter "University Studies in France".)

What are your plans after graduating?

If you are hoping to stay in Europe after completing a graduate program, you may want to select an institution where international recruiters are prevalent. Whenever possible, connect with career or employment services offices for advice, and speak with past participants for their experiences to see what paths are the most common. Consider employability rankings, such as those published by the *Times Higher Education,*[8] which highlight the universities that recruiters prefer. You may also wish to consider international rankings such as the *Financial Times, The Wall Street Journal, The Economist,* and the *ShanghaiRanking*[9] among others. Each ranking will highlight different variables, and a strong ranking will increase an academic institution's international recognition.

Fees and Financing

Financing shouldn't be an obstacle to your search. Thanks to the subsidizing of higher education by the French government, costs of attending a public university for a Master's program are particularly low, 243 € a year. (In 2019, a move to substantially increase tuition for international students was retracted following much protest, however, it is unclear at this writing what the final tuition fee will be.) The tuition at private universities or *grandes écoles,* on the other hand, ranges from 3,000 € to 35,000 € per year or more. Consult each institution directly for full fees.

Public institutions have maintained doctoral student fees of 380 € annually (not including modest application fees), whereas private institutions, including business schools, can range between 3,000 € to 10,000 € or more per year for doctoral studies. In most cases, students will need to apply for a grant. Certain doctoral programs at private institutions offer full funding for the entire five-year period.

Scholarships remain a viable option for foreign students. Of particular interest are the French Ministry for Europe and Foreign Affairs' Eiffel Excellence Scholarship Program[10] for master's and doctoral level study, which award a stipend of 1100 € to 1400 € per month for living expenses. Students are nominated for these awards based on the recommendation of higher education institutions. In addition to other merit-based scholarships, grants are available according to individual social criteria. While it is less common for foreign students to receive these grants, students who have had a tax home in France for two years prior to their studies are eligible.

Students who attend a French institution as part of a partnership agreement between universities are often exempt from the tuition fees. This is the case for the well-known Erasmus+[11] program. In many instances, students can also travel abroad for an internship. All French universities currently participate in Erasmus+, which is subsidized by the European Union.

The student may not realize that studying in France comes with significant benefits outside of the classroom. All students enrolled in French higher education are afforded the opportunity to travel openly throughout the Schengen area of the European Union. Foreign students enrolled in a long-term program are also authorized to work for the equivalent of 60% of the work year at minimum wage. A student residence permit is required in this case for non-EU students. Finally, on a day-to-day basis, know that as a student you will also receive local discounts (for museums, movies, sports centers), in addition to discount rates on public transportation.

For PhD study in particular, a doctorate that is funded in the form of a fellowship is the equivalent of a work contract. Student working contracts may be proposed for senior students within affiliated research laboratories. In these cases, students receive both a salary and access to social security for health care benefits. Contracts can be research-based or teaching-based (professional). Potential candidates should monitor professional lists for opportunities. Consult the websites of the Association Bernard Gregory (www.abg.asso.fr) or Academic Positions (http://academicpositions.com/jobs/country/france) among others for PhD and postdoc positions.

Where can you find out more about different programs?

Thanks to the abundance of offerings and educational services that guide students, you can easily find information on application offerings and procedures directly via institutional websites. Multiple educational websites offer helpful information, in particular, Campus France which provides online directories that can be searched by length of program, as well as by language of instruction, subject area, and location.[12] The French Ministry of Higher Education, Research, and Innovation provides (in French) a full listing of educational establishment types.[13] At the end of this chapter is an overview of some of the more renowned schools offering graduate degree programs.

Study abroad forums are regularly held throughout the world. International university tour operators also offer conferences where you can meet representatives from different institutions. Online resources such as *The Economist* offer forums where online chats are held with admissions officers and current students who provide information and tips on respective programs.

How to apply?

Most graduate programs encourage students to apply via their online admissions platforms. Consult websites carefully as certain standardized tests (such as the GRE, GMAT, etc.) may be required; registration for these tests necessitates advanced planning to meet respective admissions deadlines. Application criteria are likely to require a combination of elements including: essay questions, past transcripts, CVs, and in several cases, interviews. Language tests (either for English and/or French) are likely to be required.

Many global institutions will be familiar with academic credentials of international students, and may not require you to undertake any type of equivalency process. However, depending upon the institution, you may be required to provide a French equivalency of your academic background. If needed, this may be requested through the French government ENIC-NARIC Center.[14]

If you have an earlier professional experience that you'd like to validate for a degree, there are two ways to do this. *La validation des acquis de l'expérience* (VAE) will help you establish the equivalent of your past experience to facilitate access to a training program. *La validation des acquis professionnels* (VAP) process leads to a partial or full degree being awarded through the certification of your skill and knowledge.[15]

If you are applying to the university system, those students who are applying from within the EU/EEA can do so directly under the same conditions as French students. European residents without European citizenship should address the French embassy or consulate in their country of residence.

As of 2019, students from outside the EU/EEA region are required to utilize an online portal through the French government called Études en France (Studies in France).[16] This process is only for students applying to a master's-level degree (not required for doctoral programs). The Études en France platform (required for over 40 nationalities) offers a process that ensures that students meet certain enrollment conditions. It takes students through the full process leading up to the visa request and allows you to track its progress.

Pay special attention to individual application deadlines, which vary by program. As with nearly all applications, applying to three or four options is recommended. Take advantage of the opportunity to apply early to your top choices. Then, if you are not granted admission, follow up with your other program applications.

Plan your applications to coincide with the decision requirements. In the case of a rolling admissions process, good news often also comes with the requirement to make your confirmation payment in order to reserve your place. Make sure you plan the timing of your applications so that you will have an adequate period of time to consider and accept an offer if you are admitted to several programs. Remember to verify both the payment and cancellation policies of each institution's program before the application period.

Apply early, not only to potentially increase your chances of garnering an admissions offer, but also to ensure you have the time to organize your housing and potential visa paperwork. If you plan to apply for a scholarship or a study grant, the earlier the better.

Once admitted, what visa / paperwork is required?

Depending on your country of origin, you may require a student visa. In many instances, a stay of 90 days or less does not require a visa. Beyond this, a long-stay visa is often required. Consult the French consular offices for your full visa requirements. In any case, if you are a non-EU/EEA citizen and plan to stay for more than six months in France, you will have to apply for a residence permit, and prove that you have sufficient funds to support yourself.

Whatever option you choose, make sure you have insurance before venturing abroad. The most practical advice is to obtain medical, personal liability, and repatriation insurance. European students will be covered through European healthcare cards. If you are not from the European Union, however, and you plan to participate in a long-term program, you will be able to apply for national healthcare insurance. Consult the student services office of the program you are attending or check the government health services website (in English).[17]

Once you are admitted, you'll want to focus quickly on housing options. The program you are attending will likely offer campus housing, or be able to recommend local providers. You can also look into local social media networks where housing and roommate options are often provided.

Now that you are armed to undertake the admissions process in France, we hope you'll get started with confidence and enthusiasm. While studying in France can appear challenging at first glance, students who have done it have reaped exciting benefits both personally and professionally. Many a graduate will testify to the enriching educational experience and the newly opened doors the experience will offer you!

A Sampling of Graduate Schools and Programs

The following snapshot of the different kinds of graduate schools and programs offered in France is adapted from the chapter of the same title authored by Elyse Michaels-Berger, Philip Cacouris, and Stephanie Schantz in the first edition of this guide.

Science & Engineering Schools – *Écoles d'Ingénieurs*

Almost all leading French engineering schools accept applications from international students to their entire range of programs including the Master of Engineering *(Diplôme d'ingénieur)*, the MSc (Master of Science), the MS/Advanced Master's *(Mastère Spécialisé)* and doctoral studies. Admission requirements depend on the level of the student and, in certain cases, your degree of fluency in French. In addition, admissions procedures differ by school.

Many leading engineering schools now take part in research and constitute higher education consortiums or similar alliances. Several examples are cited below for your reference. Most websites are also posted in English and are highly informative. We recommend you consult these resources, as they will offer the most comprehensive, up-to-date information on programs and international admissions. Campus France[18] also publishes an online directory of engineering Master's programs. Of special note, is a network, n+i,[19] of more than 50 engineering schools, including a number of the most prominent *grandes écoles*, offering information, guidance, and support services to the international student wishing to pursue a Master's degree in an engineering field in France. The candidate may apply to schools in this network using a single online application.

ParisTech[20] is a prestigious research and higher education consortium that unites 10 *grandes écoles* of engineering. Schools included in the ParisTech consortium include:

- AgroParisTech (Institut des sciences et industries du vivant et de l'environnement)
- Arts et Métiers ParisTech (École nationale supérieure d'arts et métiers)
- Chimie Paris ParisTech (École nationale supérieure de chimie de Paris)
- École des Ponts ParisTech (École nationale des ponts et chaussées)
- ENSAE ParisTech (École nationale de la statistique et de l'administration économique)
- ENSTA ParisTech (École nationale supérieure de techniques avancées)
- ESPCI ParisTech (École supérieure de physique et de chimie industrielles de la ville de Paris)
- Institut d'Optique Graduate School (SupOptique)
- MINES ParisTech (École nationale supérieure des mines de Paris)
- TELECOM ParisTech (École nationale supérieure des télécommunications)

The CentraleSupélec[21] group includes Paris-Saclay, Metz, and Rennes campuses. The Écoles Centrale group includes the four other Écoles Centrale in France (Lille, Lyon, Marseille, and Nantes) as well as international-based schools (Beijing, Casablanca, Hyderabad).[22]

Institut Mines Télécom[23] schools include: ENSIIE (Paris/Évry); EURECOM (Sophia Antipolis); InSIC (Nancy); IMT Atlantique (Brest, Nantes, Rennes, Toulouse); IMT Lille Douai; IMT Mines Albi-Carmaux; IMT Mines Alès; Institut Mines-Télécom Business School (Évry); Mines Nancy; MINES ParisTech; MINES Saint-Étienne; Télécom Paris; Télécom SudParis (Évry, Paris-Saclay)

Information on engineering programs offered at public universities, can be found in the chapter, "University Studies in France".

Business Schools – *Écoles de Commerce*

Today's leading business schools in France (see non-comprehensive list below) include French institutions as well as foreign institutions based in France. They propose diverse offerings (Master's in Management, specialized Master's, full-time and part-time MBAs, Executive MBAs, and Doctorates) that should be considered carefully. Program length can vary from 10 months to two years for Master's programs and MBAs. Certain schools require fluent English while others require high proficiency in French for admissions. Depending on the school, coursework can be offered in English, French, or both.

Be aware of new opportunities in the business school arena as traditional structures evolve. Educate yourself about the differences between the various programs and identify the corresponding advantages (e.g., class structure, class profile, recruiter profile, etc.) for you. For example, the Master's in Management (MIM) is an increasingly attractive option for international graduates who seek to reposition themselves in the French job market. Often the MIM will offer students the opportunity to pursue one, if not two, internships during the course of studies.

Almost all business schools will offer internships, international exchanges, or dual degree opportunities, either as required or optional facets of the degree program. Investigate these elements early in the admissions process to plan your course of study accordingly.

In addition to exchange programs and dual degree partnerships, certain MBA programs have developed a strategy of multiple campuses; for example, ESCP Europe Business School campuses are based in Paris, London, Madrid, Berlin, Turin, and Warsaw. Others such as ESSEC Business School have campuses in Singapore and Morocco, while INSEAD has campuses in Singapore and Abu Dhabi as well as France.

Apprenticeship Training

While internship opportunities may be a component of specialized master's programs (M2), certain business schools and some universities also offer apprenticeship training. An apprenticeship is an innovative way to study while working; you are in effect a full-time student and a company employee at the same time. The school establishes a contract with your company, so that you are officially granted time off for your academic coursework.

Ask those schools that interest you as to whether this is an option, although it is usually clearly indicated on their websites. An apprenticeship can provide a good opportunity to balance theory and practice while maintaining a professional activity, which can also help offset the costs of your degree.

Websites for Business Programs

As it is impossible to list all the options here, we cite several examples of leading schools offering business degrees where an international educational background will be welcome. Once again, consult the Campus France website to find additional listings and business school information sources. You will find offerings as unique as an MBA in Wine Marketing and Management in Bordeaux, as well as Aviation MBAs. Depending on your long-term goals, you may want to compare French rankings with global rankings to see which schools are more internationally renowned.

- EDHEC Business School: www.edhec.edu
- ENPC École des Ponts Business School: http://www.enpc.fr/ecole-des-ponts-business-school
- ESCP Europe Business School: www.escpeurope.eu
- EMLYON: www.em-lyon.com
- ESSEC Business School: www.essec.edu
- HEC Paris: www.hec.edu
- INSEAD: www.insead.edu
- INSEEC: www.inseec.com
- Université de Bordeaux: www.u-bordeaux.com
- Toulouse Business School: www.tbs-education.fr/en

Specialized Schools: Fashion Management

Paris is one of the key cities worldwide for fashion - from traditional luxury to innovative new designs - and it is said that for a designer to show during Paris Fashion Week is the ultimate seal of approval. It is not surprising, then, that fashion education is flourishing in this city. Specialized schools, generally independent from universities or *grandes écoles,* offer high-level training in the field.

Fashion Design

Some fashion and design schools only offer undergraduate courses; graduate design programs are quite specific in requiring undergraduate degrees in garment or accessory design. Programs may be in English or French and admission requires submission of a portfolio and potentially the creation of a specific piece as well. Among the best-known schools in Paris for fashion design are Institut Français de la Mode, ESMOD, and École Duperré.

Fashion Management

This is a relatively recent discipline aimed at preparing students to work in a wide range of roles including marketing, merchandising, retailing, and product development. The program duration is approximately one year and will often include an internship. Unlike other disciplines, such as business, cross-institutional partnerships and double degree programs are not the norm in this domain.

As a prospective student, there are a number of questions you should ask yourself:

1. Type of school: Many art/design schools offer management-related courses, sometimes specifically focused on one aspect, such as merchandising or communications. Some business schools have entered the design realm, usually with a business focus on the luxury sector. The nature of the school will naturally color its approach to the subject of design. For instance, Institut Français de la Mode, a kind of hybrid of a business and design school, focuses as much on understanding the product and the culture of fashion as it does on brand management. Your undergraduate degree and your personal inclination, as well as your specific career ambitions, should guide you in your search for a program.

2. Language: Fashion management courses are given in either English or French. School websites will indicate the minimum language proficiency level required to enroll in a course. If your goal is to work in France after graduation it should be noted that it is almost impossible to secure a job offer here if you do not have at least a conversational level of French. If you have already studied French, consider an intensive language course in order to boost your level of fluency and allow yourself to do graduate study in French.

3. Reputation of school: In the absence of rankings for this kind of program, it can be hard to get a clear sense of how a school is perceived by the industry and how helpful its name will be in starting your career afterwards. Ask anyone you or your family know who works in the industry to hear his/her point of view. Otherwise look at the information the school gives about its alumni and particularly about the companies it works with; this will at least give you an idea of the school's professional network.

4. Type of degree: A number of smaller and more specialized schools offer postgraduate certificates rather than internationally recognized Master's degrees. This is a reflection on the specificity of the subject and not on the quality of a

particular program. However, be aware of this if you are thinking of returning directly to the US or elsewhere or of continuing to the doctoral level, in which case a validated diploma will be important.

As with other graduate study courses, it really comes down to being clear about what you want in terms of a study environment and how you see your post-study career path. With a range of study options available, you are likely to find the one that suits you.

Some websites for Fashion Management programs
The fashion education landscape is becoming crowded with large universities and smaller public and private institutions. Here is a sampling of reputable schools offering programs:

- Institut Français de la Mode: www.ifm-paris.com
- ESSEC Business School: www.essec.edu
- ESMOD: www.esmod.com
- HEC Paris Summer School in Fashion Management: www.hec.edu
- INSEEC U: www.inseec.com
- Mod'Art: www.mod-art.org
- Université de Paris Est – Marne la Vallée: http://ecogestion.u-pem.fr/master-innovation-design-luxe

Academic Programs in Law, Public Policy, and Administration

In contrast to the American system, a legal education in France begins after high school. French students study law for three years to become a *jurist*, a law specialist who works exclusively in a company, or five to seven years to become an *avocat*, a lawyer who works in a law firm. (See the chapter "Becoming a Lawyer in France" for further information.) There are many opportunities to study graduate-level law in France in which American students can earn graduate degrees in both the US and in France.

Master 2 in Global Governance Studies
Sciences Po Law School (Paris), offers a program in Global Governance Studies with a cohort of their own students, along with those from Columbia, Duke, Georgetown, Harvard, Northwestern, Pennsylvania, and Virginia. This one-year *Master 2* program explores legal issues within a global context. In addition, there exists a second exchange program between Sciences Po, Columbia, and Université Paris I (Panthéon Sorbonne) in Global Business Law and Governance.

JD / Master in Law –Double Diploma through Columbia or Cornell / Sorbonne
Columbia and Cornell Law Schools, in partnership with the Université Paris I (Panthéon Sorbonne), offers a three or four-year program that confers a dual degree in law (JD) and a *Master 1* and/or *Master 2* in law from the Panthéon Sorbonne. The program is designed to enable students to take the bar exams in both the US and in France. Students spend the first two years at Columbia and Cornell, followed by one to two years at the Sorbonne. Graduates may then continue to earn a *Master 2* in law from the Sorbonne.

Graduate Law Degrees (LL.M. degree)
For students interested in pursuing a LL.M. degree there are many institutions in France that offer a one-year program. Consult the following website for a detailed list: www.llm-guide.com/france. For example, the Sorbonne-Assas International Law School in conjunction with INSEAD offers an English language program culminating in an LL.M. in International Business. The Université Jean Moulin Lyon III in Lyon offers an LL.M. in International and European Law as well as a *Master 2*.

Dual Degree Programs
More and more institutions are preparing students for a professional career in the global environment through dual degrees that span disciplines.

Options to bridge law across disciplines
Sciences Po, in conjunction with the University of Pennsylvania offers a Master's in Finance and Strategy or a Master's in International Management and Sustainability along with a Penn Law LL.M.[24]

Another dual degree program follows the first year of studies at Sciences Po with the second year at Georgetown Law, culminating in a Sciences Po Master's in International Affairs combined with a Georgetown Law LL.M.[25]

HEC Paris and Georgetown Law provide an interesting option, where students spend the first year at HEC Paris for the Master's in Management curriculum, and the second year at Georgetown Law School, leading to the Master's degree in Management and Business Law from HEC Paris and the LL.M. from Georgetown Law School. Students apply to the program at Georgetown Law School during their first year at HEC Paris.

For students who wish to stay in France, HEC Paris and Université Paris 1 (Panthéon Sorbonne) also offer a dual degree. Participants earn the Master (M1 & M2) in Business Law from Université Paris 1 (Panthéon Sorbonne) and the HEC Paris / *Grande École* Master in Management & Business Law.[26]

Public Policy and Administration
There are increasing opportunities to pursue a double degree in France that spans public policy and management.

Sciences Po proposes a double degree program that culminates in a Master of Public Policy from Sciences Po and a Master in Public Administration from Columbia University's School of International and Public Affairs (SIPA). Another offers a Master in Public Policy from Sciences Po coupled with a Master in Public Administration from the Institute of Public Affairs at the London School of Economics and Political Science (LSE).

The Fletcher School of Law and Diplomacy at Tufts University in the US and HEC Paris offer another dual degree across disciplines. Students earn the Master of Arts in Law and Diplomacy (MALD)[27] at the Fletcher School and the Master in Management (MIM) from HEC Paris.

The above offerings are but a sample. These institutions and others offer myriad global dual-degree partnerships well worth further exploration as you build your international experience and expand your global network, a key to future success.

Endnotes

1. www.lafrenchtech.com/fr
2. http://e-ambassadeurs.campusfrance.org
3. For programs taught in French, see http://ecolesdete.campusfrance.org/#/main. For programs taught in English, see http://taughtie.campusfrance.org/tiesearch/#/catalog.
4. www.rncp.cncp.gouv.fr
5. www.trouvermonmaster.gouv.fr
6. https://ressources.campusfrance.org/esr/diplomes/en/mastere_spe_en.pdf; www.cge.asso.fr/formations-labellisees/liste-formation-ms
7. www.campusfrance.org/fr/comment-fonctionne-doctorat-France
8. www.timeshighereducation.com/student/best-universities/best-universities-graduate-jobs-global-university-employability-ranking
9. ShanghaiRanking's Academic Ranking of World Universities (ARWU)
10. www.campusfrance.org/en/eiffel-scholarship-program-of-excellence
11. Erasmus+: European Action Scheme for the Mobility of University Students
12. www.campusfrance.org/en/finding-a-university-programme-France; https://doctorat.campusfrance.org/en/phd/dschools/main
13. www.enseignementsup-recherche.gouv.fr/pid24558-cid49705/liste-des-etablissements-d-enseignement-superieur-et-de-recherche.html
14. www.ciep.fr/en/enic-naric-france
15. For full details on these two processes: www.enseignementsup-recherche.gouv.fr/cid21066/la-validation-des-acquis-dans-l-enseignement-superieur-v.a.e.-et-vap-85.html
16. https://pastel.diplomatie.gouv.fr/etudesenfrance/dyn/public/authentification/login.html?codeLangue=EN
17. https://etudiant-etranger.ameli.fr/#/
18. www.campusfrance.org
19. www.nplusi.com
20. https://paristech.fr/en
21. www.centralesupelec.fr
22. www.groupe-centrale.com
23. www.imt.fr
24. www.sciencespo.fr/ecole-management-innovation/en/education/dual-degrees/penn-law
25. www.sciencespo.fr/psia/content/dual-degree-georgetown-law-school
26. www.hec.edu/en/master-s-programs/dual-degree-programs
27. https://fletcher.tufts.edu/academics/masters-programs-residential/MALD

Student Anecdotes

It is a very cool experience to interact with people from all over the world. Here, in my business program, the teaching is fully international; every class has so many different perspectives, not only the French, but that of students from all the continents. It is a very special mix. I would recommend that all students learn French before coming to France, even if your coursework occurs in English. Knowing French will help you exponentially and boost your confidence at the same time. Be careful about de-prioritizing the language piece as it's critical to your success. If you go abroad for graduate study, remember that you are part of networks that will exist abroad as well; people are very welcoming and generous with their time. To help me get a foot in the door, whenever I go to a new place, I reach out to alumni by email to gain their insight and advice. Remember that European business schools will tend to attract European recruiters. — *Lauren*

At first, I was intimidated by the visa materials and administration aspects of moving to a new country but it turned out to be really easy. My friends back home were surprised that it wasn't as challenging as they had thought. With everything digitized these days, it doesn't have to be difficult. The residential housing choice comes down to your location and academic program. When I decided to focus in Finance, I knew I was better off living on campus (avoiding any time commuting) due to the rigor of the program. The first few months were also important for me to stay on campus as it was a critical time to get to know everyone. It helped me avoid the challenges of having to find a guarantor for my own apartment at first. — *Céline*

I found my housing through the student Facebook network. It was a great find that allowed me to share my residential space with French students. — *Riley*

Even if English is the primary language [in the program you choose], remember that the culture won't be Anglo-Saxon. If you appreciate the French culture and make an effort to speak the language and partake in student groups, life becomes more beautiful abroad. If you don't speak French, by all means make sure that you learn it. — *Syriash*

While completing my Bachelor's degree, I studied abroad in Paris. I truly enjoyed my time there so decided to pursue my Master's degree in art history at the same school. In the end, I completed two Master's degrees. I enjoyed both programs and believe my choice allowed me to fulfill both my academic and personal goals. Since I attended classes at the Master's level, my classes were all seminars and were generally small (30 students or less). Professors were often open to discussions with students and available to provide help on assignments. The students in the program often took classes together, which allowed us to get to know each other. I found that there were not a lot of social activities offered by the university. Occasionally, the seminars would include visits to cultural institutions in Paris and Île-de-France. I believe I adjusted well and was able to make strong connections with other students and faculty members. For international students considering this path, I would strongly encourage them to work as much as possible on their French language skills, as all of my classes and assignments were in French. I would also encourage them to involve themselves in student activities as much as possible. — *Samantha*

Through an international joint thesis agreement *(cotutelle)*, I was able to complete a double doctoral degree at both a French and an American university. Comparing these two experiences, I would describe the US experience as more well-rounded and supportive in terms of community within the department. In French doctoral programs, the focus is on individual research; a researcher will likely work closely with his or her supervisor but will often spend little time with others in the department. Upon entrance into a program, French doctoral students also move directly into the research and writing phases of their work and often finish within three years. In the US, however, doctoral students often spend the first couple years doing coursework before they pass qualifying exams, and only then do they start the research and writing portions of their work. This is beneficial in that it forces researchers to broaden their expertise in areas or topics they were not necessarily working on; however, it also means that American doctoral programs take longer to complete. Furthermore, in my American university, professional development opportunities in which doctoral candidates could learn about pedagogy, publishing, networking, and other skills they are expected to master before entering the job market, were commonplace. In either case, I would suggest that before applying to programs, know what you will be working on and which scholars at which universities are going to be the most suitable advisors for that work. While enrollment processes differ in each country, the first step in both is to identify those professors you would like to work with and contact them to discuss the possibility. Once those conversations have taken place, those professors will be very helpful in the administrative and enrollment processes.   — *Nicole*

Glossary of Terms

Admissible	Indicates success on the written portion of the competitive exams (*concours*) for entry into a *grande école*, allowing the candidate to take the oral exams (*épreuves orales*).
Admission parallèle	Alternative admissions process; usually for entry into *grandes écoles* for students who have not studied in a *prépa*. For example, students holding a university degree may apply to a *grande école*.
Alternance	A study program alternating on-the-job training with classroom studies. Work may be remunerated.
Baccalauréat général	A secondary school program covering a range of subjects with relative emphasis on one of three domains: scientific, economic/social studies, or literary. The *bac* is an exit diploma from secondary school and qualifies the student for guaranteed admission to university in France.
Baccalauréat technologique	Technological secondary school program offered in seven fields combining concrete professional experience and general education. Leads to the technological *bacs: bac* STAV, *bac* STD2A, *bac* STHR, *bac* STI2D, *bac* STMG, *bac* STL, or *bac* ST2S, or *bac* TMD. Leads to either immediate employment or continuation of studies.
Bac STAV	*Baccalauréat technologique: sciences et technologies de l'agronomie et du vivant;* agricultural studies offered by a *lycée agricole.*
Bac STD2A	*Baccalauréat technologique: sciences et technologies du design et des arts appliqués;* for design and applied arts.
Bac STHR	*Baccalauréat technologique: sciences et technologies de l'hôtellerie et de la restauration;* for hotel and restaurant industry studies.

Bac STI2D	*Baccalauréat technologique: sciences et technologies de l'industries du développement durable;* emphasizing sustainable development and industrial science and technology.
Bac STMG	*Baccalauréat technologique: sciences et technologies du management et de la gestion;* technical *bac* for management, marketing, and finance.
Bac STL	*Baccalauréat technologique: sciences et technologies de laboratoire* divided into two specialities, biotechnology and applied laboratory science.
Bac ST2S	*Baccalauréat technologique: sciences et technologies de la santé et du social*; for studies leading to careers in the health and social sectors.
Bac TMD	*Baccalauréat technologique: techniques de la musique et de la danse*; music and dance *bac*.
Baccalauréat Pro	A *baccalauréat professionnel* is awarded from a *lycée professionnel*; vocational training in one of almost 80 different specialties offered; possibility to pursue further studies, usually for a BTS, or direct entry into the work force.
BCPST	*Biologie, chimie, physique et sciences de la terre* (biology, chemistry, physics, and earth sciences); a scientific *prépa* track.
BDE	*Bureau des étudiants:* student-run office on school campuses that organizes extra-curricular activities and social events, and serves as a student information center.
BEP	*Brevet d'études professionnelles:* Intermediate vocational qualification earned while working towards a *baccalauréat professionnel*.
Bienvenue en France	"Choose France"; the student welcome and support strategy for international students in France, launched in 2019, and designed to substantially increase the enrollment of foreign students.
Binôme, Trinôme	Study groups of two or three students.
Bizutage	Hazing. Officially outlawed and punishable by law in France, this practice unfortunately, continues somewhat during the WEI (*Weekends d'intégration*, the "welcome" weekend) at some of the *grandes écoles*.
Bologna Process	European wide initiative harmonizing the structure of higher education systems in order to facilitate credit transfer, validation of coursework, and mutual recognition of diplomas across participating European countries.

Bourse	Grant (scholarship) allocated to students based on need and sometimes merit to help finance studies. *Boursièr(e)* refers to the student who receives the grant.
BTS	*Brevet de technicien supérieur*: Technical diploma awarded after two post-*bac* years of vocational training. Studies focus on specific technical skills either for direct entry into the workforce or continued studies.
BTSA	*BTS Agricole: brevet de technicien supérieur* in agriculture, often after a *bac* STAV.
BUT	*Bachelor universitaire de technologie:* a new three-year university based technology program to start in 2021, coinciding with reform of the DUT. To eventually replace the *licence professionelle*.
Campus France	The French national agency for the promotion of French higher education throughout the world; www.campusfrance.org – in French, English, and Spanish. Applications from international students to institutions of higher learning in France are made through the Campus France website.
CAP	*Certificat d'aptitude professionnelle*: a national vocational training diploma signifying entry level qualification in some 200 specialties.
CEFDG	*Commission d'évaluation de formation et diplômes de gestion*; the national agency that accredits diplomas in management, including the label, *"grade de master"*.
CGE	Conférence des grandes écoles: the federation of French *grandes écoles*, businesses, and affiliates promoting the development and influence of its members in France and abroad.
CIDJ	*Centre d'Information et de Documentation Jeunesse*: A branch of the education ministry which provides young people with information relevant to many aspects of their lives (internships, employment, housing, health issues, leisure activities, etc.) via a network of local, regional or national outlets, and online at www.cidj.com.
CIO	*Centre d'information et d'orientation*: Information center within a local school district and under the aegis of the French education ministries; provides extensive documentation and information for young people on education and vocational opportunities.
Cité universitaire	Student residence hall(s). Allocation of student housing is based on financial need and the distance between the student's family home and school.

CNOUS	*Centre national des œuvres universitaires et scolaires*: the national public agency, under the aegis of the ministry of higher education, that oversees the network of regional offices (CROUS) providing social services for students, ranging from student grants to housing and student dining services.
Colles	Also spelled as *khôlles*. Term referring to oral practice tests given at regular intervals in *prépa*, checking the student's understanding of course content.
ComUE	*Communauté d'universités et établissements*; a consortium of institutions of higher education, which may include both public and private entities, designed to reinforce, coordinate, and promote higher education and research within a given region.
Concours	Competitve entry exam(s) for entry into most of the selective higher education programs. Examinees are ranked according to their results.
Contrôle continu	Regular testing of a student's understanding of course content over the course of a semester.
Convention de stage	Internship agreement; a specific government-regulated contract signed by the intern (a registered student), the intern's school, and the employer.
Conventionné	Government subsidized and/or government regulated.
Cours magistraux	Large group lectures, often in amphitheaters.
CPGE	*Classes préparatoires aux grandes écoles/prépa*: two, sometimes three years of intensive study preparing students for competitive entry exams (*concours*) for the *grandes écoles*.
CTI	*Commission de titres d'ingénieur*; the national commission for engineering degrees. 200 engineering schools in France are currently accredited by the CTI to award an engineering degree.
Cuber	Repeating the second year of *prépa* to increase chances of obtaining a better ranking in the *concours* for entry into a *grande école*.
CVEC	*Contribution vie étudiante et de campus*; fee (about 90 €) paid before university registration is finalized. For cultural, social, and sport activities, and preventive health care.
DAEU	*Diplôme d'accès aux études universitaires*; an equivalency diploma enabling those without a *bac* to enter university or take the French civil service exam.

DALF	*Diplôme approfondi de langue française*; official certificate of advanced French language proficiency, validating levels C1 to C2 of the Common European Framework of Reference for Languages (CEFR).
DAP	*Demande d'admission préalable*; pre-application request necessary for non- EU international students wishing to apply for first-year university studies (L1) in France. Through Campus France website as from Nov 1 of preceding year and until mid January.
DE	*Diplôme d'état*; state diploma delivered by a public institution of higher learning mostly for allied health professions, social work, and sports. For example, DE *d'infirmier* - diploma of nursing.
DELF	*Diplôme d'études en langue française*; official certificate validating French language proficiency at levels A1, A2, B1, and B2.
DEUST	*Diplôme d'études universitaires scientifiques et techniques*: two-year diploma aiming to facilitate gainful employment via apprenticeship and/or an internship.
DNM	*Diplôme national de master*; master's degree, a French national diploma awarded by universities for two years of studies after a *licence*. Called *"le master"*.
Double licence	Double undergraduate degree in two complimentary disciplines such as math and computer science, history and political science, law and English, etc. Admission is selective.
DRT	*Diplôme de recherche technologique*; a collaborative diploma validating the completion of technological research within a company or laboratory.
DSE	*Dossier social étudiant*; application procedure for financial aid (bourse) and university housing
DU	*Diplôme d'université*; university diploma specific to each university (not to be confused with the DE). Usually after a short-term period of study on a specific subject.
DUT	*Diplôme universitaire de technologie;* professional diploma granted upon completion of a two-year training program in a university-based technological institute (IUT). Graduates enter the work force directly or continue their studies. Curriculum directly related to business and industry; internships are an important component of the program.
Écoles de commerce	*Grandes écoles* specializing in business management, marketing, and finance.

ECTS	European Credit Transfer and Accumulation System; permits credits earned in one program within the three-cycle European system to be applied for study in another school or country within the EU. One year of study usually equals 60 credits.
EFTS	*Établissement de formation en travail social;* Social Work school. Three-year program.
ENIC - NARIC	ENIC (European Network of Information Centres) and NARIC (National Academic Recognition Information Centres). Promotes policy on recognition of foreign diplomas and degrees, and provides assistance for study abroad, financial aid, and practical advice between member states.
ENS	École normale supérieure; prestigious higher education institution for advanced undergraduate and graduate studies with teaching and research departments in the humanities and scientific disciplines. There are four ENS campuses in France: Paris, Paris-Saclay, Rennes, and Lyon; students are called "*normaliens*".
ENSA	*Écoles nationales supérieures d'architecture;* the national schools of architecture that award state recognized degrees: *licence - master - doctorat.*
Épreuve	Evaluation, test, exam.
Erasmus+	European Region Action Scheme for the Mobility of University Students. Formerly "Erasmus"; the expanded Erasmus+ program encourages and facilitates academic exchanges for students and faculty, internships, and vocational and volunteer opportunities for youth across EU countries.
ESPE	*École supérieure du professorat et de l'éducation;* graduate school that trains teachers and other education professionals. University based, it confers the *master*. See MEEF.
Études en France	The centralized application and enrollment platform open to nationals of 44 non-EU countries wishing to pursue study at institutions of higher learning in France.
Fac	Short for *faculté*, or French university.
Filière	A student's main track of study.
Formation continue	Continuing or ongoing education in view of professional development or skills training. May offer recognized validation or diploma. Often paid for by employer.
Foyers	Relatively inexpensive residences for students; some offer food services as well.

Grandes écoles	Prestigious post-*bac* schools with selective admissions; usually recruiting students based on rankings obtained on competitive exams *(concours)*.
Grand établissement	Status awarded to a limited number of public institutions of higher education and research, allowing them to negotiate particular rules of governance within the ministry to which they adhere. A *grand établissement* may also be a *grande école* or a university.
Greta	Public adult continuing education. Programs provide training and education for adults in many vocations.
Hypokhâgne	Term traditionally denoting the first year of studies in a literary *prépa* devoted to preparing students for the *concours* for entry to the École normale supérieure (ENS).
IFSI	*Institut de formation en soins infirmiers;* nursing school. Three-year program leading to national diploma of nursing (level of *licence*). Application made through Parcoursup website.
IEP	*Institut d'études politiques;* institute of political studies, internationally-oriented specialized schools with programs that include political and social sciences, economics, history, and law. "Sciences Po" schools are IEPs.
Inscription cumulative	Procedure in which students enrolled in *prépa* register simultaneously at a university in order to accrue credit for course work completed in *prépa*. These credits, usually 30 per semester, may be transferred to other programs should the student not complete the two years of *prépa* or otherwise not pursue study at a *grande école*.
Interne-externé	Refers to the student, usually in *prépa*, who is entitled to eat meals at the school in which he/she is enrolled.
IUT	*Institut universitaire de technologie;* university institute of technology offering professional or technological training programs. There are many types of programs and each institute usually specializes in a specific domain. The degree conferred is a DUT.
Khâgne	Term traditionally used to denote the second year of study in a literary *prépa* devoted to preparing students for the *concours* for entry to ENS (École normale supérieure).
L.AS	*Licence avec une option accès santé*; one of two paths followed for first year of medical studies at the start of university.
LMD	*Licence - master - doctorat*; often referred to as LMD. French terms denoting the three cycles of study under the Bologne Process reform. European standardization of equivalencies for undergraduate-graduate-doctoral studies: *licence* (3 years of study), *master* (5 years of study), *doctorat* (8 years).

Licence	Three-year undergraduate university degree in France, similar to the bachelor's degree in the US.
M1, M2	Terms denoting the first and second year of the French *master* (post-*licence*) program.
Master	French national diploma awarded by universities for two years of study after a *licence*. See DNM.
Mastère Spécialisé (MS)	Specialized master's diploma (sometimes called Advanced Master's) granted by a *grande école* for in-depth study in a specific area. A full-time, one-year program primarily for young professionals who have already earned a Master's.
Maths Spé	*Mathématiques spéciales;* second year of study in a scientific *prépa*.
Maths Sup	*Mathématiques supérieures;* first year of study in a scientific *prépa*.
MBA	Master of Business Administration.
MEEF	*Métiers de l'enseignement, de l'éducation et de la formation*; a master's degree (*master* MEEF) conferred by a university graduate school of education for teachers and education professionals.
MESRI	Ministère de l'Enseignement supérieure, de la Recherche et de l'Innovation; the French Ministry of Higher Education, Research, and Innovation.
MPSI	*Mathématiques, physiques, sciences de l'ingénieur;* math, physics and engineering science: a first year scientific prépa curriculum.
MSc	A science Master's; a graduate-level program at a *grande école*. Geared to international students and often taught in English; in science, social science, or specialized areas of business and management. A minimum of three semesters and a thesis (*mémoire* or *thèse*) is required.
Onisep	Office national d'information sur les enseignements et les professions; public information arm of the French education ministries, providing national and regional information on education programs, and vocational and professional training. Extensive outreach, publications, and online resources (www.onisep.fr).
PACES	Common first year of medical studies, phased out in 2019 and replaced by PASS and L.AS in 2020.
Palmarès	Ranking of institutions published in widely circulated magazines and/or the internet; term used to designate rankings of educational institutions based on multiple criteria such as starting salaries of graduates and percentage of students who repeated a year.
Parcoursup	The national online application platform for the first year of study in higher education, or reorientation for a subsequent year.

ParcoursPlus	A new application within Parcoursup reserved for non-students holding a *baccalauréat* who wish to change career or embark on a new study path.
Partiel	Similar to a mid-term exam; graded evaluation of material covered during a certain period.
PASS	*Parcours spécifique santé*; one of two paths for first-year medical studies, taken at the start of university studies.
Passerelle	Literally "bridge" between two different kinds of post-*bac* institutions in France to facilitate transfer from one kind of school to another, (e.g., from French university to a *grande école*).
PCSI	*Physique-chimie et sciences de l'ingénieur*; physics, chemistry, and engineering science, a first-year scientific *prépa* curriculum.
Portes ouvertes	Open Houses held by individual schools for prospective students to tour, learn about programs offered, and meet administrators, teachers, and students.
Prépa BCPST	*Biologie, chimie, physique, sciences de la terre*; biology, chemistry, physics, and earth sciences, a *prépa* for entry into biology or veterinary studies.
Prépa commerciale, ECE	French business school *(école de commerce) prépa* for those who studied social science subjects in *lycée*.
Prépa commerciale, ECS	French business school *(école de commerce) prépa* for those who studied math and science subjects in *lycée*.
Prépa HEC	Vernacular for *Classes préparatoires économiques et commerciales*; prepares the student for entry exams *(concours)* into the *grandes écoles* business schools.
Prépa ENS Lettres A/L classique	2nd year literary *prépa* program: literature, history and geography, Latin, Greek, modern foreign language, philosophy.
Prépa ENS Lettres A/L moderne	As above, second year literary *prépa* program without Latin and Greek requirements; emphasis on modern literature and civilization.
Prépa LSS (B/L)	*Prépa lettres et sciences sociales*. Literary *prépa* for humanities studies, social sciences (e.g., economics, sociology), and math.
Prépa scientifique	*Prépa* program emphasizing science and math subjects.
PSI	*Physique et sciences de l'ingénieur*: physics and engineering sciences, one of the second-year *prépa* curriculum tracks.

PTSI	*Physique, technologie et sciences de l'ingénieur*; physics, technology and engineering sciences, a first-year scientific *prépa* track.
RNCP	*Répertoire national des certifications professionnelles;* the national register of professional certifications. These certifications are recognized throughout France.
Salon Postbac	A major school fair held in Paris, usually in January, where *lycéens* can speak with representatives from a variety of schools and programs, including universities, *grands établissements, prépas,* specialized schools, and vocational training and apprenticeship programs.
Stage	Internship. Many study programs in France require internships; these are strictly controlled by French labor laws.
STS	*Section de technicien supérieur;* curriculum in technology fields offered in some *lycées* by which students can acquire skills for a specific trade without committing to long-term studies. (See BTS.)
SCUIO–IP	*Service commun universitaire d'information et d'orientation et d'insertion professionnelle;* university information and guidance center for academic orientation and career placement.
TCF	*Test de connaissance du français;* standardized French language test overseen by the French education ministries. Scores matched to six proficiency levels (A1 – C2).
TD	*Travaux dirigés;* tutorial classes, exercises or experiments in small groups supervised by an instructor.
TP	*Travaux pratiques;* practical classes or lab work, generally hands-on exercises or experiments as opposed to theoretical work.
VAE	*Validation des acquis de l'expérience;* process for certifying work experience as a barometer of knowledge and capacity to enter a study program.
Vœux	Literally "wishes"; choices a *lycéen* selects on the Parcoursup website, indicating the schools and programs he/she aspires to attend.
Voie	Literally "path"; a curriculum path or specific study track.
Voie royale	Literally "royal pathway"; the CPGE – *grande école* education route which, historically, virtually guaranteed top-notch employment after graduation. Today, as elitist symbolism holds less currency, the term is less commonly used.
"X"	Moniker for the renowned French engineering school, École Polytechnique.

Higher Education Opportunities Abroad

Undergraduate Study in the United States

Laura Vincens

The United States is a mecca for university students from all over the world. US universities consistently rank among the best in the world and are widely perceived to be among the most prestigious. Moreover, the variety of institutions and degrees available in the US is unparalleled. From two-year community colleges to large research universities, there is a niche for just about every student. Notwithstanding high tuition fees, uncertain financial aid, and widely varying application procedures, pursuing higher education in the United States offers students a unique educational, social and cultural experience.

In the US, the terms "college" and "university" are used interchangeably. Readers should note that the word "college" in the US is both a general term including community college, college and university and "college" as a specific category of higher education institution (though there are exceptions too like Dartmouth College which has graduate schools in addition to its undergraduate college). A college is primarily an undergraduate institution while a university also offers graduate degrees. Thus, for example, Yale College is the undergraduate school of Yale University. There is no inherent difference in selectivity between a college and university. Colleges constitute some of the most prestigious schools in the United States.

Most American universities provide students with a foundation in the liberal arts, fostering knowledge and appreciation of multiple disciplines, including the humanities, social sciences, and natural sciences. The focus is on developing communication, analytical thinking, problem-solving, reasoning, and research skills, all of which are critical in today's world. Along with a broad education, students must define a "major", an area of specialization in an academic field, as part of their degree program. The range of majors offered varies from institution to institution and can include pre-professional options, such as business and engineering, as well as more traditional fields of study such as history or biology. A major is traditionally chosen at the end of the second year of college and constitutes approximately one-third of the course work a student will complete in the four years leading to a bachelor's degree. In some cases, a student will choose to double major in two areas of concentration. The educational structure in American institutions allows young people the opportunity to sample and explore diverse and intriguing subjects as part of their undergraduate experience.

Another distinguishing characteristic of American universities is the diversity of students one will encounter on campus. Universities seek to build a community of students coming from different racial, ethnic and socioeconomic backgrounds, and geographical regions of the United States and countries around the world. They also strive to create a multi-talented student body in order to enrich the experience for students, opening them up to differences, preparing them to live and work in a global society and becoming more concerned and caring human beings.

American colleges seek to promote a cohesive and dynamic campus community. Housing and dining facilities are available on campus. Many require first-year students to live in campus dormitories and eat in student dining halls. Some have adopted the residential college system by which students and faculty live and eat together in a shared residential facility. A residential college may also sponsor cultural and recreational events. On a broader scale, it is commonplace for a university to hold lectures, exhibits, concerts and theatrical performances on campus. American universities strongly encourage students to become active and innovative participants in campus life by supporting myriad clubs and organizations, athletic events and facilities, entrepreneurial initiatives, and community service endeavors. Career advising services are likewise prominent on college campuses, assisting students with obtaining internships, summer jobs and employment upon graduation.

While there is much to be gained from attending an American university, it is not necessarily the ideal path for everyone. The business of providing such a comprehensive education is expensive, and tuition and housing fees are high for students. Public universities tend to have a lower price tag, especially if one is a resident of the state in which the institution is located. Financial aid is available to both American citizens and international students, although it may not cover the full cost of attendance, particularly for non-US citizens. Before making a decision to attend an American university, it is essential to determine if you have the adequate resources. (See the chapter, "Financing Your Education in the US".)

One should be mindful of other factors when considering applying to an American university. If, upon completing high school, one is very clear about what one wishes to study, a four-year liberal arts program with general education requirements may prove to be unsuitable. Moreover, it is important to know that one cannot study law or medicine as an undergraduate in the United States as these are considered graduate-level courses. The lack of accessibility to many of the most selective US institutions may also deter students. Applications have soared in the renowned Ivy League and equivalent schools such as Stanford or MIT. In 2018, Harvard admitted 1950 students from an applicant pool of 43,330 candidates, that is, 4.5%. By the same token, Stanford offered admission to 2,071 students or 4.36% of 47,450 candidates. It is, nevertheless, important to keep in mind that there are more than 2,600 accredited colleges and universities from which to choose!

Evaluating the Applicant

US colleges and universities make admissions decisions using the following criteria. The school record alone, no matter how outstanding, is not the only factor considered.

Academic record
All colleges give major importance to the quality of the student's academic record, including the rigor of courses taken and grades earned, most often beginning with 9th grade (3ème).

Standardized tests
Many schools require students to submit scores on either the SAT or ACT as a prediction of future academic success. Some institutions may also ask for SAT Subject Test scores. However, a number of universities are now either "Test Optional" (not required for admission) or "Test Flexible" (allowing students to choose from a list of acceptable options). International students or American citizens living overseas, attending a school where the language of instruction is not English, may be asked to submit scores from an English language proficiency exam such as the IELTS, TOEFL, or the Duolingo English Test.

It is essential to be aware of the testing requirements for each institution to which you are applying. Do not lose sight of registration deadlines. Keep in mind that late registration for the SAT and ACT is not available for overseas testing. One can only register as a stand-by candidate if the registration deadline has passed.

Test preparation is essential and even more so for the student who is not practiced in taking exams comprised of multiple-choice questions. This is often the case for those educated in the French system. Additionally, the math sections can be confusing to the French educated student, as there are differences between the American and French way of presenting math operations. Diligent self-study with prep books and mock/practice tests (including free online prep from Khan Academy[1] in partnership with the College Board) are very beneficial. If possible, enrollment in a test prep course may be a worthwhile investment. It is not unusual at all to see a significant improvement in scores after study and practice. If possible, it is advisable to take the SAT a second time to potentially improve scores.

Extracurricular activities
Schools seek to admit students who will contribute to campus life. Applicants will be asked about the school and community activities they have participated in throughout grades 9-12 (*3ème-terminale*).

School or community service
Community service, which reflects responsibility and a sense of commitment, is valued and colleges will look for evidence of meaningful and sustained volunteer work.

Essays
The college essay is a crucial element of the admissions process as it is an opportunity for an admissions committee to discover something more about you than has been learned from grades, scores, activities, and recommendations.

"The purpose of the American-style college essay is to tell the admissions committee something interesting, sincere, enlightening, and compelling about you that they would not know from the application itself. It's a story; everyone likes stories. Write about your real passions, fears, dislikes, unique experiences, or failures. Show. Don't tell. Use anecdotes. Avoid clichés. Be sensitive to the reader."[2] The essay should be written in your voice, not that of your parents, teachers or other adults. Don't write about what you think a committee wants to hear. The topic does not have to be dramatic or life-changing. You can write about an ordinary, daily, real life activity. Be yourself.

There are numerous examples of "successful" student essays that can be found online or in books devoted to the topic. For references to further information on this key component of the application, see the section at the end of this chapter, Resources for US College and University Admissions.

Summary and teacher recommendations
While grades communicate the level of academic achievement of a student, they do not tell the whole story. Colleges therefore request teacher recommendations to learn more about a student's intellectual curiosity, motivation, participation in discussions, collaborative interaction with classmates, etc. A head teacher or administrator may be asked to provide a summary recommendation, which is intended to provide information about a student's overall academic performance, character, and contribution to the school community, as well as any extenuating circumstances which may have had an impact on a student's achievement at a given time.

Individual factors
There are individual factors that can play a role in college acceptance such as unusual talents or achievements, athletic distinction, alumni affiliation, and ethnic or cultural background.

The Application Process

1. The **application** includes an online application form, consisting of a multi-page summary of essential biographical information, a detailed list of extracurricular activities, and personal essays. Many institutions now use the Common Application allowing applicants to apply to any of the participating institutions with a single application. If appropriate, the student may also submit an additional résumé of extracurricular activities, portfolios of art work, or music recordings. Note that there is a separate, unique application to the University of California system.

   The Coalition Application is another pathway for applying to colleges. There are approximately 130+ colleges that use the Coalition Application. The majority also use the Common Application. The goal of Coalition institutions is to provide lower income and underrepresented students with greater accessibility to higher education. The application allows for students to build a portfolio of achievement beginning in 9th grade through an online "locker", which contains examples of projects, essays, videos, art work, extracurricular accomplishments, etc.

2. The **scores** earned on the College Board SAT and SAT Subject Tests, the American College Test (ACT) and the required English proficiency test must be sent directly from the testing service at the request of the applicant to the colleges to which he/she is applying. This can be done at the time of registration (four SAT score reports may be sent free up to nine days after receipt of scores or at a later date for a fee; or four ACT score reports may be sent free up to five days after receipt of scores). Note that in some cases, colleges will allow you to self-report scores and will only ask for an official score report if you are admitted and choose to matriculate.

3. The **official transcript** of the student's grades/marks (grades 9–12 / *3ème–terminale*), sent directly by the school. Some institutions may require that the transcript be translated into English by an officially accredited translator. Plan well in advance when that is the case.

4. A **secondary school report** (evaluation form) and **summary letter of recommendation** by a school administrator or head teacher.

5. Letters of **academic recommendation** from one or two of the student's current or recent teachers. It is the responsibility of the student to request letters of recommendation from his/her teachers and to follow up and ensure they are submitted on time. Recommendation letters must be written in English.

6. An **optional letter of recommendation** from someone outside the school, usually in connection with the student's extracurricular involvement, may be submitted if additional recommendations are accepted by the university. An optional recommendation should only be requested if it will add something significant to the file.

7. A **personal interview** may be required, but most often an interview, if offered, is optional. Overseas students are often interviewed by alumni.

8. For non-US citizens, **certification of financial support**, or proof of the ability to pay for the costs of the university and living expenses.

9. If applying for financial aid, the required **financial aid forms**. (See the chapter, "Financing Your Education in the US".)

10. The **Application fees** must be paid when submitting applications. There are no fees for registering with the Common Application; however, there are application fees for submitting a Common Application plus a supplement to individual colleges.

NOTE: A guide for help preparing documentation from French schools is available in French at the Franco-American Commission: https://fulbright-france.org/fr/etudier-usa/documentation.

Getting Started:

9th Grade / Troisième: Academic Performance
This is the beginning of the US high school record. All grades from *troisième* onwards will need to be reported on official transcripts sent to American universities, so keep carefully on file.

10th Grade / Seconde
September/October: Begin researching US colleges/universities. Attend the CIS International University Fair Paris,[3] held annually in late September or early October, as an excellent starting point. Representatives from numerous US colleges and universities are present to provide information and advice.

February/March/April: Take the PSAT 10 (Preliminary SAT) at least as practice for the SAT. For US citizens, this test is the qualifying exam for the National Merit Scholarship Program. Contact the College Board for more information. www.collegeboard.org

11th Grade / *Première*

Academic Performance
Première/11th grade is a crucial year. Although it is possible to apply successfully to US universities having begun the process as late as the autumn of *terminale*, students can avoid unnecessary stress by beginning to think ahead in *seconde* (see the chapter "Thinking Ahead"). Even though US universities look at the entire high school record (grades 9–12 / *3ème–terminale*), the junior year is the last complete year of study before colleges will be making decisions and one where they will have at their disposition essential credentials: the initial results of the IB, the French *bac*, or OIB *(Option internationale du baccalauréat)*.

Selecting a College
The time is here to begin choosing institutions to which you would like to apply. This can be an exciting and revealing experience, but also a demanding one as it necessitates a great deal of research into the different universities to determine which ones you find to be a good fit. This will require you to take a look at who you are, what you value, aspire to study, and even future career goals.

You will want to explore the following resources as you research institutions:

- University websites
- Guidebooks and online resources
- College campus visits / tours including virtual tours on school websites
- Summer programs on a college campus
- Talk with alumni, friends, relatives, contacts.
- Participate in meetings with visiting university representatives if available.
- Attend the annual CIS International University Fair Paris.

You will want to consider the following factors when selecting colleges:

- Academic environment: majors, core curriculum, pre-professional, traditional liberal arts, internships, year abroad programs, etc.
- College type: size, private, public, co-educational, single sex, religious affiliation or Historically Black Colleges and Universities (HBCUs)
- Location: urban/suburban/rural, geographic location, proximity to family
- Campus life: housing, social life, Greek life, school spirit, political orientation, the traditional beautiful college campus grounds.
- Costs/Financial Aid
- Entrance requirements: expected credentials for admission

There is no single, official ranking of higher education institutions in the US. There are, however, many private rankings and surveys which are widely reported in the popular press. These rankings are usually based on such criteria as selectivity (defined by the average SAT scores, class rank, or average grades in high school of students accepted to a school), professional qualifications of the teaching staff, success of graduates, etc. In spite of these seemingly objective criteria, the rankings can be very subjective. When referring to a ranking, make sure that you understand the criteria used. You can consult rankings to see groups of colleges similar in selectivity and other characteristics, but not for absolute individual hierarchical rankings. Never rely on a single ranking to determine your choice.

The Education Conservancy,[4] a group of admissions professionals from Harvard, MIT, University of Chicago, Smith, and the University of Washington, have advised students to keep the following guidelines in mind:

> "Know that what you do in college is a better predictor of future success and happiness than where you go to college."

> "Resist the notion that there is one perfect college. Great education happens in many places."

> "Resist attempts to turn the process into a status competition."

Testing

By the end of 11th grade, students should have taken the appropriate standardized tests; however, retakes and subject tests can still be taken into the autumn of 12th grade. An academically strong US citizen may take the PSAT / NMSQT in October to qualify for a National Merit Scholarship.

> *It is essential to plan ahead as not all tests are available at all test sites or dates.*

The SAT is offered internationally only four times in a calendar year, and although the Subject Tests are available on five occasions, not all subjects are offered on each test date. Some Subject Tests, such as Latin or language tests with listening, are only offered once or twice a year outside the US. As there are a limited number of test centers and seating capacity in Paris, register well in advance! This also pertains to the ACT, which is now offered at only two sites in Paris and one in Nice.

- PSAT 10, PSAT / NMSQT: Offered in February, March, or April for the PSAT 10 in 10th grade and October for the PSAT / NMSQT in 11th grade at selected school examination centers throughout France. This is similar to the SAT, but shorter. It is an excellent opportunity to practice taking the multiple-choice type test under actual testing conditions, and for US citizens, it is the qualifying exam for the National Merit Scholarship Program. Contact local schools to register.
- SAT: Offered internationally on four occasions: October, December, March, and May. Registration online: www.collegeboard.org
- SAT Subject Tests: Offered internationally on five occasions: October, November, December, May, and June. www.collegeboard.org
- ACT: Offered internationally in September, October, December, February, April,

June. Registration on-line: www.act.org

- English proficiency exams: These can be taken either in the junior or senior year on multiple occasions. Consult websites for examination dates. TOEFL: www.ets.org/toefl; IELTS: https://ieltsregistration.britishcouncil.org. The Duolingo English test is accepted at over 500 US institutions. This online test can be taken at any time: https://englishtest.duolingo.com.

Essay / Personal Statement
Make a list of possible topics for your college essay and begin writing drafts and revising.

Recommendations
Inform teachers from whom you will be requesting letters of recommendation.

12th Grade / *Terminale*—Priorities

August / September
- Establish final list of colleges and select application round: Early Decision, Early Action, Regular Decision. (See Glossary of Common US Educational Terms at the end of this chapter.) Be aware of the application deadlines in all cases.
- Register for the standardized tests you are certain to be taking in the fall.
- Continue drafting and revising essays.
- Establish a timetable so that you are working on applications on a regular basis.
- Contact those teachers and the school official you have asked to write recommendations, and provide them with the necessary information for how to access forms and submit the recommendation. You and/or your parent may need to meet with them to explain the application procedures you are following and the importance of the recommendation letter. Arrangements should be made to have the letters translated if necessary.
- Attend the annual CIS International University Fair Paris if representatives of the schools to which you are applying will be attending. (Usually held at the end of September or the beginning of October.)

October
- If you are applying Early Decision (ED), Early Action (EA), or to a school which admits on a rolling basis, complete the appropriate applications and supplemental forms. In most cases, the deadline for early applications is between November 1st and 15th. Check school websites for precise deadlines.
- Request predicted IB, *bac* or OIB scores from your teachers.
- If need be, register for future standardized tests.
- If applying for financial aid, complete the required institutional forms. (See the chapter "Financing Your Education in the US".)

November
- Submit your ED / EA early application(s) and any other required documents.
- If you have not done so already, send test scores to the universities from the testing service, if required.
- Ensure that all required letters of recommendation and documents have been submitted along with predicted IB, *bac* or OIB scores if they have been requested by the university or will prove to be advantageous.

December
- Most notifications of early application decisions will arrive by December 15th. If need be, prepare to submit additional applications by the regular decision deadline.
- Students applying regular decision will prepare to submit applications by the deadlines.

January / early February
- Ensure that your 1st trimester or mid-year grades have been submitted by the administrator or the teacher who is writing the recommendation letter along with IB, *bac* or OIB predictions.

Late March / Early April
- Admissions decisions will be released.

May 1
Respond to schools to which you have been admitted or placed on a wait-list. At that time you must select the one institution you plan to attend, but may remain on the wait-list for any of the other schools to which you have been wait-listed.

Glossary of Common US Educational Terms

Associate's Degree – This is the first degree one can earn at the higher education level, usually requiring two years of full-time study.

Bachelor's Degree – This degree typically requires four years of coursework. Each institution sets the credit requirements leading to the degree, a certain number of which must be earned in a student's chosen area of study, referred to as a major. The rest of the student's course work is divided between general requirements, which may be established by the college or university, and electives, which the student may choose from the school's catalogue. Depending on the academic discipline, a student earns a Bachelor of Arts degree (B.A.) or a Bachelor of Science degree (B.S.) in a specific area, such as a B.A. in Comparative Literature or a B.S. in Physics.

Credit – A credit or "unit" is awarded for a determined number of hours of study. Most academic courses "carry" (are worth) three or four credits. At the undergraduate level, full-time students take four to five courses per semester. Some courses award only one or two credits, and some up to six credits, so the number of courses can vary. But it is unusual for a student to carry more than 15 or 16 credits per semester. Thus, students typically earn 30–32 credits per year (two, 15–16 credit semesters), and it takes four years to earn the credits necessary for a bachelor's degree. Students who earned a French *bac général* or an IB or took AP classes in high school may be awarded college credit and thus may be able to graduate in less than four years.

College – Refers to a public or private institution of higher education that confers a bachelor's degree. Historically, colleges in the US were small (300–2,500 students), four-year institutions where one went to get a well-rounded undergraduate education with a major in a broad area such as science, history, or literature. Today, most colleges offer a wide range of majors and many have graduate programs. Smaller colleges generally emphasize teaching more than research. Most universities comprise a number of "colleges" or "schools"; hence the terms "college" and "university" are often used interchangeably.

Early Decision (ED) – A plan under which a student may apply to a single college of his/her first choice, usually by November 1st or 15th of the senior year. ED is a legally binding contract by which the student agrees to matriculate if offered admission. Decisions are usually rendered in mid-December. If not admitted in the ED round, a student may receive a deferral and be reconsidered for admission with the regular decision applicants.

Early Action (EA) – This application plan follows essentially the same application/notification calendar as Early Decision but does not include the binding contract. The institution allows the accepted candidates until May 1st to accept or decline the offer of admission.

ETS – The Educational Testing Service handles all of the registration and score reports for the College Board tests (PSAT, SAT, SAT Subject Tests).

Graduate-level degree – This refers to degree programs beyond the four-year bachelor level, generally called master's or doctorate degrees.

Higher education – Higher education refers to post-secondary education, including both undergraduate and graduate studies.

Major – In the four years leading to a bachelor's degree, a student will be required to pursue a major, a specialized course of study in a single discipline. Some students will choose to double major or specialize in two disciplines.

Rolling Admissions – Instead of reviewing the total pool of applications after the deadline, schools will review applications as they receive them until the available places are filled.

Secondary Education – Secondary education refers to the four years of high school, grades 9–12, also known as the freshman (9th), sophomore (10th), junior (11th), and senior (12th) years, which correspond to *troisième, seconde, première*, and *terminale* in France.

Social Security number (SSN) – Identification number assigned to American citizens by the US government. Non-Americans who have been admitted to study in the US and have been issued an I-20 form are eligible to apply for a SSN.

Undergraduate level – Includes all of the academic programs leading to a bachelor's degree.

University – A large (5,000 to 50,000 students) institution typically composed of several schools, such as a School of Education, Business, or Engineering. Universities typically offer a wider variety of courses than do colleges, and all have both undergraduate and graduate programs.

Resources for US College and University Admissions

- *Barron's Profiles of American Colleges*
- College Board Publications: https://store.collegeboard.org/sto/enter.do
    - *College Handbook*
    - *International Student Handbook*
    - *Book of Majors*
    - *Trends in College Pricing*: https://trends.collegeboard.org/college-pricing
    - *Trends in Student Aid*: https://trends.collegeboard.org/student-aid
- College Confidential: www.collegeconfidential.com
- *Colleges that Change Lives,* Loren Pope
- *The College Finder,* Steven Antonoff
- Crafting an Unforgettable College Essay/The Princeton Review: www.princetonreview.com/college-advice/college-essay
- *Fiske Guide to Colleges,* Edward B. Fiske
- *Fiske Guide to Getting Into the Right College,* Edward B. Fiske
- Franco American Commission for Educational Exchange: www.fulbright-france.org. For documentation in French: https://fulbright-france.org/fr/etudier-usa/documentation.
- *Guide to the College Admission Process,* National Association for College Admission Counseling (NACAC)
- *The Insider's Guide to the Colleges,* Staff of the *Yale Daily News*
- *Looking Beyond the Ivy League,* Loren Pope
- *On Writing the College Application Essay, 25th Anniversary Edition: The Key to Acceptance at the College of Your Choice,* Harry Bauld
- Peterson's college search website: www.petersons.com
- U.S. News and World Report, "Best Colleges Rankings": www.usnews.com/best-colleges
- 35+ Best College Essay Tips from College Application Experts: www.collegeessayguy.com/blog/college-essay-tips

Endnotes

1. www.khanacademy.org/sat
2. Red Brick Writers
3. The Council of International Schools sponsors the CIS International University Fair Paris with logistical support from the Association of American Women in Europe (AAWE): www.aaweparis.org/university
4. http://educationconservancy.org

Student Anecdotes

The American university I attended as an undergraduate was my first choice (I applied Early Action), although I think I would have been happy almost anywhere. The academic environment was relatively rigorous, but some students were aware of classes that were "easy A's" and intentionally loaded up. I did not, and was more of a dilettante, taking classes that interested me across departments. The university is Jesuit and relatively conservative although skewing towards a liberal campus environment. I adjusted easily to the school environment, although the drinking culture caught me off guard. Thanks to my OIB, I placed out of the introductory writing class, which I would have greatly benefited from. That class would have given me a better understanding of the writing expectations of American university professors, since I never really felt confident in my writing. Take the intro writing class! Do research with a professor! Go to office hours! Explore off campus! – Zöe

I chose my university because it was a top school with solid programs across subjects (good for an undecided student like myself at the time), a beautiful campus, and I wanted to be on the East Coast. I enjoyed the academics and the social life. There was a lot of work but help is available (office hours, peer study groups). Professors are generally very accessible but less so for larger classes. Most people take academics seriously. Fraternities and sororities are very visible and are an important part of campus life even though a majority of students are not in them. My *lycée* prepared me for the academics, but socially it was very different. I adjusted to the school environment by attending events, joining clubs and making friends. My advice would be to talk to students at the places you are contemplating going to and be aware of the downsides of each place, both academically and socially. – Daniel

I chose the American university I attend because I just felt that "click". After attending half a dozen Admitted Students Days, it was the only one that stood out for me and I have no regrets. The academic environment is pretty rigorous and known for it being difficult to obtain "A"s, but I definitely think that if you work hard you will get the grades you deserve. My high school more than adequately prepared me through the International Baccalaureate program, making my first semester of college seem relatively easy. The social/cultural environment is definitely different than back in Paris with "going-out" referring to spending an hour in a frat-house basement instead of going out to bars or clubs. Our campus and the city does offer a variety of other things to do like going to student musicals or to museums, which are free for students. Adjusting to this new environment didn't feel very difficult as I luckily made a very good group of friends early on. Some advice I have for students thinking of coming to the US is to be open to a variety of schools, go to office hours (they do actually help), and don't stay in the campus bubble all the time. – June

I chose this school because it provided the best balance between academics and sports. The program has exceeded all my expectations. The academic environment is rigorous, but not overly competitive, and the social life is diverse and dynamic. My advice is to be sure to make the right decision because what happens in college determines a lot of where your life will lead afterward. – Adrien

I chose this school for my bachelor's degree because I wished to attend university in an urban setting. I felt that this would allow me to learn as much outside of school as I did in the classroom. As I studied art history at university, it was important to me to have access to the museums and cultural environment of New York City. Academically, the school offered a large number of classes and diplomas in both the sciences and liberal arts. With few exceptions, the classes I attended were generally small (30 students or less) and involved a lot of participation. While largely a commuter school, there were a number of clubs and activities that allowed students to meet in social settings, and the school even had its own art gallery. If you go to a large university, I encourage students to get involved in clubs or other activities to meet people and find a place for themselves. – *Samantha*

I was admitted Early Decision to my university; it was my top choice, as well as my only choice. I chose it due to its location, its lack of a campus which I thought would give me a greater sense of "living in the real world", though ultimately what made me choose it was the feeling I got when I visited. I can't fully explain or quantify it; I felt as though I was at home there and I would not be anywhere else. I still feel that this is the truth, not only due to the academic environment but through the truly remarkable people I've encountered. The academics are rigorous, though this depends entirely on the program to which one is admitted. There is, however, a go-getter sentiment which permeates throughout my school and while this is motivating to some, others will crack under the pressure. My secondary school in France adequately prepared me for university, perhaps too much so, as the full IB diploma as a whole was, in my opinion, far more difficult than my college curriculum, though I feel that the work I do in school now requires far more of my own thought and willpower than the formulaic IB. The social environment is composed of a crossroads of individuals, mostly American, many of whom are first generation or bi-national. You can truly find every kind of person at my school, though what we all have in common is passion and motivation. Starting school was definitely an adjustment, as naturally it is overwhelming to start over somewhere and have to create a new life for yourself. I was homesick at times, though frankly my life in this new city just seemed to fall into place without having to exert much effort. For the most part, everyone at university is starting over, you are all in this together and you will be welcomed if you welcome others. Take your time getting to know people; they may surprise you. Talk to your professors, they are here to help you. Find places and things to do that you enjoy in your new city in order to make it your home. – *Amélie*

Financing Your Education in the US

Caroline Bouffard

Figuring out how to finance a college education in the United States is a primary concern for many families. Along with the usual aspects of determining the right match college to attend — location, size, type, etc., the financial fit should also be one of the factors that drives the college search process. Keep in mind that today, more than two-thirds of all students attending college in the United States receive some form of financial assistance.[1] That's not surprising given that the average out-of-state tuition and room & board at a four-year public institution for the 2018–19 school year was $37,430. For a private, non-profit university, the average price was $48,510 for 2018–19.[2]

While there are certainly colleges that cost upwards of $70,000 per year, the good news is that with careful planning and an open-mind, a US college education can be affordable. Once students identify their universities of interest, a good place to start is to investigate the "Cost of Attendance" (COA), or the average total cost for a year. After determining the COA, consult the school's Net Price Calculator, found on its website. The calculators are more or less sophisticated depending on the institution, but can provide a good estimate of what the net price will be based on your family's financial situation. When filling out the calculators, be as accurate as possible and remember that your focus should be on the NET PRICE (out-of-pocket expense) and not the STICKER PRICE (COA) published on the university website.

Assessing Student Need

A student's financial need is calculated as the difference between the Cost of Attendance (COA), minus the amount the student and their family is expected to pay, referred to as the Expected Family Contribution (EFC).

How your EFC is calculated

Your family's financial strength in terms of paying for college is calculated according to a formula established by the federal government, otherwise known as Federal

Methodology (FM). Taxed and untaxed income, assets, benefits (such as unemployment), family size, and number of family members attending college during the year are all considered. All American students applying from France are encouraged to use the FAFSA4caster tool to determine their eligibility for federal financial aid. The Free Application for Federal Student Aid (FAFSA) is the application that students must submit to receive any type of federal aid.

The FAFSA in detail

- Only US citizens or eligible residents are qualified to file the FAFSA.
- Male students over the age of 18 must first register with the Selective Service System to be eligible for federal financial aid. There is no such requirement for female students.
- The FAFSA opens on October 1st and should be submitted for the first time during the student's senior (12th grade / *terminale*) year. The earlier the student files, the earlier they will learn of their financial aid offers.
- Apply using the web-based version of the FAFSA at www.fafsa.ed.gov. It includes step-by-step instructions for completing the online FAFSA as well as pre-application worksheets. Obtain a Federal Student Aid (FSA) ID at https://fsaid.ed.gov/npas.
- In order to continue receiving financial aid through the four years of undergraduate studies, the student is required to file the FAFSA every year.
- The tax information that is submitted on the form is from the "Prior Prior Year" (PPY), which permits you to submit tax information from two years ago.
- All income and tax information, including from French or other foreign tax forms must be submitted. Some universities might require an unofficial translation of the foreign tax return.
- The FAFSA is free to file.

The CSS Profile

The CSS (College Scholarship Service) Profile is the tool developed by the College Board to allow students to apply for institutional (non-federal) aid and uses the Institutional Methodology (IM) formula to calculate need. Besides Federal grants, aid in the form of scholarships and grants from the universities themselves are the biggest sources of aid available to students.

Details:
- The CSS Profile can be filled out by both US domestic students and international students; applicants use their College Board login details to submit the form.
- Close to 400 private universities use the CSS Profile to distribute institutional need-based aid and some require it to also grant merit scholarships.
- The form becomes available on October 1st.
- In addition to the standard information asked on the FAFSA, the CSS Profile asks for more detailed information including that of non-custodial parents, home

equity, net-worth of small family businesses, non-qualified annuities and medical expenses, among other items. Also, student income and assets are assessed higher on the CSS Profile than on the FAFSA.
- The cost to submit the CSS Profile is $25 for the first school and $16 for each additional form to be submitted.

> *An American citizen who was educated abroad is considered a domestic student when it comes to financial aid.*

As an international student, non-US citizen, will I be given any need-based aid or merit scholarships?
- Some universities flat out state that they cannot provide any type of aid to nonresident alien students while others can be quite generous. (Please note that an American citizen who was born, raised, and educated in France is considered a domestic student when it comes to need-based and merit-based aid).
- The Resources section of www.personalcollegeadmissions.com lists approximately 480 universities and their average aid awards to nonresident alien undergraduates.
- In my experience, students who are accepted to institutions and whose grades and test scores fall within the top 25% of the applicant pool, receive some form of merit scholarships.
- It is helpful to note that Ivy League universities do not offer merit scholarships but rather need-based aid only.

Anecdote: Last year, a French family from the suburbs of Paris approached me to help their daughter with her US college application process. They supported her desire to study in the US but gave me a strict budget to work with — 35,000 € per year for tuition and cost of living expenses. I knew this would be challenging because their student had not been particularly motivated throughout high school, did not have significant extracurricular activities, had very average SAT scores and was still working to get her TOEFL score above a 90. She did, however, have a strong will to achieve her goal of pursuing her Bachelor's degree in an American university. I focused the search on *Colleges that Change Lives*[3] and *Great Colleges for B students*[4] as well as some state universities that met her specific criteria. In the end, 'Jennie' was accepted to 6 colleges with an average of $15K worth of scholarships per year. She is now happily attending SUNY Binghamton University in New York where her yearly cost of attendance is $37,800.

Types of Financial Aid

Financial aid can come in the following forms: loans, work-study, grants, and scholarships. Note, only institutional aid is available for the non-US citizen international student.
- **Federal loans** are borrowed directly from the US Department of Education, must be repaid, and the terms and conditions are set by law.

    Direct Subsidized Loans are made to eligible undergraduate students demonstrating financial need and have slightly better terms than unsubsidized loans. The US Dept. of Education pays the interest during the student's time in college, during the first 6 months 'grace period' after graduation and during a period of deferment.

Direct Unsubsidized Loans are made to eligible undergraduate, graduate, and professional students and there is no requirement to demonstrate need. Students are responsible for paying interest during all periods. The 2018–19 interest rate is set at 5.05%. (See chart at the end of this chapter for maximum loan thresholds.)

Direct PLUS Loans are made by the Department of Education to parents and graduate and professional students. Applications are made through www.studentloans.gov.

- **Work-study:** students eligible for need-based aid may also be granted access to the federal work-study program for US citizens and qualified resident aliens. Students can earn money to pay for school through part-time jobs on campus. Participating schools offer qualifying jobs to students usually on a first-come, first-served basis but the student still needs to apply and interview for the jobs. Earnings from these jobs are not applied directly to the tuition and fees or housing, but rather are meant to cover day-to-day expenses.

- **Grants and scholarships** are considered 'gift aid' because they don't have to be repaid.

    Federal grants are 'need-based' awards including:

    Federal Pell Grants: destined for students with substantial financial need; eligibility is based solely on the EFC calculated by the FAFSA. The maximum Pell Grant award for the 2019–2020 award year was $6,195. The corresponding maximum Pell Grant eligible Expected Family Contribution (EFC) was $5,576.

    Federal Supplemental Educational Opportunity Grants (FSEOG): granted to students with exceptional financial need — not all universities participate in this program and the range of awards goes from $100 to $4000 based on various factors determined by the financial aid office at the university.

    Teacher Education Assistance for College and Higher Education (TEACH) Grants: Eligible students have to participate in the TEACH program, be enrolled in an undergraduate, graduate or post-graduate eligible program, and achieve certain academic requirements.

    Iraq and Afghanistan Service Grants: Students who are not eligible for a Pell Grant based on their EFC, but meet the other eligibility criteria and whose parent or guardian was a member of the US armed forces and died during their military performance in Iraq or Afghanistan after the events of 9/11 and who were under 24 years old or enrolled in college at least part-time at the time of parent's death, could receive this grant up to $6,195 for the year 2019–2020.

- **Institutional Aid:** Financial aid that is offered by the school the student plans to attend. This can be in the form of need-based aid or merit-based aid.

    Sometimes colleges offer their own loans, but more commonly, colleges give aid in the form of grants and scholarships to students who either demonstrate financial need or qualify academically. Special artistic or athletic talents may also qualify students for certain grants or scholarships. Please see the section devoted to athletic scholarships at the end of this chapter.

Some schools are more generous than others when giving institutional aid depending on the size of the pool from which they can draw money.

Need-blind vs. Need-aware schools: when it comes to making admissions decisions, schools fall into one of these categories. Need-blind schools will not consider the student's financial situation at all when making a decision. Conversely, schools that are need-aware, when deciding between two students with identical credentials, may award admission to the student with no financial need.

Tips
If you are 100% sure you do not need financial help to pay for college, not applying for financial aid will be to your advantage.

If financial aid is required for you to be able to attend college in the US, be sure you are aware of each school's admission policy.

Non-institutional scholarships

There is a popular misconception that "millions of dollars of scholarship money goes unused every year." The truth of the matter is that researching and applying for outside scholarships is very time-consuming and usually doesn't lead to more than a small amount of award money that may barely make a difference in the overall cost of attending college. One note-worthy opportunity, however, is the #YouAreWelcomeHere national scholarship initiated in 2018 destined for international students who are not US citizens. Fifty-seven participating universities offer two annual scholarships each covering at least 50% of tuition to students who are committed to furthering the #YouAreWelcomeHere message through intercultural exchange that bridges divides at their future campuses and beyond.[5]

A few words about private loans: Sallie Mae is the largest private student lender in the US market today offering both undergraduate and graduate student loans with fixed and variable rates.

Parents should also check with banks in their home countries for local student loan options. For example, BNP Paribas currently offers a competitive student loan at a 1.5% fixed rate on 15,000 € for seven years, eligible to be spent on international studies. In general, the parents should be clients of the bank and a qualified adult must co-sign for the loan.

A note about Early Decision (ED): Some universities allow students to apply 'Early Decision', a binding agreement whereby if the student is accepted, he or she must attend. There are several disadvantages to this arrangement for students counting on financial aid: 1) They will not be able to compare financial aid packages from multiple colleges. 2) When you commit to a college through Early Decision, your chances of receiving merit-based aid might be reduced, given that the schools do not have as much incentive to attract students who have already committed. 3) If you do apply ED and the financial aid offer is insufficient, most schools will release the student from the ED contract. In this case, students should make sure they are prepared to send off other applications.

Financing Graduate School

As with the undergraduate financial aid process, students will be required to file the FAFSA form and in some cases the CSS Profile. The good news is that if they have already graduated from college, they will be considered 'independent' and their parents' income and assets will not be factored into the formulas for determining eligibility for financial aid. Also, the thresholds for taking out federal student loans, is much higher for graduate students. For example, the graduate loan limits for an Direct Unsubsidized Loan is $20,500 each year, with a lifetime maximum of $138,500 for graduate or professional students.

One of the best-kept secrets in higher education is that graduate students in STEM fields are typically fully supported. However, it's not the school, or the department, per se, that picks up the tab. Rather it's the research grant of the faculty member that supports the student, perhaps with the additional aid of a fellowship or scholarship. The quid pro quo for the financial support is the (seemingly unlimited) number of research hours that the student will put in on the path to acquiring his/her PhD. A student will not be accepted into a PhD program if there aren't research monies to support him/her; it is imperative that the student contacts faculty BEFORE submitting applications.

Medical School Special Notes

- Average four-year cost of public out-of-state med school is $250,222; for private medical school the average four-year cost is $330,180.
- The median debt for a medical school graduate in 2018 was $202,000.
- Some universities require non-US/nonresident alien students to place the entire four-year tuition in escrow prior to enrollment in a medical school. This does not apply to US citizens living abroad.
- NYU's Langone Health/School of Medicine offers free tuition to all students in the MD degree program.
- In addition to need and merit-based grants and scholarships, and loans (Direct Unsubsidized, Direct Plus, Perkins), other sources of aid can come from service-based aid (e.g., National Health Service Corps) and repayment/forgiveness options.

Law School Special Notes

- LSAC-Law School Admission Council[6] is a reliable resource for all things related to law school admissions.
- Most law schools accept applications on a rolling basis so it's important to apply early in the fall of the year prior to enrollment. This is also the best way to obtain merit scholarships from the universities that offer them.
- Given that law school rankings are fairly transparent, students can use scholarship offerings to leverage better offers.
- Law schools participating in the Loan Repayment Assistance Program (LRAP) offer JD graduates who enter into certain legally related public interest or government employment following graduation, the possibility to receive funds, in

the form of interest-free forgivable loans which assist them in paying for all or part of their monthly loan repayment obligations.

Business School Special Notes

- Most MBA students rely on a combination of personal savings, grants, scholarships and employee sponsorship to pay for their degree.
- Most business schools offer both need-based and merit-based aid for both domestic and nonresident aliens but in order to qualify, sometimes additional applications are necessary and specific deadlines have to be respected.
- The French-American Chamber of Commerce Foundation provides multiple, merit-based scholarships for French students pursuing a business degree in the US and to American students looking to pursue an MBA, Master's or *mastère spécialisé* in a business-related program in France.

Certificate of Finances

All international students who require a student visa will need to provide financial documentation to the university demonstrating the availability of funds equal to or exceeding the standard Cost of Attendance (COA) at that university. Generally, this is required after being accepted, but sometimes this requirement must be met during the application process. The documentation can be in the form of a standard certificate signed by the student and the parents with copies of bank statements, or as a letter signed by the family's bank.

References and Resources

- Federal Student Aid: www.studentaid.ed.gov
- College Board CSS Profile: https://cssprofile.collegeboard.org
- FastWeb: www.fastweb.com
- Education USA: https://educationusa.state.gov/find-financial-aid
- Franco-American Fulbright Foundation: https://fulbright-france.org/fr/etudier-usa
- French-American Chamber of Commerce: www.faccnyc.org/facc-foundation
- International Scholarship Data Base: www.internationalscholarships.com
- College Board's *International Student Handbook*
- Princeton Review's *8 Steps to Paying Less for College*

Annual and Aggregate Limits for Subsidized and Unsubsidized Loans[7]

Year	Dependent Students	Independent Students
First-Year Undergraduate Annual Loan Limit	$5,500—No more than $3,500 of this amount may be in subsidized loans.	$9,500—No more than $3,500 of this amount may be in subsidized loans.
Second-Year Undergraduate Annual Loan Limit	$6,500—No more than $4,500 of this amount may be in subsidized loans.	$10,500—No more than $4,500 of this amount may be in subsidized loans.
Third-Year and Beyond Undergraduate Annual Loan Limit	$7,500—No more than $5,500 of this amount may be in subsidized loans.	$12,500—No more than $5,500 of this amount may be in subsidized loans.
Graduate or Professional Students Annual Loan Limit	Not Applicable (all graduate and professional students are considered independent)	$20,500 (unsubsidized only)
Subsidized and Unsubsidized Aggregate Loan Limit	$31,000—No more than $23,000 of this amount may be in subsidized loans.	$57,500 for undergraduates—No more than $23,000 of this amount may be in subsidized loans. $138,500 for graduate or professional students—No more than $65,500 of this amount may be in subsidized loans. The graduate aggregate limit includes all federal loans received for undergraduate study.

Endnotes

1. https://trends.collegeboard.org/sites/default/files/2018-trends-in-student-aid.pdf
2. https://trends.collegeboard.org/sites/default/files/2018-trends-in-college-pricing.pdf
3. https://ctcl.org/
4. Tamra B. Orr, *America's Best Colleges for B Students: A College Guide for Students without Straight As*, 8th edition, (Belmont, CA: SuperCollege, LLC, 2019).
5. www.youarewelcomehereusa.org
6. www.lsac.org
7. https://studentaid.ed.gov/sa/types/loans/subsidized-unsubsidized

Athletic Scholarships: The Basics, by Robynne Pendariès

Contrary to the common perception that many students receive athletic scholarships, the reality is that only about 2% of all bachelor's degree candidates earn one (and even less for students from foreign countries).[1] A "full ride" scholarship is extremely rare and usually only occurs in sports such as American football and basketball for men and basketball, volleyball, tennis, and gymnastics for women. Besides athletic skill, good grades and motivation contribute strongly to obtaining an athletic scholarship.

There are basically five "levels" or "Divisions" of college sports, each with its own academic requirements:

NCAA (National Collegiate Athletics Association) Division I: usually large or midsize universities with significant financial resources allocated to athletics. These schools offer a wide array of opportunities for athletic participation while requiring a high academic standing of their student athletes.

NCAA Division II: usually small schools with fewer financial resources for athletics. These schools follow a partial scholarship model of financial aid involving a mix of athletic scholarships and other types of aid (need-based grants, academic merit scholarships and/or campus employment earnings).

NCAA Division III: mix of small to large institutions with strong academics that do not give athletic scholarships, however, the students' high achievement in a specific sport may benefit their application. Normal financial aid restrictions apply. There are no NCAA-specific eligibility requirements for admission to these schools.

NAIA (National Association of Intercollegiate Athletics): typically smaller schools with less financial resources, hence fewer athletic scholarships. Eligibility requirements are less strict than NCAA.

NJCAA (National Junior College Athletic Association): Athletic scholarships are available to over 500 two-year junior and community colleges in a variety of sports. Like the NCAA, the NJCAA is divided into Divisions I, II, and III. Division I schools may offer full scholarships, including room and board and travel expenses. Division II schools may grant scholarships that include tuition, books, and fees. Division III member institutions may not offer athletic scholarships.

All of the above levels award athletic scholarships EXCEPT NCAA Division III, NJCAA Division III, and Ivy League universities. The Ivy League (although in the NCAA Division I) and NCAA Division III institutions do not give "athletic scholarships" per se, however, after the student athlete meets the academic criteria for acceptance into these schools, they often offer competitive financial aid packages as a means of recruiting high-level athletes.

It is important to plan ahead and investigate opportunities as from *3ème*. Coaches from institutions with considerable financial resources will attend sports competitions to spot potential recruits, however, it should be noted that any direct contact with students is highly regulated and also very restricted. Competing in a sport event in the US during the early *lycée* years will often put the student on the radar screen of schools seeking student athletes. One should not wait until the year of *terminale* to report athletic accomplishments and expect the awarding of financial aid! The groundwork must be laid well before then.

When calculating the cost of an American university, note that full athletic scholarships are extremely rare, except in football and basketball (revenue-generating sports). Most athletes receive 50% scholarships, but if your child is an American citizen he/she may be granted additional financial aid such as federal Direct loans or work-study to cover total costs. All students, regardless of nationality, may qualify for academic merit scholarships, as these are determined by the institution, or private bank loans to supplement their athletic scholarship.

Another reason to start the process early is that, aside from each university's individual academic requirements, the NCAA has its own set of core-course requirements. It's actually the NCAA that determines and administers the scholarship that is awarded by each individual university. It is essential to familiarize oneself with the eligibility criteria for students applying from France specifically (or another home country) before moving forward. Since the French school system, including the OIB, as well as the IB programs, are so rigorous, the student-athlete usually has no problem becoming NCAA eligible.

The NCAA website provides a wealth of information on securing athletic scholarships. See the Resources section at the end of this chapter for further details.

Similar criteria are required for the NAIA and NJCAA, although these may be less academically rigorous. Further information can be found on their website (see References and Resources).

Steps to becoming NCAA Eligible

- Register online with the NCAA Eligibility Center (previously known as the NCAA Clearinghouse).
- Take the SAT or ACT and have the scores sent directly to the NCAA (important: even if the universities you apply to are "test-optional", the SAT or ACT is required for NCAA eligibility).
- Upload your translated school transcript to the NCAA Eligibility Center website (important: there are very specific instructions as to how the translations are transmitted—see website link in the Resource section for details).
- Meet core-course requirements specific to your school's athletic "level": Division I or Division II.
- Meet the GPA average/sliding scale with SAT and ACT test scores minimum requirement. Division I and Division II criteria are listed on the links provided in the Resource section.
- Complete the "amateurism" questionnaire found within the registration procedure of the Eligibility Center (set of questions which ensure that the student-athlete has not earned any money through playing their sport, which could render the student-athlete "ineligible" to receive any scholarship money!).

Timeline: Aiming for an athletic scholarship

- *Troisième*: Familiarize yourself with the recruitment calendar for your specific

sport; sign up on the NCAA Eligibility Center.
- *Seconde*: Promote yourself, send your CV to coaches; gain visibility by competing in your sport in the US; take the PSAT.
- *Première*: Take the SAT or ACT, several times if necessary; contact college coaches by phone (see NCAA rules on their recruitment calendars link in the Resource section); take the TOEFL (often required if you have been schooled in any language other than English); and hopefully you can make a "verbal commitment" to a scholarship offer by the end of this academic year.
- *Terminale:* Fill out college applications; once the scholarship has been awarded by the school, the student-athlete must sign a National Letter of Intent (NLI) anytime between November 14th and the following August 1st. The NLI is an agreement between the university and the athlete. Even if you sign the NLI, you will still need to complete your NCAA Eligibility process and be accepted by the university. Keep in mind that athletic departments and admissions offices work together and schools will not propose a NLI to an applicant unless admission is almost certain.

References and Resources
- NCAA (National Collegiate Athletics Association): www.ncaa.org
- Information for International Student-Athletes: www.ncaa.org/student-athletes/future/international-student-athletes
- Eligibility Center: web3.ncaa.org/ecwr3
- Translation procedures: https://ncaa.egain.cloud/kb/EligibilityHelp/content/KB-2183/What-are-the-requirements-for-submitting-translations?query=transcript%20translations
- General Eligibility Requirements: www.ncaapublications.com/productdownloads/INTEB18-19_single.pdf
- Division I Eligibility Requirements: www.ncaa.org/sites/default/files/2018DIEC_Requirements_Fact_Sheet_20180117.pdf
- Division II Eligibility Requirements: www.ncaa.org/sites/default/files/2018DIIEC_Requirements_Fact_Sheet_20180117.pdf
- Student Athlete Recruiting Calendars: www.ncaa.org/student-athletes/resources/recruiting-calendars
- National Letter of Intent (NLI): www.nationalletter.org
- NAIA (National Association of Intercollegiate Athletes): www.naia.org, and its Eligibility Center: play.mynaia.org
- NJCAA (National Junior College Athletic Association):http://njcaa.org

Endnote
1. www.usnews.com/education/best-colleges/paying-for-college/articles/2017-10-04/4-myths-about-athletic-scholarships

Graduate School in the US for International Graduates

Céline Ouziel

Graduate-level study in the United States generally starts the fifth year of higher education, at which point students work towards earning master's and doctoral degrees. Both usually involve intensive coursework and research. Graduate programs in American universities are more specialized than undergraduate programs offered by US colleges. As graduate students are expected to be more focused on their program of study they generally have fewer opportunities for extracurricular activities. Depending on the program, courses can be in the form of lectures by faculty members and/or seminars with fewer students per class so as to foster discussion. Class participation, research papers, and examinations may carry the same weight. Degree requirements are stated in terms of "credits" (sometimes called "units", "hours", or "points"). Each program has its own degree requirements.

Masters' Degrees

The Master of Arts (M.A.) and Master of Science (M.S.) degrees are usually awarded in the arts, sciences, and humanities disciplines. The M.S. is also awarded in technical fields such as engineering and agriculture. These programs are often research oriented and may lead directly to doctoral studies. Many master's programs offer a thesis and a non-thesis option. The degree is the same in both cases, but the academic requirements are slightly different. Non-thesis programs are usually more coursework intensive. Students in degree programs that include a thesis component generally take a comprehensive examination covering both their coursework and thesis.

Professional master's degrees aim at training students for a particular profession and at a higher level than undergraduate degrees offering the same discipline. These degrees are considered "terminal" degrees in that they don't lead to a PhD. Credits earned in terminal master's programs may or may not be transferable toward a doctoral degree later on. Such master's degrees are often designated by specific descriptive titles, such as Master of Business Administration (MBA), Master of Education

(M.Ed.), Master of Fine Arts (MFA) or the Master of Laws, also known as LL.M. that students can pursue after a three-year law degree called the JD (Juris Doctor).

For both kinds of master's degrees, the duration of full-time programs varies from one to three years. For example, Master of Science degrees are often one-year programs; Master of Arts and Master of Business Administration (MBA), two years; Master of Fine Arts (MFA) and Master of Architecture can be three years. Again, the duration of programs varies with each university and even between departments within the same university.

Doctoral Degrees

At the doctoral level, the PhD (doctor of philosophy) is the most common degree awarded in academic disciplines. Other doctoral degrees are awarded primarily in professional fields, such as education (Ed.D. or Doctor of Education), business administration (DBA or Doctor of Business Administration) and law (SDJ or Doctor of Juridical Science). Doctoral programs are research oriented and are aimed at training researchers and university professors.

Unlike the French *doctorat*, American doctoral program requirements include coursework and seminars in addition to the writing of a dissertation based on the student's original research. A comprehensive examination, known as the preliminary examination, is usually given after three to five years of study and completion of all coursework. Successful completion of this examination marks the end of the student's coursework and the beginning of concentration on research. When the student has completed writing his or her dissertation, he/she is required to defend it before a jury composed of faculty specialized in the field.

Doctoral programs can recruit holders of master's degrees but also holders of bachelor's degrees. Please check the websites of each graduate program to verify admissions requirements before applying.[1]

Choosing the US for Graduate School

Students living in France and wishing to study in the United States might consider applying at the graduate level rather than at the undergraduate level. Depending on the program, American graduate curricula can be quite complementary to the French *1er* and *2ème cycle*. In some cases, it is more advantageous to wait a few years and apply at the graduate level. For example, if a student would like to specialize in a certain field of study and does not want to go through the "general education" courses imposed by most American undergraduate programs, he/she may study in France at the undergraduate level and then apply to graduate school in the United States.

US higher education is renowned worldwide but is often better recognized in France at the graduate level. Bachelor's degrees corresponding to the first four years of higher education studies are often equivalent to no more than a *licence* in France, unlike most US master's degrees which often have a high reputation among French employers. For the most part, the French system does not see liberal arts education in a very positive way and prefers a more specialized curriculum. If you wish to study law or medicine in the United States, instead of going right after high school you can choose to obtain a first law or medical degree in France and then go to the US for law or medical school. It is important to know that US law and medical degrees are not automatically recognized in France, and therefore a decision to follow this route must be taken only after careful consideration.

Finding a Program and a School

There are more than 30,000 graduate programs in the United States offered by thousands of institutions. Setting your own criteria and taking the time to find a good fit are of the utmost importance. Apart from selecting programs that offer your field of study, other criteria should be taken into account:

Type of institution: It can be a college, a university, or an institute. Colleges are generally smaller and concentrate on undergraduate studies but they might also offer master's programs. They usually don't have doctoral degree programs and research centers in contrast to larger universities that offer all kinds of graduate degrees. Institutes are often more specialized, for example, art institutes or institutes of technology. Both private and public institutions offer graduate programs of the same value. State universities receive funding from the state and have lower tuitions, especially for US citizens that are residents of the specific state. On the other hand, private institutions may offer better funding opportunities especially for non-US citizens.

Accreditation: Unlike the French system, the US government is not involved in higher education accreditation. Rather, private non-profit agencies are commissioned by the federal government to approve institutions and programs. They can be regional accrediting agencies located in the same geographic area or professional associations (accrediting programs offering specific fields of studies, e.g., business, engineering, architecture, etc.). Don't choose an institution that is not at least regionally accredited. For professional master's degrees, professional accreditation can guarantee recognition among peers and is even sometimes a requirement for licensure purposes.

Region/environment: This might seem insignificant, but if you have the choice between hundreds of graduate programs, choose one that is located in a region where you will feel comfortable and where you will be able to engage in activities that you like.

Admissions requirements: Some programs are more selective than others. Many university websites provide current student statistics (average test scores or GPA, average number of years of work experience, etc.) and publish alumni testimonials. This information enables you to check if you correspond to the kind of profile they are looking for. Don't apply if you feel that you don't match.

Financial aid opportunities: Not all US universities provide financial aid, especially for non-US citizens. American students themselves often have to take out loans to pay for their graduate studies. If you don't have personal funds and cannot find any external support, don't apply to an institution that clearly won't provide financial aid to you. This information is often indicated on their website.

Faculty: You may wish to study with a particular professor teaching at a specific university because you are familiar with his or her publications. This is especially important for prospective doctoral students.

Beware of rankings: Rankings can help guide a decision but they can also be misleading. Before relying on a ranking, check to see which criteria were considered and if your specific field of study is included. Big names don't always offer the kind of program you may be seeking.

The educational advising center of the Franco-American Commission in Paris can help you identify graduate programs matching your criteria. You can meet with an adviser at their office in Paris or through Skype sessions (services and hours are described on the website: https://fulbright-france.org). The Commission's Advising Center is part of the EducationUSA network of educational information centers affiliated with the US Department of State's Bureau of Educational and Cultural Affairs, and thus guarantees a high level of quality and objectivity. EducationUSA members advise prospective international students on university study in the United States and provide accurate, complete, and unbiased information about all accredited US higher education institutions.

The internet is a useful tool but there is no real quality filter. Some websites serve as university search engines and may specialize in graduate studies (for example, www.gradschools.com or www.petersons.com/graduate-schools.aspx). Websites often display ads featuring schools; one should bear in mind that these are paid for by the advertising schools and do not necessarily mean that they are better known or endorsed by the website.

It is advised to visit professional association websites, especially those associations that accredit specific professional programs. Some examples:

- For business: www.aacsb.edu (The Association to Advance Collegiate Schools of Business)
- For law: www.americanbar.org/groups/legal_education/resources/aba_approved_law_schools (American Bar Association)
- For architecture: www.naab.org (National Architectural Accrediting Board)
- For engineering: www.abet.org (ABET - Accreditation Board for Engineering and Technology)
- For international affairs: www.apsia.org (Association of Professional Schools of International Affairs)

The complete list of national accrediting agencies can be found on the Council for Higher Education Accreditation's website: www.chea.org.

How To Apply

Pay attention to deadlines! Application deadlines for fall enrollment range from November 30th to March 15th. Each institution and even each graduate school within the same institution will have its own application form (generally online) and its own application procedures. It is therefore important to check each graduate school website before starting the application process. Graduate admissions decisions often involve two steps. First, your application including grades and test scores will be evaluated by the graduate school admissions office. If you fulfill the eligibility requirements, your application is then transferred to the department to which you are applying. Your first contact during the admissions process will then be with the graduate admissions office.

Traditionally, most US admissions offices will request other information and documents in addition to the application form itself. These are described below:

Testing Requirements
Many graduate programs will require applicants to take admissions tests such as the GRE (Graduate Record Examination) or the GMAT (Graduate Management Admission Test). The GRE is administered and developed by ETS (Educational Testing Service), an American organization based in Princeton, New Jersey.[2] The GMAT is administered in Europe by the Graduate Management Admissions Council.[3] Graduate programs and business schools use GRE and GMAT scores to evaluate your readiness for graduate-level work.

The GRE General Test and the GMAT measure verbal reasoning, quantitative reasoning, critical thinking, and analytical writing skills that are not related to any specific field of study. The GRE Subject Tests measure your aptitude in eight different subjects: Biochemistry, Cell and Molecular Biology, Biology, Chemistry, Computer Science, Literature in English, Mathematics, Physics, and Psychology. If you are majoring in one or more of these disciplines you might be asked to take the corresponding subject test or tests in addition to the GRE General Test. The scoring for the Verbal Reasoning and Quantitative Reasoning sections are on a scale of 130-170. For more information on scoring and revisions of the GRE General Test, see the Educational Testing Service website.

M.A. and M.S. programs will generally require the GRE test while most MBA programs will require GMAT scores. Both exams consist of three main parts, the Analytical Writing Assessment, the Quantitative section, and the Verbal section. The last two parts are multiple-choice questions. The quantitative section of the GMAT test is generally more challenging than the GRE quantitative section.[4]

Very few admissions offices will indicate a minimum score to be considered for admission. Generally, the more selective the university is, the higher the scores should be. However, applicants should not focus too much on test scores. For example, the Wharton School at the University of Pennsylvania (one of the most selective business schools in the world) has accepted MBA program candidates who have had GMAT scores ranging from 500 to 790 out of 800.[5]

For international applicants who have completed their undergraduate studies in a non-English institution, an English test is required. Most US universities will require TOEFL scores (Test of English as a Foreign Language), but more than 3,000 US institutions will also accept IELTS scores (International English Language Testing System).

Both TOEFL and IELTS measure your ability to use the English language in an academic setting. Skills in four language areas are evaluated: listening, speaking, reading, and writing. The main difference between the two tests is that the administration of the entire TOEFL test – even the speaking part – is via internet (however, candidates still take the test in a secure testing center), while IELTS is paper-based and the oral part consists of an interview by an evaluator. Please check with the admissions offices of the institutions you've chosen to apply to before taking one or the other. Most US universities will indicate a minimum score needed to be considered for admission. For TOEFL, the majority of US universities require a minimum of 80 out of 120; more selective institutions require a minimum of 100 out of 120. For IELTS, the minimum scores necessary vary from 6.5 out of 9 to 7.5 out of 9 for the most selective universities.[6]

You can take these tests several times and almost everywhere in the world, but each test costs between 100 € and 250 € so it's best to be prepared. It is possible to study for the tests alone with books (there are many publications that you can order online or buy in English-language bookstores). You can also pay to take preparation courses with private entities in France or in the US, but there are now more and more free test prep programs offered online. For example, ETS has launched a free TOEFL six-week online preparation program.[7]

Academic Information
Each admissions office will request academic transcripts of all your coursework as from your first year of higher education. If you studied in France, it corresponds to the *relevés de notes*. If these are in French, they must be translated into English by an official translator *(traducteur assermenté)*. Admissions offices often require that transcripts be sent directly from the school where you completed your studies. If this is not possible, you can generally provide certified copies of your credentials. The admissions office might also ask you to go through a "credential evaluation service", a private company providing objective evaluations of the US equivalents of foreign credentials. In that case, you will need to plan for additional fees (around $100).

Some admissions offices will also ask for a GPA (Grade Point Average), corresponding to the average grade you've received at the end of your program. However, this GPA is on a 4.00 scale and it is not always obvious to translate the French *moyenne* into a GPA. We advise applicants to keep their grades out of 20. Check the Fulbright Commission's website at: https://fulbright-france.org/fr/etudier-usa/etudes-usa/systeme-universitaire, to learn more about the grading system in the US.

Letters of Recommendation
You will be required to provide letters of recommendation (or reference letters) written by a teacher, professor, employer, or anyone who has supervised you for a certain period of time. This letter should be very informative and provide specific examples of your academic/professional abilities as well as some aspects of your personality, such as ability to work on a team, leadership skills, etc. This is why it is important to ask someone who really knows you instead of someone who is well-known but has only met you once or twice. Of course this letter should be written or translated into English. More and more admissions offices require online reference letters. In that case, candidates have to provide the email address of each referent who will receive instructions to fill out an online recommendation form.

Personal Statement / Statement of Purpose
The applicant is also required to write a personal statement or statement of purpose. This is a kind of letter of motivation, but not completely like the French model. You

should include information that generally answers the following questions: Why do you want to study in the US and why that particular field of study? Why at this university in particular? What are your academic and professional goals? Why do you think this program would be a good complement to what you've learned so far? What is unique about you? What sets you apart from the others? What are you going to bring to the program? Why do you think you are a good fit for this particular graduate program? Do not repeat your résumé, but elaborate on things you have done that are not detailed in the résumé. Don't hesitate to include personal information and write in a narrative style.

Applications Fees / Financial Statement for Non-US Citizens
Each admissions office will require application fees (from $40 to $150) that will not be reimbursed even if you are not admitted. It is thus advised to apply to a maximum of five programs. Some graduate offices might grant fee waivers depending on candidates' background but each school/program has its own policy in that matter.

Non-US citizens who will need to apply for a student visa will have to show proof of financial support for their studies in the US. Find out which documents (e.g., bank letter, affidavit of support) you will need to provide. This information is often requested at the end of the admissions process, once you are admitted. US citizens are not required to provide proof of financial support.

Additional Documents According to Departments
Within the same university or graduate school, individual departments might require additional material. For example, if you are applying for an MFA (Master of Fine Arts), the department will probably ask for a portfolio of your artwork. If you are applying to a master's program in Journalism, you will need to provide samples of your work (clips, articles, videos).

Interviews
Interviews are often conducted after the school has received your application; in some cases an interview is optional or not required. If you live outside the US, you can meet with one of the school's alumni living in your region or the admissions office can conduct phone or online interviews. If a school asks for an interview, it might mean that they are interested in your profile and would like to know more about you.

Financial Aid

Studying in the US can be rather expensive, but financial aid exists, especially at the graduate level.

One option is the Fulbright Scholarship Program, created in the aftermath of World War II with the hope that educational exchange could help lay the foundation for a lasting peace. It was thanks to the initiative of Senator J. William Fulbright that the American government was able to create a program of educational and cultural exchange between the United States and participating countries (about 155 today). The Franco-American Fulbright Commission administers the Fulbright program between France and the United States and gives grants to French citizens who go to the US to study or research or to American citizens who come to France for academic purposes. Information about the Fulbright program from France is available at https://fulbright-france.org. Please note that Franco-American dual citizens are not eligible to apply to the Fulbright program from or to France.

Some private foundations offer scholarships or fellowships especially for US or international scholars who are in PhD or post-doctoral programs. A partial list is available on the Fulbright Commission's website.[8] US citizens who have a US social security number can apply for federal student aid. (See chapter "Financing Your Education in the US".)

At the graduate level, departments may offer Teaching Assistant (T.A.) or Research Assistant (R.A.) positions. In exchange for services that you provide to your department (teaching, administrative, or research tasks), you will obtain a tuition waiver and possibly an additional stipend. Each department has its own budget for T.A. and R.A. positions, so it is important to contact the department chair to ask about eligibility. These kinds of opportunities are also open to non-US students.

Many US universities offer scholarships and/or fellowships to graduate students. These can be need-based, need-blind, or merit-based. Check the financial aid office of the university to which you are applying to know more about their policy on financial aid. A list of US universities offering financial aid to international students can be found at: https://educationusa.state.gov/find-financial-aid.

References and Resources

- Franco-American Fulbright Commission: https://fulbright-france.org
- EducationUSA network: https://educationusa.state.gov
- US Department of Education, US Network for Education Information (USNEI): https://www2.ed.gov/about/offices/list/ous/international/usnei/us/edlite-index.html
- Council for Higher Education Accreditation: www.chea.org
- Free Application for Federal Student Aid: https://studentaid.ed.gov/sa/fafsa
- Federal Student Aid – An Office of the US Department of Education: https://studentaid.ed.gov/sa

Endnotes

1. Information taken from the website of the EducationUSA network affiliated with the US Department of State: https://educationusa.state.gov
2. www.ets.org/gre or www.takethegre.com
3. www.mba.com
4. Information taken from the following websites: www.mba.com; www.ets.org/gre
5. Wharton class profile 2020: https://mba.wharton.upenn.edu/class-profile
6. Information taken from the following websites: www.toefl.org and www.ielts.org
7. www.edx.org/course/toeflr-test-preparation-insiders-guide-etsx-toeflx-4
8. https://fulbright-france.org/fr/etudier-usa/etudes-usa/financer-votre-sejour/niveau-graduate

University Study in Canada

Catherine Godard and Jude Smith

Canada is over 10 times the size of France but with half of its population. The country has over 37 million inhabitants, of whom almost 32 million reside in the provinces of Ontario, Quebec, British Columbia, and Alberta. Thus, over three quarters of Canada's population is concentrated in these four provinces, leaving the vast remaining territory more sparsely populated. With such wide-open spaces, Canadians have developed a symbiotic relationship between nature and man. Canada is a leading country in ecology, wild life preservation, and natural resource conservation. From their earliest schooling students are taught to respect their surroundings and to use their natural resources wisely. The United Nations has repeatedly voted Canada in the top 15 countries with an admirable quality of life due to relatively high life expectancy, high educational achievement, above average national income, a public health care system, and a low violent crime rate. Canada's natural resources and beauty add to the country's highly desirable living standards.

The sparse population in so many areas has also led to more liberal immigration policies. International students may be allowed to work on campus and up to 10 hours per week off campus. After having finished their studies, they may seek a permit to work for one year in Canada. These pathways also may lead to permanent residence status. Canada is a young and diverse country that is developing in its own way and at its own pace.

Over 370,000 international students study at nearly all of the more than 100 public and private institutions of higher education in Canada. According to the OECD, of all G7 countries, Canada has the highest proportion of college or university degree holders, with over 57 % of Canadians aged 25 to 34 completing tertiary education. The quality of life, the mosaic of diversity, and the access to higher education are some of the reasons that continue to make Canada a most attractive option. As most major cities in Canada are very close to the American border, fear of cold should be put into perspective. Winter sports and activities such as the annual Montreal Snow Festival, cross-country skiing in the countryside, sledding, the Quebec Winter Carnival in Quebec City, the maple syrup "sugar shacks", and the lakes and national parks for sailing and sport activities year-round, all add to the distinctive quality of life that is found in Canada.

Internet research makes it easy to explore the different higher education options in Canada through the following websites:

- EduCanada (official government website): www.educanada.ca
- Universities Canada: www.univcan.ca
- Canadian Education Centers – StudyCanada: www.studycanada.ca
- Moving2 Canada: https://moving2canada.com/study/
- Maclean's Guide to Canadian Universities (profiles, rankings): www.macleans.ca/education-hub

Advantages to Studying in Canada

Generally speaking, Canadian institutions have three fee schedules for tuition: residents of the province, citizens of Canada, and international students. Reciprocal agreements between the province of Quebec and France make it possible for French citizens to attend Quebec institutions under the fee schedule for Canadian students from other provinces. Thus, tuition fees for French students total less than 8,000 Canadian dollars (CA$) per year. This is significantly less than the tuition paid by other international students, which may be as high as over CA$18,000 per year, but is more expensive than the rate paid by Quebecois students of just over CA$2,500.

> *Reciprocal agreements between the province of Quebec and France make it possible for French citizens to attend Quebec institutions under the fee schedule for Canadian students from other provinces.*

Another advantage to studying in Canada is "transfer credit", granted for high *lycée* exam results on the French *baccalauréat*, IB, or AP, up to the equivalent of one year of university study. For example, high achieving students may earn a four-year BA Honours with a full liberal arts component, including a major and minor concentration, in three years. Remember, the awarding of transfer credits or advanced standing cannot be determined until the final *bulletin de notes* (report cards) and the results of the French *baccalauréat*, IB, or AP have been received by the Registrar in July.

In Canada, unlike Europe, there is more freedom to delay choosing a major. Students must choose a faculty or school of study, but their major remains undeclared until they have had the chance to explore different courses, usually towards the end of their first year study. It is even possible to change faculties or schools after the first year of study, so students are not locked into their original choice.

Admissions

Most Canadian universities will ask only for the student's transcript *(bulletin scolaire)* from French and international institutions. These report cards do not need to be translated, as long as they are in English or French as Canada is bilingual. As an example, McGill will want to see all of *première* and the first trimester of *terminale* report cards before making an admissions decision. In addition, Concordia and most other Canadian institutions will also want to see the *bulletins* from *seconde*. Those applying from international schools may be required to submit transcripts for the entirety of their secondary education, e.g., US grades 9-12. In most cases, transcripts/*bulletins* are uploaded online to the institution. If this is not possible, students or schools may mail them directly to the institution. If you do need to mail transcripts, you may need to photocopy the reports and have your school stamp and sign each page, along with stamping and signing the flap of the sealed envelope before you or the school sends them off.

Most universities do not require essays or recommendations, although the trend towards having students submit a personal statement is growing. Students can also write about special circumstances that they wish to explain, such as a dip in grades due to an illness. Generally, standardized exams (ACT or SAT) are not required of students pursuing the French *baccalauréat*, IB, or A-levels, however, verify the program requirements of the school you'd like to attend. Certain programs, such as engineering, may require standardized exam scores. Institutional online applications are very straightforward and can be completed quite easily. Concerning grade requirements, students should aim at keeping their individual subject scores above 12/20 on the French *baccalauréat* and over 5/7 on the International Baccalaureate.

In addition, a test of English language proficiency may be required, either the TOEFL or IELTS, and minimum score requirements can be very stringent. For example, McGill currently requires a score above 21 in each of the four sections of the TOEFL iBT (internet based test) and 100 overall depending on the program of study. This is not required for students pursuing the French *baccalauréat* with an American or British option (OIB).

Quebec

Quebec universities begin reviewing applications in January and will send decisions by email on a rolling basis. Offers are contingent on students continuing to work in the same manner as when the offer was made. Students have until May 1 to accept their offers. However, they should not wait too long as they will want to process their student immigration papers, apply for housing, and be ready to register for classes.

Some universities to consider (all under the French/Quebec tuition agreement):

Instruction in English
- McGill University (Montreal), with its Desautels Faculty of Management and other faculties and schools of architecture, ecology, and liberal arts, continues to be very popular with our graduates in France. Entrance to law school is possible after completing at least two years of undergraduate studies. The McGill Faculty of Law is excellent preparation for international law careers as it provides instruction in both Napoleonic Code and Common Law.
- Concordia University, (Montreal), is renowned for its John Molson School of Business, Mel Hoppenheim School of Cinema, as well as fine arts, political science, and liberal arts curriculum.
- Bishop's University, (two hours from Montreal in Sherbrooke), a small liberal arts college that is on the Vermont border, providing top-notch opportunities for study in small classes with excellent professors.

Instruction in French
- Université de Montréal, considered as a major research institution
- HEC Montréal with its special three-track business degree in French, English, and Spanish—students from outside of Quebec enter into a preparatory year
- UQAM, Université de Québec (in Montreal)
- Université de Sherbrooke (two hours from Montreal)

Ontario

With the most universities in its province, Ontario has its own application system: OUAC, Ontario University Application Centre (www.ouac.on.ca). Students apply online and the system forwards their applications to the different universities, but supporting documents (*bulletins*, references, TOEFL scores), must still be sent to each institution by the *lycée* either online or by mail as explained above.

The application deadline depends on the school, but generally falls at the end of December, allowing the students sufficient time to make their choices and apply. Students must be responsible for checking on the deadline for the institutions they are applying to, as they may change from year to year. While Quebec offers a financial incentive to French citizens, Ontario and the other provinces of Canada treat them and other non-Canadians as international students with corresponding higher tuition fees. Although costs vary at each institution in Ontario, tuition fees range in cost from CA$30,000 to nearly CA$60,000.

Some institutions to consider:

- University of Toronto with its three campuses: St. George Campus, Scarborough, and Mississauga. The University of Toronto has a college system reminiscent of Oxford and Cambridge in England. Students are assigned a college when they are admitted.
- York University: especially the Glendon Campus for its charm and the Keele campus for their School of the Arts, Media, Performance & Design. Students arriving speaking only French or English leave speaking both.
- University of Ottawa: numerous majors and prides itself on a bilingual education.
- Queen's University with the Bader International Study Centre at Herstmonceux Castle for study in the UK the first year of entry.

All of the universities in Ontario have an excellent reputation, but here are some other schools of note: University of Guelph (veterinary medicine), Carleton University, University of Western Ontario, University of Waterloo (engineering), McMaster University, Brock University (oenology), the Ontario College of Art and Design (OCAD University), and Ryerson University for fine arts.

Other Provinces

Although more than a third of all universities in Canada are in Ontario, each of the western provinces has a major university (e.g., University of Alberta, University of Manitoba, and University of Saskatchewan) with an excellent level of education. Many of these institutions accept applications through June. More and more students are turning to the Maritime Provinces (New Brunswick, Nova Scotia, and Prince Edward Island). Dalhousie University in Nova Scotia is just one of many.

The University of British Columbia (Vancouver and Okanagan campuses) is also very attractive to English-speaking international students. The area is absolutely beautiful with the ocean and mountains allowing for all sorts of summer and winter activities. Fine Arts institutes are also interesting, such as the Emily Carr University of Art + Design, or the Visual College of Art and Design (VCAD). Simon Fraser University also has much to offer, particularly their Institute for Performance Studies.

Immigration Procedures

For all Canadian universities, students must obtain a Canadian Study Permit online through the Canadian Embassy. In addition, applications may be submitted at a government-authorized private VAC (Visa Application Center) located in Paris or Lyon. This is your only option if biometrics (fingerprints and a photograph) are required. Biometrics are needed for those who have only French nationality. US citizens do not have this requirement. Other foreign nationals must check the Canadian government website, www.cic.gc.ca/english/visit/biometrics.asp, to determine if biometrics are required to secure a study permit. While it may only take three weeks to acquire your study permit through the online process, it may take longer if biometrics are necessary.

To apply for a study permit, students must a have a letter of acceptance from a Designated Learning Institution (DLI). These institutions are approved to host international students by each Canadian provincial or territorial government. A valid passport or travel document is also required prior to the application. In addition, students will need to provide proof of financial support to cover all costs related to their study, including housing and all other related expenses. With a valid study permit, full-time students may have the possibility to work on or off campus.

To study in Quebec students must obtain additional documentation prior to the study permit application. Students are responsible for applying to the Quebec Delegation for a CAQ *(certification d'acceptation du Québec)*; and then applying to the Canadian Embassy or VAC for a study permit. In addition, all Quebec university students must be registered with the Quebec Ministry of Education. Upon completion of all of the above permits and certifications, students apply through their institution of higher learning to acquire a "Permanent Code", assigned by the Canadian Ministry of Education. This code is required for student status in Quebec and may be necessary for French citizen students to receive the Canadian student tuition rate. Check your target university for application procedures.

Arriving at University

While some students are completely self-sufficient, it is advisable for a parent to accompany the student to university towards the end of August for the international student orientation week. School will usually begin in September. In December there is a three-week break and school usually ends in late April. Students need to open a bank account in Canada (preferably one that has low/no fees for wire transfers), arrange for a cell phone, get bedding and curtains for the dorm room and generally settle in. Note that textbooks (which are very expensive) can be rented by semester via online services. Going off to college is a big step. Do consider the distance involved, the freedom of choice in the curriculum, and the maturity of your student.

Students should be aware that their grades from 10th grade onwards will be pivotal in the decisions about their future. Internet virtual visits are good, but if you have the opportunity, it is very inspiring for students to actually visit campuses to understand exactly what they are working towards. Take advantage of summer camps and university programs to improve English, not only for the TOEFL, but to be able to face the required work at university in the best possible conditions. Remember that students will be expected to do at least three hours of reading for each class, about 15 to 20 hours per week, and they need to be prepared to submit their research papers in English, (the exception being attendance in a French language university), although some Canadian universities will accept student research papers in French. It is an exciting time for young people and Canada provides wonderful options for study and quality of life. Canadian diplomas can lead to graduate studies in most countries throughout the world.

References and Resources

- Statistics Canada. Table 17-10-0009-01 Population estimates, quarterly (www150.statcan.gc.ca/t1/tbl1/en/tv.action?pid=1710000901)
- http://hdr.undp.org/sites/default/files/2018_human_development_statistical_update.pdf
- https://cbie.ca/wp-content/uploads/2018/08/Student_Voice_Report-ENG.pdf; www.educanada.ca/programs-programmes/university-universite.aspx?lang=eng
- www150.statcan.gc.ca/n1/en/pub/81-604-x/81-604-x2018001-eng.pdf?st=5LWIZdME (pg. 24)
- www.canada.ca/en/immigration-refugees-citizenship/services/study-canada/study-permit.html
- www.canada.ca/en/immigration-refugees-citizenship/services/study-canada/study-permit/prepare/designated-learning-institutions-list.html
- www.immigration-quebec.gouv.qc.ca/en/immigrate-settle/students/index.html

Student Anecdotes

I chose a Canadian university since I wanted to be free and live away from home. Even though my first instinct was to look into American universities, that option would have meant taking out an astronomical amount of student loans. Having a French passport means lower tuition fees in Quebec, so choosing a university in Montreal was a good "middle ground". After all, Montreal was voted the #1 student city in the world a few years ago! It was very hard to adjust to my new school environment. During my first semester, I, and most of my friends almost failed all of our classes. It was hard to learn to manage your own time, coming from a French *lycée* with such a tight schedule. All of a sudden in university I only had 16 hours of class time per week; it's so easy to get lost in all the "free time" you have. So when the syllabus specifies that "you will need to work on average xx amount of hours outside of class to keep up", take this seriously! You will fail if you don't put the work into it and nobody will reprimand you if you don't do your homework. I only truly managed to adapt once I understood this. – *Loren*

The university I attend in Montreal was my first choice as it offers great programs and I always wanted to live the North American university experience. Also, Montreal is a bilingual city, so it is always nice to have the opportunity to speak French from time to time. I am very satisfied with my choice, simply because I love the culture. The academic environment is intense, depending on the program. Naturally, engineers have it harder than other faculties. Personally, in Management the environment is relatively rigorous, but extremely different than it was in high school *(terminale* S*)*. Workloads are more concentrated in the middle and then at end of the semester, meaning you have calmer periods followed by intense studying. My high school definitely prepared me adequately for university, as it required me to be rigorous in my studying. The culture of my school is very liberal, and everyone is very welcoming. To any student debating between going to *prépa* or abroad, definitely try a change of environment! You won't regret it! – *Nathalie*

I applied to several universities in Canada, Scotland, and England. My final decision was to study Bioresource Engineering at a university in Montreal for the following reasons: I was interested in the degree, the university is prestigious, but I also like the campus. It is crucial that I mention that the latter is not the main "downtown campus", but the smaller and more rural campus, which hosts agricultural, environmental, and food-related studies. Indeed, the campus I attend hosts a significantly smaller student population and therefore, there's a tighter community. I still had some trouble making friends at first, but what helped me the most was living in a residence, group projects, and clubs where you can meet people that share similar interests, such as music in my case. The system also offers plenty of opportunities for students to take on important responsibilities, get involved, and manage these clubs, societies, and events. For instance, during my second year I founded the first ever archery club on campus, which I believe would have been much harder on a larger campus and maybe impossible in France (from what my friends have told me).

My campus was more of a typical North American campus and also has a tighter community where you can literally "know everyone" and have a more human relationship with your professors. However, there are things that both campuses share. They are all very international, accepting, and tolerant (I find the people here much more respectful than in France). I have to say I am very satisfied with my choice because of the experience I gained from being here and the amazing people I've met. I've noticed that French students tend to stick together. It is also the case for people of other nationalities, however, I really recommend you try to mingle with everyone. I've seen people become great friends despite language and cultural barriers, and I believe you will be missing out on a lot of opportunities if you don't go out of your comfort zone. Forget about the boundaries and limits set by the French system and think outside the box. If you have any innovative ideas, don't be afraid to make them happen. The ultimate goal is to grow and evolve after all. – *Alex*

Undergraduate Study in the UK

Joumana Ordelheide

The United Kingdom is world renowned for the quality of its higher education. With approximately 130 universities in the UK offering over 50,000 courses, it is a highly desirable destination for many students. Approximately 400,000 international students study in the UK and 120,000 of them are EU students. French students are the second most represented students in the UK amongst the EU students, with around 13,000 students currently studying in the country.[1]

There is a wide range of courses available to students wanting to study in the UK. (Note that the British term "course" is the same as the American "program".) Currently, the most popular courses are Business and Administrative studies, Engineering and Technology, Social Studies, Creative Arts and Design, Law, and Biological studies. However, with a diverse course offering available, students can find degrees that will suit any interest, from courses in medicine or criminology to psychology and product design.[2]

Why international students flock to the United Kingdom

The United Kingdom not only offers a great diversity in courses but also in campuses. Whether it is an urban campus nestled in one of London's vibrant neighborhoods, or one of the traditional campuses that dot the lush countryside, students can find an educational environment that suits both their academic needs and their lifestyle. This, in combination with the close proximity to continental Europe and easy and affordable travel options, is often cited by students and parents alike as one of the main reasons France-based students decide to study in the UK.

Furthermore, the application process gives students the opportunity to reach their full potential and demonstrate to universities that they are capable of attaining marks that may not currently be reflected in their transcripts or grade reports. France being a country known for its difficult grading, students often worry about how their marks will be perceived but, with very rare exceptions, students do not need to submit transcripts when applying to the UK. This allows students to work with their teachers and guidance counselor to come up with a predicted grade that corresponds to their potential academic achievements and not solely based on their current grades. As admissions responses are conditional, universities are thus more likely to take a chance on students that show the potential to do well on their baccalaureate, allowing them to access more prestigious universities than they would in France.

Different types of undergraduate programs to meet student needs

There are three main categories of courses that students graduating with the French *baccalauréat* can access. Most students can access the Bachelor programs directly after having graduated from the *lycée* system; however, other options are also available to students.

Foundation programs
Foundation programs aim to prepare students for succeeding in undergraduate studies, allowing students to access a program for which they do not yet have the academic level or the required English language proficiency. These one-year programs help students acclimate to a different system of education and to prove their ability to join the more competitive programs. However, most of these programs are not credit bearing, so they would add a year to the duration of the studies.

Foundation programs exist both as integrated programs and as independent programs. Integrated programs allow students to apply to a program with foundation directly; for example, a student would be admitted into a specific university program with foundation (e.g., Business and Management program with foundation). Although students can apply to other universities during their foundation program, the aim would be for them to progress into the degree course at their chosen university. Independent foundation programs can be offered by a university as well as by other educational providers such as high schools, language schools, or other accredited educational institutions. Students are accompanied in the application process during the foundation program, but their course and university destination is not pre-set as they are in the integrated programs.

Some foundation programs are very specific to the course they will be preparing. Many art schools will encourage students to complete foundation programs before applying to their degree of choice, as the foundation program will refine both the student's artistic abilities and will also accompany them in the preparation of their artistic portfolio, which is essential in the evaluation of applications to art degree courses.

Bachelor programs
Bachelor programs are the first and most logical step to take for any student who does not need a preparation program after the *baccalauréat*. Typically, Bachelor courses last three to four years and subsequently give students access to master's degrees or the job market.

"Sandwich" programs
A classic undergraduate degree in the UK is programmed to run for three years. However, there are more and more programs, called "Sandwich" programs, that

allow students to complete a year abroad (typically called "with international study") or a year of work/internship (typically called "with industry experience"). This special year is typically "sandwiched" between the third and fourth years of study and extends the program to four years. As placement and study abroad spots are limited, students need to apply directly to a program that has this feature. It is still possible to request to study abroad or to complete an internship during the duration of the studies if the student did not apply to a "Sandwich" program. However, the availability and the spots at prestigious universities and companies are not guaranteed.

Admission to top programs is highly competitive

There are three primary types of highly competitive programs that exist in the UK. These universities and programs not only limit the amount of students they recruit from abroad, but also have very specific and more complicated admissions requirements that set them apart from the regular UCAS admissions processes.

Oxford and Cambridge (Oxbridge)
Not only are the applications to Oxford and Cambridge notable due to their early deadline of October 15th, but the extremely high entry requirements, testing, and interview process make their admissions process even more selective than that of most other well-ranked universities in the UK. Students seeking admission to Oxbridge should generally be at least in the top 5% of their class and must complete specific admissions tests for most programs in order to be qualified for an interview. Generally, less than 10% of applicants are admitted, making it a strong reach for even the highest achieving students.

Medical and Dentistry Programs
Medicine and dentistry programs also have an early deadline of October 15th. As it is a general rule for the UK to give priority to students from the UK, students from other countries have a very low chance of being offered an interview and eventually a place. The invitation for an interview is based entirely on the student's BMAT (BioMedical Admissions Test) or UCAT (University Clinical Aptitude Test—formerly known as the UKCAT) score, which are the medical school examinations required for everyone applying to study medicine in the UK. Students are also expected to have had experience in the medical field, for example, by shadowing a medical professional, working in a laboratory, or volunteering with first aid services, making it a challenge for students who are of high school age. In addition, students may only apply to four medical programs; their fifth UCAS choice can be in a science program. Traditionally, less than 5% of students are granted an interview for medical school in the UK, making medicine the most competitive program to gain entry to in the UK. However, it is possible to gain entry to medical and dentistry programs at the graduate level after having completed a program in the sciences, which is often a suggested path for students who are not admitted at the undergraduate level.

Conservatory, Arts, Design and creative programs requiring portfolios or auditions
Although each of these courses is unique, it is important to point out that many creative courses have a requirement of a portfolio or audition process, which requires students to be prepared ahead of time as the submission of these documents

or invitations to the auditions follow very shortly after the application deadline. It is important to be mindful of these dates, often available on the university's website, so as to not be surprised by specific requirements. Oftentimes, students should already have content for these applications, as the expectation is that an artist has been developing his/her craft over the years. It is also important to be mindful that specific subject entry requirements may be requested that are not accessible with the traditional *baccalauréat* curriculum, requiring the student to complete and prepare extra qualifying examinations independently.

Choosing the right course and university

When applying to the UK, students are not only applying to a university but also to a specific program of study. This program must correspond to the student's career goals and to his or her profile. It is highly discouraged to submit an application to different courses unless they have a similar foundation, as it will be very difficult to complete a personal statement that is coherent and that relates to the different courses. It is also not advisable to submit applications to different courses at the same university, as unless the entry requirements differ dramatically, the chances that a student is refused from both programs are very high. Hence, it is very important to first choose the degree course of interest to the student before preparing a list of universities. The next step would be to determine if the student has the entry requirements needed to enter the program at specific universities, and finally assembling the list of universities based on supporting elements such as location, duration of program, and accessibility to value-added features such as study abroad opportunities.

UCAS: The first and essential step

The UK's online application system is called Universities and Colleges Admissions Service, UCAS for short, and it centralizes all UK university applications. Although students can in some cases apply independently to universities through other platforms, UCAS centralizes the responses and the admissions offers, so it is highly advised to use UCAS as the primary application platform. The UCAS system allows students to apply to five universities in one application process and all the elements transmitted will be the same to all universities.

Important deadlines:

- Music Conservatory courses: October 1st of the final year of secondary school.
- Oxbridge, Medical, Dentistry programs: October 15th of final secondary school year.
- All other programs: January 15th of the final year of secondary school.
- It is possible to submit applications once the January 15th deadline has passed, however, these may not be considered until after all the applications submitted before January 15th have been evaluated.

The UCAS application is a simplified application process, with five main components:

1. Biographical information: The first part of UCAS will gather basic information on the student, his/her nationality and address, and basic information on the student's academic background and employment history.

2. Personal Statement: The personal statement is perhaps the most important piece of the application. Detailed later in this chapter, the personal statement is the occasion for students to showcase their academic background and extracurricular activities, and to differentiate themselves in order to convince admissions officers that they should be admitted.

3. Reference: The reference is a unique letter of recommendation submitted by a teacher, counselor, or school director. This reference letter aims to support the student in their application and to confirm to the university that the student is suited for the course they have chosen. There are many ways to write an impactful letter of recommendation, and the author should be someone who fully supports the student's project and who is familiar with the student's academic achievement, extracurricular activities, and career aspirations. It is important to note here that this is a very difficult document to obtain from many French *lycées*, so it is important to work ahead of time with the person writing this letter to ensure it has the content that the universities are seeking.

4. Predicted grades: Submitted alongside the reference, predicted grades are another essential element of the UCAS application. Apart from in very rare cases (Cambridge supplemental application, or foundation programs, for example), students do not submit transcripts or grade reports to UK universities in the application process. The only academic elements submitted to the universities will be completed examinations (for example, the results of the *épreuves anticipées* completed at the end of *première*, or the results of admissions or language examinations) and a predicted grade.

A predicted grade is a prediction of how well students will do in their final examinations at the end of their secondary school studies. In the case of the French *baccalauréat*, the referee will provide a predicted grade for the overall average expected for the student *(moyenne générale)* as well as a predicted grade by subject. As all admissions responses for students currently in high school are conditional, it is important that this predicted grade be ambitious but realistic, and it is equally important that students choose their university and programs based on this predicted grade (see details on conditional offers further in this chapter).

5. University choices: The five university and course choices are listed in the choices section. There is no order of preference at this point of the application. The order is set once students receive their admissions results, where they will keep two offers, one "firm" and one "insurance".

The UCAS application is then sent in electronic format via UCAS Apply, with a small fee depending on the number of applications the student has chosen. There are no attachments or documents to be sent to the universities. All of the admissions requirements will be verified once the student has completed his/her examinations. At that point, students will need to send in their official examinations results as well as any other component detailed in the admissions offer on UCAS.

What needs to be done after the application is submitted

Responses and final admissions decisions are then received and followed up on via UCAS Track, the secondary UCAS application portal. However, certain universities will also have their own university portals that they will use to manage and request supplemental application elements. It is important to keep an eye out on any potential emails, on UCAS Track, as well as on any messages that appear in the admissions portal.

Admissions offers

Once the application is submitted, admissions offices can take between two weeks to several months to respond to the students, with the latest responses coming in at the end of June. Traditionally, most students will have heard back from universities by the end of March.

Once all offers are received, students will have to choose two universities from their list of positive responses, one firm choice and one insurance choice.

Firm choice: The firm choice is the student's first choice university to attend, and should also be the university that has higher admissions requirements than the student's insurance choice. It should be ambitious when it comes to entry requirements and fit all of the other academic and quality of life criteria the student has listed. It is very important to consider all criteria when making this choice, as once the selection is made, it is locked in and cannot be changed once the *baccalauréat* results are received. If a student meets the admissions conditions of the firm choice, the plan must be for them to attend that university.

Insurance choice: The insurance choice is a back-up choice in case the student does not meet the offer from their firm choice; therefore it must have lower entry requirements than their firm choice.

Clearing

If a student does not fulfill their admissions requirements, or does not receive any admissions offers, there is an opportunity to participate in the clearing process, which allows students to receive offers of admission to a university that has entry requirements that match their final admissions results. Students will either be automatically eligible for clearing as both their firm and insurance choices have refused their applications, or they can release their application into clearing themselves though the UCAS portal.

Adjustment

If students have received higher admissions results than expected, they may contact the universities to find out if they will participate in the adjustment process. Adjustment allows students to be considered for a course with their final results. This is a good process to consider if the student obtained a final grade that was significantly higher than his/her predicted grade.

Deciphering entry requirements: Conditional offers

As entry requirements are pre-set by admissions officers ahead of time, it is very simple and easy to find out what the university is looking for in a student's academic profile. These requirements will vary by, and will often have a requirement for, an overall average in the examination results, as well as a condition in subjects that are related to the course the student wishes to pursue. A third requirement will often refer to required admissions and language tests, and/or portfolios and auditions. This information is in the majority of cases clearly indicated in the entry requirement section of the course to which the student is interested in applying. This section will also indicate whether or not supplementary examinations and other elements are required, what the minimum language requirements are, and whether or not students will be going through an interview process.

In most cases, the universities will provide the academic entry requirement based on the UK A-Level examinations that will be shown in a series of three letter grades. You will find below an informative chart of the traditional equivalencies of these grades to the French *baccalauréat*, based on this author's experience, discussions with universities, and offers her students have received. However, it is essential and of the upmost importance to contact the university and verify the specific university equivalencies, not only in general terms, but most importantly for the targeted course.

A level requirement	French *bac* approximate equivalent
A*A*A*	17 to 18/20 and above
A*A*A	
A*AA	16/20
AAA	13.5 to 15/20
AAB	
ABB	12.5 to 13/20
BBB	
BBC	11.5 to 12/20
BCC	
CCC	10-11/20

This equivalency table is a guide to help the student understand the elements listed on the universities' websites. It is very important to verify these scores with the universities directly.

In some rare cases, universities will present the entry requirements using UCAS Tariff Points. The approximate equivalencies of these points can be found on the UCAS website; however, they are not as accurate at the A-level equivalencies. In any case, it is best to contact the universities who will indicate the minimum offer they are looking for.

In order to have a chance to receive a positive response from the universities, a student's predicted grade needs to match the entry requirements. It is extremely rare to see a student receive an offer of admission to a course whose entry requirements exceed the predicted grade.

As the admission responses are conditional upon obtaining a specific score on the *baccalauréat*, it is strongly advised that students vary their university choices based on entry requirements in order to raise the chances of receiving positive responses, but also to have a backup school with lower requirements in case they underachieve in the final examinations.

For example, a student with a predicted 15/20 as a general average in the *baccalauréat* should consider choosing:

- 1-2 universities requiring 15/20
- 1-2 universities requiring 14/20
- 1 university requiring 13/20

When students follow this tiered admissions strategy, they tend to receive approximately 3 positive admissions responses out of 5. This will of course also depend on the strength of the other application components.

Language and admissions tests

Admissions tests required for entry to university in the UK can be categorized by two types: English language examinations to demonstrate sufficient language skills to complete an undergraduate degree in English, and admissions tests, which test things such as general knowledge and cognitive capabilities. In most cases, students will have a minimum level to attain to qualify for the program, which will be indicated in the conditional offer if a student is admitted.

English language tests

The aim of the language test is to ensure that a student can follow their chosen course of study. As part of the conditional offer, students will have to attain a minimum score to be able to start their studies. Oftentimes, this will be a general average and a minimum score per section. Although the universities in the UK accept a wide variety of examinations, the preferred examination is the IELTS delivered by the British Council. Details on the minimum requirement for entry is detailed on the university website, and can vary depending on the degree the student hopes to complete. In either case, contrary to many other systems of education, students have until the end of their final year of secondary studies to prove their language level, and can continue to take a language test until the summer of their graduation from school.

Recently, some universities have started allowing students to replace the IELTS or other English language examination with a score on the LV1 foreign language exam ("LVA" on the new *bac*) for students completing the classic *baccalauréat*, or on the English Literature portion of the OIB. However, this approach is not guaranteed, and students should allow for enough time to prepare and take the IELTS or other English language examinations.

Admissions tests

There are courses that require an additional admissions test to be eligible for admission. Without this test, a student's application will not be considered. These tests will be subject specific, and verify a student's subject knowledge as well as other soft and hard skills. These tests need to be completed during the same year as the student is applying to university and, in most cases, students need to have registered and/or taken this test by the time they submit their application. Most of these tests are taken with an external provider and registration for the test takes place online. Some of the tests will be administered on campus when the students are invited for an interview.

Primary personal statement: the key to success

The personal statement and application essays allow admissions officers to get an understanding of the student's profile and personality and his/her motivations to attend university. Usually, the admissions officers deciding on the student's file, as well as the faculty advisors from the department they are applying to, will read the statement. These people decide whom they want on their campus and in their course, so it is imperative to draw and retain their attention throughout the statement and to demonstrate that the student is a good fit for the program and the university.

Things to consider for the statement:
- Only one personal statement is submitted via UCAS for all universities. Students should therefore not name a specific university in the statement unless they are only applying to one university.
- Content needs to be 60% about the subject and why the student wants to study it, and 40% about their personality, their skills, and ambitions. For very highly academic and highly ranked programs and Oxbridge, the expectation is that 80% of the personal statement be about the subject and why the student wants to study it, and 20% about their personality, their skills, and ambitions.
- The statement needs to be geared towards the degree that the student wants to study.
- A UCAS personal statement can be a maximum of 4000 characters (including spaces) and 47 lines.
- Students need to show that they want to learn. What they are looking for is not just statements, but proof of the student's character through the lens of different experiences that they have had.

  - Prepare and work on the statement ahead of time and for a long time; a good statement is never written overnight and requires reflection and thought.
  - Make it personal. Admissions staff will want to know about the student, his/her personality, and who they want to become.
  - Go into detail and explain. Do not create a list of things a student has done without giving an explanation as to who they have become or how it has impacted them. If they don't go into detail the statement won't have any impact.
  - Why you? If a student reads his/her essay and realizes that they could replace their name with anyone else's, then they haven't completed the task.
  - Do not overcorrect. Although it is important to get feedback and correct a student's statement, if the level of linguistic ability significantly exceeds the English language scores they have achieved, admissions officers will know that it is not the student's work.

Elements to Include:
Why this degree?
- Why does the student want to study the chosen subject?
- What are the specific courses in this subject that attract the student?
- What aspect of this degree do they find will be valuable for their future?
- What about the subject encourages them to find out more?

Academic experience
- How have the student's current studies prepared them for this course?
- What are important courses that they have taken at school or outside that show that the student can be successful in this course?
- What are the projects that they have completed at school that show they have an interest in this course?

Work experience
- What internships have they done? What were the tasks and achievements and what have they learned from them?
- Are they in any way linked to what they have studied? If so, how?
- What skills does the student have, and what experience shows they have these skills?

Other interests
- Does the student read about the course outside of school? If yes, in what form and what does it bring to them?
- Do they do community/volunteer work?
- Has the student participated in any other extracurricular activity that shows a skill that can be either linked to the course, or demonstrates a specific skill or capacity?

Why this university/your future?
- What will studying in the UK bring to the student and what will he/she bring to the school?
- Where does the student see himself/herself in a few years?
- How will this degree and university help them with their career goal?

Additional personal statements / essays / questionnaires
There is a trend among universities to request additional personal statements for certain competitive courses. These statements will be requested following the first application submission and sometimes a student will only have 10 days to submit the work. Similar to an interview, this exercise is requested to understand the specific interests and motivations of the student.

Tuition, cost of living, and scholarships

Tuition
Tuition for undergraduate students varies depending on the nationality of the student. EU students currently have the advantage of paying the same fees as UK students, while international students are required to pay a higher fee. However, this may change in the future because of the evolving relationship between the United Kingdom and the European Union. Each university's website will indicate the exact fees that the students will need to pay based on the year they will start their studies. One interesting consideration is that universities in Scotland offer the same low tuition fees as local Scottish students to students coming from EU countries, while they charge higher fees for other UK countries and international students.

Cost of living
It is important to consider the difference in costs based on the location of the

university. Accommodation and living expenses can more than double in larger cities such as London, as daily life is considerably more expensive than in smaller cities or at universities with more on-campus facilities and services.

Scholarships

It is rare to find scholarships for non-UK students at the undergraduate level. The British Council and some institutions may offer some help with tuition, but competition for these scholarships is high and they rarely cover full tuition fees. Currently, EU students can benefit from the student finance loan that the UK government offers, which defers payment of tuition fees (and adds interest) until the student starts working.

Conclusion

Higher education opportunities in the UK are numerous and are of particular interest to the French bilingual student because of the UK's close proximity to France and reasonable tuition fees. As arrangements evolve concerning the relationship between the UK and EU, any impact on student visas or tuition fees for non-UK students may change. It is therefore advisable to keep abreast of developments in this regard prior to the application process.

References and Resources

- General application information and rankings:
  - www.ucas.com
  - https://study-uk.britishcouncil.org
  - www.thecompleteuniversityguide.co.uk/league-tables/rankings
  - https://concourse.global/c4/United_Kingdom
  - www.theguardian.com/education/ng-interactive/2018/may/29/university-league-tables-2019
- Medical school application guide: www.medschools.ac.uk/media/2357/msc-entry-requirements-for-uk-medical-schools.pdf
- Admissions tests: www.ucas.com/undergraduate/applying-university/admissions-tests
- Finance and scholarships: www.gov.uk/student-finance

Endnotes

1. www.ukcisa.org.uk/Research--Policy/Statistics/International-student-statistics-UK-higher-education
2. Ibid.

Student Anecdotes

I am a second-year student in Politics and International Relations at a university in Bath. At the beginning of my last year of high school, I started considering going to university abroad. Indeed, after doing all my schooling in France in the exact same location, I felt the need to discover other cultures. Though I first considered going to Montreal, the UK appeared clearly as the best option due to the short travel distance, its educational system, and its sport culture that really appealed to me. I immediately knew I wanted to study in a campus university and did not really think of going to London. Bath, being a dynamic and historical city that combines an easy access to all kinds of services and a truly beautiful architecture, corresponded perfectly to my expectations.

As I never visited the UK before my first day at university, I felt a big cultural shock the first weeks but got used to it quickly since I was the only international student in my flat. Moreover, the university demonstrated several times during the year its will to integrate all the students and not to leave anyone behind. During the fresher's week, everything was done in order for us to meet our future fellow students, while during the first lectures, members of the staff talked about the easy accessibility of psychological support for students. I was happily surprised about all the efforts the university showed in order to make our educational experience the best possible. Thanks to the enormous amount of societies and the organisation of several events and activities during the year, I am really satisfied about the social life I have in Bath. The academic expectations at Bath were considerably different from France. While most of the academic work I had in *lycée* consisted of acquiring knowledge, in Bath, research and analytical skills were at the forefront. I encountered some difficulties understanding the lecturers' expectations for my first assignments, and my first semester at university did not show good results at all. However, thanks to the great support the university provides, whether it is from the peer mentors, the personal tutors, the lecturers or simply from older French students, I made great progress and was able to improve my average by 13 points in a year.

Overall, the quality my university excelled in was the constant availability of the teaching staff to answer any of our questions. By allowing closer relations between students and teachers, they made studying not only more enjoyable but also more motivating. I am really satisfied about my experience in England so far.   – *Charles*

As university in Scotland is free for Europeans, and my school in Edinburgh is quite high in the rankings, I went for it. However, coming from a top Parisian *lycée*, I'm disappointed by the quality of teaching. Although there's a large European and foreign population, it feels very British. I have often felt non-white here, which I never felt in France. The city itself is interesting and has some things to do. Some students go out every night and there's a nightclub for each night of the week. The social life is a bit "cliquey". I'd tell a *lycéen* that they're probably over-prepared; in my opinion, university starts around *première* level, but it requires a lot more initiative and works very differently from France.   – *Quentin*

I chose my UK school because it is highly ranked in my subject area and is near my home (Paris). I'm very satisfied with my choice: my course is amazing and the friend group I've made here is extremely supportive. The academic environment of my *lycée* was a semi-strict Catholic French education, with a high emphasis on excellent *bac* results and high success rates, but the social environment was not very diverse and it was a bit closed culturally. My university environment in London suits me much better as it is the most ethnically, culturally, and humanly diverse environment I've ever lived in, and it's a breeding ground for positive interactions. I adjusted almost immediately; the main change is the workload, which is much more start-and-stop (extremely light at times, and occasionally very heavy). I would advise French students considering going to the UK to study to leave their comfort zone a little: integrate into the culture! Don't just hang out with French students on campus, and don't take the Eurostar home every weekend (not only is it expensive, but you won't adjust). Try the culture; meet new people; throw yourself out there.   – Alex

I chose my university in England because it holds a sound reputation despite being a relatively young institution; it's consistently well-ranked, and has a prestigious reputation in certain fields such as the social sciences. On a different note, the quality of life on campus surpasses the urban competition in Birmingham, Manchester, Edinburgh, and London. Students and lecturers share both a physical and symbolic proximity, as new and stimulating relations tend to flourish amidst the beautiful, natural scenery. I am utterly thrilled to be studying at my university as well as grateful towards all the wonderful professors and students who have enlightened my way in both academia and life.

The English international section of my Paris area public *lycée* was arguably one of the best decisions undertaken by my parents throughout my childhood. To this day, as a fourth-year undergraduate student, I find myself drawing upon the cultural references of our English literature class and the practical knowledge of our History and Geography lessons.

The adjustment aspect in the UK was perhaps more challenging at first, though I would not single out my school in this regard (despite having a well-founded reputation for being a more privileged, 'posh' environment). In the end, most of the issues of adjustment on both an academic and sociocultural level tend to be brief and surmountable, according to the experiences of my foreign peers and my own. The university is well aware of the adaptational phase that international students go through, and they provide a number of tailored services, such as the student mentor programme.

Overall, it has been both an exhilarating and challenging experience. Without a doubt, the United Kingdom harbours some of the most advanced institutions of higher education in the Western hemisphere, and the full English immersion is a tremendous source of personal growth and linguistic empowerment. This being said, I would urge students to equally consider the merits of Dutch and Scandinavian universities (myself having nearly ended up in Maastricht). Not only are the tuition fees considerably more affordable, but the universities have strong academic standards in a number of fields and departments. Ultimately, however, what matters most is your own connection to the institution, that is, whether you identify with it on a personal and academic level.   – Edouard

Higher Education in the Netherlands

Mariët Robert

It ain't much, if it ain't Dutch! If this is the first time you are hearing this expression, it definitely will not be the last. The Dutch are proud of their small country and why wouldn't they be?

The Netherlands is home to 13 public research universities, offering international programs. Seven are among the top 100 *Times Higher Education World University Rankings*.[1] All of the Dutch research universities appear among the top 250 global universities. Some programs are even ranked #1 in the *QS World University Rankings* and other world rankings.[2]

The oldest university in the Netherlands is Leiden University, founded in 1575. One of the newest, Maastricht University, founded in 1976, is ranked among the top 10 of the best young universities in the world.[3] Whether the universities are new or old, they offer a high quality education with a personal touch. The Dutch are friendly, straightforward, and practical so it is no surprise that these characteristics are embedded in their educational system.

The Dutch speak English fluently and are widely recognized for such. In fact, they are known to be among the best non-native English speakers in the world. Dutch higher education thus offers a large number of programs in English. Furthermore, the language of instruction in all of the University Colleges is English. While the study of Dutch as a foreign language is optional it may become a requirement for other European and international students. Dutch tuition fees are considerably lower than those in English-speaking countries, which make the Netherlands an attractive option for the Anglophone student.

With all these qualities, more and more European and international students find their way to the Netherlands. So, what kind of education is offered in the Netherlands that is attracting these international students?

The Dutch Higher Education System

There are 13 public research universities, 10 University Colleges (honors colleges of the research universities), and 36 universities of applied sciences known as HBO *(hogescholen)*, offering international programs. Together they offer a wide range of more than 2,000 programs that are taught entirely in English. Diplomas granted from all of the research universities and the University Colleges are recognized worldwide for the excellent education they offer.

The Research Universities

These come in all different shapes and sizes. It is important to first choose the program one is interested in and then select the university. The student population can vary from 12,000 to 32,000 bachelor, master, and PhD students. Some universities are very international while others are less so, and some are located in city centers while others are in the suburbs. Some are known for their excellent business, political science, agriculture, or engineering programs. Many of the universities offer a large variety of programs. The duration of the bachelor programs is typically three years and master's programs range from one to two years.

The 13 public research universities are:
- TU Delft
- Eindhoven University of Technology
- Erasmus University Rotterdam
- Universiteit Leiden
- Maastricht University
- Radboud University
- Tilburg University
- University of Amsterdam
- University of Groningen
- University of Twente
- Utrecht University
- Vrije Universiteit Amsterdam
- Wageningen University & Research

Nyenrode Business Universiteit is a small, private business university that offers programs in English.

The University Colleges

The University Colleges are a more recent concept inspired by the liberal arts and sciences programs in the United States with the strong student community atmosphere that is also found in some of the UK universities. The first University College was established in 1997 as an honors college of a research university. Today there are 10 University Colleges; each college has its own specialization.

University Colleges offer a three-year liberal arts and sciences bachelor's program proposing a wide variety of subjects from humanities and social sciences to the physical sciences. Academic advisors help students choose courses and thus design their own interdisciplinary curriculum. All courses are taught in English with a strong international focus, and classes are small and interactive. In most cases, students live on campus for at least the first year, which fosters a strong community atmosphere where lifelong friendships are formed with students from all over the world and with different backgrounds and cultures.

The 10 University Colleges are:
- Amsterdam University College (University of Amsterdam and Vrije Universiteit Amsterdam)
- Erasmus University College (Erasmus University Rotterdam)
- University College Fryslân (University of Groningen)
- Leiden University College the Hague (Universiteit Leiden)
- University College Groningen (University of Groningen)
- University College Maastricht (Maastricht University)
- University College Roosevelt (Utrecht University)
- University College Tilburg (Tilburg University)
- University College Twente (University of Twente)
- University College Utrecht (Utrecht University)

The Universities of Applied Sciences (UAS / HBO in Dutch)
The universities of applied sciences, called HBO in Dutch, are not to be confused with the research universities. The universities of applied sciences offer a professional-oriented education principally for bachelor degree programs, some master's, and very rarely the PhD level. Students gain practical work experience through internships, which are an integral part of these programs. The bachelor programs take four years to complete.

There are 36 universities of applied sciences, all of which are government-funded and offer a range of programs given in English. It is strongly advised to check if the program/university of interest is internationally recognized and accredited.

Some universities of applied sciences in Art and Design, Music, and Hospitality Management are world-renowned, including the Design Academy Eindhoven, the ArtEZ University of the Arts, and the Hotelschool The Hague.

Many research universities, University Colleges, and universities of applied sciences offer interactive and personalized education. Teamwork plays an essential role in the Dutch education system, especially within the Problem-Based Learning method. Problem-Based Learning, or PBL, offers a different way of learning. Students learn more about a certain subject by approaching problems from different angles. They learn to be independent and open-minded, acquiring knowledge by doing, working together as a team, and speaking up. This small group work is guided by a tutor.

Tuition Fees, Scholarships, and Housing

Tuition Fees
The tuition fees for EU students start at 2,087 €. For international non-EU students, the fees are higher but still remain very reasonable, ranging between 6,000 € and 15,000 € for bachelor programs and between 8,000 € and 20,000 € for master's programs.

Please note that the cost of living varies between 800 € and 1,100 € per month.

Scholarships
A complete overview of scholarships offered in the Netherlands can be found at these websites: www.studyinholland.nl and the www.nuffic.nl/en website.

Housing
Finding a room in some Dutch cities can be daunting. Students usually do not live on the campus but rent their own room. Some universities offer housing for EU and international students; however, there is always more demand than supply. The Golden Rule is that if housing is offered by your university, sign up for it as early as possible!

Almost all University Colleges guarantee at least one year of housing, with some offering three years of guaranteed housing.

Establishing a List of Preferred Universities

Creating a list of prospective universities is an important starting point and is based on what one WANTS and what one can OFFER as qualifications. This step is essential for optimizing one's chances of future success. The final list of preferences should consist of three categories: the "dream" or "reach" universities, the "realistic possibility" universities, and the "back-up" or "safety" universities.

1. You first need to decide what you want to study. No worries, there is a large choice of English programs ranging from Political, Environmental, and Aeronautical Sciences to Business Administration, Psychology, and Media and Communication. If you prefer to study a variety of subjects, the liberal arts and sciences programs of the University College would be a good choice. The most important thing to consider is a subject or a major you are passionate about—keep in mind that 65% of jobs of the future have not been created yet!

2. Once you know what you want to study, you should decide where you want to study. City or suburban setting? Or Randstad (the megalopolis of Amsterdam, Rotterdam, the Hague, and Utrecht). Furthermore, you need to decide if you want to study at a research university, a University College, or at a university of applied sciences.

3. An important step is also to find out if your qualifications match with the selection criteria. For example: what overall grade average, eventually specific subject grades, and what English tests are required? Please note, not all Dutch universities accept completion of the OIB British or American sections as proof of English language proficiency.

4. Rankings are important, but it is even more important for you to feel at home at the university. Each university has its own personality, atmosphere, culture, and method of teaching. The best way to find out is to attend "Open Days" and "student-for-a-day" events, and go talk with teachers and students. You can also sign up to attend the CIS International University Fair in Paris, or the UIS Dutch University Fair, "Etudier aux Pays-Bas", held each year in partnership with the Dutch Embassy in Paris. Think about the criteria that are important to you, read up on the program and course offerings, and prepare a list of pertinent questions. Ideally, you want to start researching and visiting universities during

the spring preceding your final year.

5. Find out if your university or program is international. Will it be easy to make international friends? How many students stay on campus for the weekend instead of going home? Many Dutch universities are international. In Amsterdam alone, there are 10,000 international students from 130 different countries. The German student population in the Netherlands is the largest group with 22,584 (2018-2019 figures). Italy is second, and China is third. France is 9th with 2,759 French students enrolled in bachelor and master programs combined.[4]

Dutch Application Procedure

Check the application deadlines of your programs! Deadlines can vary for European and international students and range from January 15th until May or June. Sometimes you can apply even earlier via "early deadline". For almost all programs you first need to register via Studielink, the official Dutch registration platform for higher education institutions. It is not an application platform like UK's UCAS or the US' Common App. Once you are registered and you have selected your programs in Studielink, the Dutch platform will inform your preferred universities. The university will contact you with the link to their application platform. Each university has its own application platform and the application procedure may vary between different programs. One can choose up to four programs in total of which no more than two are numerus fixus programs.

Numerus Fixus Programs

The numerus fixus programs have a quota, limiting the number of spaces available. The procedure will become selective if the number of students requesting that school exceeds the number of places available. The deadline for all numerus fixus programs is January 15th. The selection procedure takes place between January 15th and April 15th and all students are given a ranking. If there are, for example, 600 places, all the students who are ranked between 1 and 600 will receive an offer. If offered a spot, a student must confirm the offer within two weeks. If an offered spot is declined, the next student, number 601, will be offered the spot and so on. All the students with a ranking number 600 and above will be on the waiting list. Do not despair as you can still get admitted during the summer! Thus, it is very important that you DO NOT CANCEL your program in Studielink!

Please note that for the programs in medicine, dentistry, dental hygiene, and physiotherapy, you can only choose one numerus fixus program.

Selective Programs
Small or well-known programs can be selective and, in general, all University Colleges are selective. The faculty will select students based on grades and on a wide range of other criteria.

Non-Selective Programs
Some very highly ranked programs are non-selective. This could happen with courses that are less popular or "à la mode" or are offered for the first year in English. In order to be selected for the course, you need to obtain a diploma equivalent to the VWO (pre-university Dutch secondary school diploma). Furthermore, you need to check

if any specific subjects are required and fulfill any necessary English language entry requirements.

Some universities have a rolling admissions process, which may mean that applications can be assessed on a first-come, first-served basis. Due to the rising popularity of the Dutch education system, the admission procedures may change each year.

Dutch Selection Criteria

Each faculty/department and each University College sets their own selection procedure and the criteria by which an applicant will be assessed. The admission procedure for selective and numerus fixus programs can be very challenging and confusing. READING and UNDERSTANDING the application procedure beforehand are absolutely essential.

The admission procedure for numerus fixus and selective programs takes the whole person into consideration. Students are assessed on academic skills plus evidence of motivation, ambition and relevant experiences; thus, a very important component of the application is the letter of motivation or personal statement.

For both the research universities and the University Colleges, a secondary school diploma equivalent to the Dutch VWO[5] is required. The *bac général* with or without the OIB, and the IB are equivalent diplomas. Sometimes a *bac technologique* may be accepted. If you are not directly eligible, check to see if having completed one year of study at a university of applied sciences could qualify you for entry as a first year bachelor at a research university.

In order to be considered for a university of applied sciences you need to obtain a diploma equivalent to the Dutch MBO-4, or HAVO; in the case of French diplomas, these are the *bac professionnel* and the *bac technologique*.

Motivation Letter
This is your chance to sell yourself; no one else will do it for you! Now is your time to shine and tell the admissions officers how qualified you are and how your past experience can show why you have such an interest in their program. You will need to come up with EVIDENCE!

How do you do this? Have you read any current, related articles or books; watched documentaries or online talks? Have you attended lectures, related classes or, for example, attended a criminal hearing? What about internships? Is your TPE *(Travail personnel encadré)*, IB Extended Essay or independent study project on a related subject? If you have not yet done any of this, you need to! This is what the admissions officers are looking for – EVIDENCE. Do you perform, play a musical instrument or compete in sports? Have these passions taught you any skills that could be applied to your studies such as time management, communication, team building, public speaking and leadership skills? ADVICE: start writing all this down on a piece of paper, organize a brainstorming session with your parents and, yes, siblings can join in too!

It is extremely important to READ the content of the program very carefully. You will need to explain why you are so excited about this specific course. Which parts do you like best? Furthermore, it is very important when applying to a Dutch university to demonstrate your strong interest in that particular institution.

Again, understand exactly what is required, follow the guidelines and start on time.

BE CREATIVE, BE POSITIVE, and never ever plagiarize!

What Universities May Request

- Transcripts 11th grade/*première*, and sometimes 12th/*terminale* 1st and 2nd trimester transcripts
- Diploma (an official school copy with signature)
- Diploma Statement (if you do not yet have your diploma, this official statement from your school confirms you meet the requirements to receive one by 1 September).
- Curriculum vitae; universities may supply their own template.
- Letter(s) of Recommendation
- English Language Proficiency: IELTS / TOEFL results, or IB, and for certain schools, OIB British or American section. Please note, British or American nationality does not prove proficiency in English.
- Letter of Motivation, Questionnaire, Test, … Dutch universities can be very creative! READ the exact requirements, follow the guidelines, and start on time.
- An assignment
- Personal Study Plan
- Interview
- Some programs, such as art, will ask for additional information or a portfolio.

OIB British / American Section

Please note that not all Dutch higher education institutions accept the OIB British or American section as a proof of English proficiency. If this is the case, ask your school, English teacher, or guidance counselor to contact the university in order to give them further information on the OIB British/American curriculum and your level of English.

IELTS / TOEFL / Cambridge

The IELTS and TOEFL are both English language proficiency tests and are valid for two years. Both tests are recognized by universities worldwide. The Cambridge C1 Advanced is an English exam that qualifies the student for university-level studies in English; this certificate does not expire. Preparation courses for this exam are offered at the British Council and at some schools.

This author recommends the IELTS test, as students have reported feeling more comfortable with it; there is an oral portion with an examiner. The British Council in Paris organizes many instructive and high-quality courses for perfecting one's English. They offer free resources, MOOCs, and videos online. One can sign up for a free placement test at the British Council.

Binding Study Advice (BSA) and European Credit Transfer and Accumulation System (ECTS)

After being accepted to a bachelor's program in the Netherlands, the universities can keep track of how one is doing and how motivated one is toward one's studies.

Many Dutch Universities use a system called BSA or Binding Study Advice to ensure that only the most motivated and successful students will be allowed to continue after their first year of studies. A BSA can either be positive or negative. How does it work?

Each year a student can earn up to 60 ECTS credits. ECTS stands for European Credit Transfer and Accumulation System, and 60 ECTS points represents between 1500 and 1800 study hours within classes and outside the university. Each university sets its own minimum requirement; some universities expect you to earn 45 out of the 60 while others require 60 out of 60 ECTS. If you receive a warning (a "conditional negative BSA") in December for not meeting the ECTS requirements, you can withdraw before February 1st and are permitted to resume your studies in September of the same year. If you decide not to withdraw before February 1st, and you receive, again, negative BSA advice (feedback) from the university at the end of the study year, you will then be asked to leave your studies. ADVICE: if you do find yourself getting a warning in December, do not feel ashamed — but, take it seriously and discuss the issues at hand with your parents and your university study advisor.

A three-year bachelor's degree is worth 180 ECTS points and a one-year master's degree is 60 ECTS credits. In general, 1 ECTS point represents 25 to 30 study hours inside and outside the university. These ECTS credits will allow a person to continue studies in the EU or in other international countries. Liberal Arts and Sciences graduates most often pursue a master's degree after their program. Please inquire with your study advisor and/or the master's program you are interested in and check if there are specific course requirements (ECTS).

Tips

Never EVER assume anything! If you do not find the minimum required *bac*, OIB, or English grades on the university website, CONTACT the Admissions Department! You will avoid wasting precious time and even better, you will be able to determine if you are going to be eligible.

Each year more and more European and international students are learning about the excellent Dutch education system. As a result of this increased interest, the entry requirements tend to change each year and admission is becoming more competitive. Check and re-check the selection criteria at the beginning of October when all universities will have updated their websites.

Applying to universities is both exciting and stressful: it is like being on a roller coaster. The rails are always there, even if you cannot see them. You will definitely go down a couple of times, maybe hit some scary bumps, but you will go up again. My best advice to students, after years of university counseling, is always believe in yourself, never give up, and work hard until the very end.

References and Resources

- Study in the Netherlands: a very rich information website - www.studyinholland.nl
- Research Universities - www.studyinholland.nl/study/dutch-institutions/research-universities
- University Colleges - www.studyinholland.nl/study/dutch-institutions/university-colleges
- Universities of Applied Sciences - www.studyinholland.nl/study/dutch-institutions/universities-of-applied-sciences; www.vereniginghogescholen.nl/english
- Dutch organisation for internationalisation in education - www.nuffic.nl/en/
- Finding programs - www.studyfinder.nl; www.bachelorsportal.com; www.mastersportal.com
- IELTS tests, more information on the British Council website - www.britishcouncil.fr/en/exam/ielts and www.ielts.org
- CIS (Council of International Schools) annually organizes an International University Fair in Paris, usually in September - www.cois.org
- In partnership with the Dutch embassy, ULYSSES International Studies (UIS) annually organizes in Paris, the Dutch University Fair, "Étudier aux Pays-Bas" - www.ulyssesinternationalstudies.com
- Studielink, where your adventure begins - http://student.sl-cloud.nl
- Atelier Néerlandais: Platform of the Dutch Embassy in Paris for creative industries - http://atelierneerlandais.com

Endnotes

1. www.timeshighereducation.com/world-university-rankings/2020/world-ranking#!/page/0/length/25/locations/NL/sort_by/rank/sort_order/asc/cols/stats
2. www.topuniversities.com/university-rankings/university-subject-rankings/2019/agriculture-forestry and www.topuniversities.com/university-rankings/university-subject-rankings/2019/communication-media-studies
3. www.timeshighereducation.com/student/best-universities/best-young-universities-world
4. www.nuffic.nl/en/publications/incoming-degree-student-mobility-dutch-higher-education-2018-2019
5. VWO (voorbereidend wetenschappelijk onderwijs) - Dutch secondary school scientific preparatory program/diploma

Student anecdote

I applied to the most selective schools on my horizon in early applications, and once I received offers, I made pro and con lists and realized that most of the final programs were similar. My university in the Hague was the best choice for me as it's located in the international peace center of the world, which would give me more internship and job opportunities. After being submerged in the Dutch culture, surrounded by so many international students, as well as studying with highly trained teachers who are always available to help and guide you, I realized that being anywhere else would've been a wrong choice.

From the beginning, it was made very clear what was required to succeed in the first year, striking a balance between the amount of contact/class hours and personal workload outside of class. Hence, it was pretty easy to adapt because expectations were made clear and when you were unsure about assignments, the teacher's office hours allowed us to easily follow a path similar to a French OIB program.

Furthermore, other students are very helpful. Even second year students guide you and help you choose the courses for the rest of the year by sharing their experiences. I think this is due to a culture that emerges from all the students living in the same building, where there is always someone to assist you, to keep you company, or just to be kind. My transition was really easy from living at home in Paris with my family to living alone in a student/academic building. If I could go back and change how I chose, applied, and moved to the Netherlands for my studies, I'd start the process earlier. I would plan ahead for administrative issues prior to moving, make sure to be well researched, and visit the universities if you have the opportunity, even if you don't end up attending those.   – *Chiara*

Higher Education in Australia

Henrietta Flinn

Why would the Franco-American, Franco-British, or Franco-French student consider studying in Australia, a country on the other side of the world and in the Southern Hemisphere, when there are so many excellent choices of colleges and universities in the US, the UK, France, and elsewhere?

Firstly, Australian educational institutions deliver an open and flexible pedagogical style and offer high-tech campuses similar to those found in the US. In contrast to the more formal French-style pedagogy, Australian teaching reflects the country's egalitarian nature, in which students are encouraged to think for themselves and to express their opinions freely. There is a great deal of emphasis placed on continuous assessment, rather than end-of-course[1] examinations.

Secondly, due to its geographic location, Australia has positioned itself to meet the growing demand for higher education in English for students from the emerging world economies of India, and in particular, China. The city of Perth is a five and half hour flight to Singapore, the gateway to Southeast Asia and a global financial hub. International students studying in Australia can benefit not only from their professors' and instructors' knowledge of countries in the Asia-Pacific region, but can make contacts with future business and government leaders from these countries.

Thirdly, over 85% of Australians live in urban areas and nearly 70% live in the state capital cities, making Australia one of the world's most urbanized countries.[2] As a result, most Australian educational institutions are situated in urban areas, close to city facilities and an international airport.

Finally, Australia is a safe and democratic country; political unrest is limited, crime rates are low, and there are strict gun control laws. Australians are an open and friendly people who value the diversity that international students bring to campuses and communities. Universities provide comprehensive support services to all first-year students (and to international students in particular) to help them adjust to university life. Most universities offer dormitories or residences for students and campuses in Australia are similar to those in the US: good facilities, student activities, clubs, sports fields, bars etc.

International Student Population

Australia has the third highest number of international students in the world behind only the US and the UK. It has more international students per capita than any other country, with over 800,000 in 2018. Of this number, there were about 2,400 French students enrolled in technical vocational education and training programs[3] (Australian acronym VET); and about 1,100 students in university degree programs. A further 1,100 were studying in non-award classes (not for credit).

The majority of international students in Australia come from China, accounting for about 38% of the international student population in 2018.

Higher Education Structures

Australia's higher education sector is similar in structure to that of the UK. It consists of universities and Vocational Education and Training (VET) institutions, the majority of which are vocationally oriented post-secondary institutions.

Universities
There are currently 43 universities in Australia: Australian universities, two international universities, and one private specialty university. The Group of Eight (Go8) is a coalition of Australia's most prestigious universities, which have an excellent reputation internationally, and are comparable to the Ivy League in the US.

VET Institutions
VET is education and training that focuses on providing work-related skills. VET courses are primarily offered by Registered Training Organizations (RTOs). These can include technical and continuing education institutions (TAFEs - Technical and Further Education) as well as private colleges. Some universities may also offer VET courses in addition to higher education courses.

Choosing an Educational Institution

Comprehensive information on all aspects of studying in Australia is available on the easy-to-navigate government website, Study in Australia (www.studyinaustralia.gov.au). In France, Australie Mag is the official representation and advising center for Australian universities, and its website offers a plethora of information in French about the education system and institutions of higher learning throughout Australia (www.australiemag.com).

The Australian higher education system consists of public and private universities, Australian branches of overseas universities, and other higher education providers. Qualifications offered include associate degrees, bachelor degrees, and advanced diplomas at the undergraduate level, as well as postgraduate certificates and diplomas, master's, and doctoral degrees.

Only those educational and vocational training institutions registered by the Commonwealth government may enroll international students who are holders of a student visa. These institutions and the degree or diploma programs they are certified to offer are listed on the Commonwealth Register of Institutions and Courses for Overseas Students (CRICOS). Prospective students can search for programs and institutions via the CRICOS website.

Regulation and Quality Control

The Tertiary Education Quality and Standards Agency (TEQSA) is Australia's independent national quality assurance and regulatory agency for higher education. All organizations that offer higher education qualifications in or from Australia must be registered by TEQSA. Higher education providers that have not been granted self-accrediting authority (almost all of the non-university providers) must also have their courses of study accredited by TEQSA.

The Australian Qualifications Framework ensures that Australian degrees and diplomas meet established standards. It comprises ten levels, and links school, vocational, and university education qualifications into one national system, allowing students to move easily from one level of study to the next, and from one institution to another, as long as they satisfy student visa requirements. In addition, VET institutions are regulated via the Australian Skills Quality Authority (ASQA).

Recognition of Australian Degrees and Diplomas

Although Australian degrees and diplomas are recognized via agreements with most countries (including France), prospective students intending to work elsewhere after graduation are strongly advised to contact the professional associations in the country concerned to determine if their Australian qualification will allow them to practice professionally.

The Qualification Recognition Agreement between France and Australia covers all institutions which are members of the French Conférence des Présidents d'Université (CPU), the Conférence des Directeurs des Écoles Françaises d'Ingénieurs (CDEFI) and the Universities Australia. The aim of the agreement is to encourage mutual recognition of qualifications, periods of study, and higher education awards in order to facilitate student exchange and continued study in the partner country. However, it does not cover courses of study in healthcare nor does it cover diploma recognition in either country for the purpose of undertaking a professional activity.

Australian business and economics undergraduate degrees in business/commerce/economics are recognized for entry into prestigious MBA programs in France; however, professional experience is as important as an undergraduate degree, if not more so. Many Australian-educated students have gone on to study at highly reputable schools in France such as HEC and INSEAD, and some Australian universities offer exchanges with a number of these institutions.

Students with an Australian degree may need to go through accreditation processes and may also have to undertake additional studies. For information on the recognition of Australian qualifications in France consult the ENIC-NARIC (European Network of Information Centres - National Academic Recognition Information Centres) website.

Academic Year

Australia is in the Southern Hemisphere, so the academic year runs from late

February or early March to late November. The academic year is divided into two semesters; however, some institutions offer a trimester system and/or run summer schools from December to February.

Undergraduate and graduate students enroll for courses at the beginning of the calendar year, however, the starting date of classes may vary. Australian universities do allow mid-year enrollment (around July) for certain programs. Students studying towards a doctoral degree or doing postgraduate research may be able to negotiate an alternative starting date with their study supervisor.

Undergraduate exchange programs must be coordinated with the student's home education institution. For example, a student based in France could study for a semester in Australia, starting in July. Also, a French *lycée* graduate could envision taking a short gap year before starting university in Australia in February/March of the following year.

Degrees and Diplomas

Qualifications that can be obtained at Australian universities and other higher education institutions include the bachelor degree (three years); bachelor honours degree (four years); graduate certificate (six months following a bachelor degree); graduate diploma (one year following a bachelor degree); master degree (one to two years following a bachelor honours degree or bachelor degree); and doctoral degree (typically three years following a master degree). In addition, students can undertake an associate degree, a short-cycle degree taken in conjunction with employment.

Vocational education and training (VET) institutions offer certificates (duration of study ranges from four to six months and 12 to 18 months), diplomas (24 to 36 months), and advanced diplomas (24 to 36 months).

> *The academic year in Australia runs from late February to late November.*

Australian degree programs can be very flexible, depending on the field of study. Students can spend a semester abroad, or opt for distance learning if they prefer following online courses. In addition, there is latitude in class selection similar to the US liberal arts model.

The Melbourne Model, instituted by the University of Melbourne (one of Australia's oldest universities), aligns degrees conferred by Australian universities with those offered by Asian, European, and North American institutions. The model aims to internationalize academic programs and match degree structures with the Bologna Process (see "Glossary of Terms" page 123).

There are over 200 exchange programs between French and Australian universities/ *grandes écoles*. For example, Sciences Po has exchanges with ten Australian universities. Credit transfer between an Australian university and an institution abroad is usually agreed upon between the two universities concerned.

Course Structure and Assessment

An undergraduate has a mix of lectures and tutorials, with some technical subjects also including laboratory classes. A lecture might be attended by up to 200 students, while up to 30 students are in a typical tutorial.

Students may be assessed continuously throughout the year as well as at the end of each semester and/or academic year. The final grade for a class is based on performance in assignments (written and/or practical, depending on the course) and exams, as well as class participation, attendance, and group exercises.

For example, as part of a Bachelor of Advanced Computing at the University of Sydney, in the intermediate-level course "Data Analytics: Learning from Data", students have three hours of lectures and one hour of computer laboratory time per week. Students are assessed through computer practicals (10%), online quizzes (15%), group work assignment and presentation (15%), and a final exam (60%)

TAFE programs, with their emphasis on providing students with direct industry experience, very often include internships and work placements.

English Language and Entrance Requirements

A satisfactory level of English is required in order to obtain a student visa from the Department of Home Affairs. Educational institutions set their own English language requirements for admission including the minimum language proficiency test scores required for each program. These may be different from the score needed to secure a student visa so it is important to check on both the Department of Home Affairs and the institution's websites for all requirements.

The academic requirement to gain entry into an Australian tertiary education institution is the foreign equivalent of the Australian Senior Secondary Certificate of Education (Year 12), i.e., the French *baccalauréat*, International Baccalaureate (IB), A-Levels, or US high school diploma. Some programs may also have specific prerequisites.

Graduate studies in Australia require the satisfactory completion of at least one undergraduate degree. Institutions may take research ability or relevant work experience into consideration.

Applying to University

Prospective international students in an International Baccalaureate (IB) program can apply through the Universities Admissions Centre (UAC) that processes applications for admission to tertiary study at universities and colleges in the state of new South Wales (NSW) and the Australian Capital Territory (ACT).

Students with a French secondary or tertiary school background will need to either apply directly to each targeted school or complete a common application through Australie Mag, enabling application to multiple institutions in a single procedure. See www.australiemag.com for details.

Standard university application deadlines
- Semester 1 (usually starts in February) – deadline is 31 October of the preceding year
- Semester 2 (usually starts in July) – deadline is 30 April; but may vary depending

on the institution.
- Some universities offer a trimester system of intake for international students with start dates in February, July and November, so deadlines for applications are October, May, and September.

Tuition Fees and Scholarships

Tuition fees for international students at Australian higher education institutions vary depending on a number of factors, such as location (capital or regional city), length of program, and ranking. They generally compare favorably with those in the US.

Scholarships, grants, and bursaries are available for international students and are offered by the Australian Government, education institutions, as well as some other public and private organizations. For more details see the Study in Australia and Australie Mag websites.

Admission Requirements

A student visa must be obtained online from the Department of Home Affairs website for anyone planning to study in Australia for more than three months.

Australia requires international students to show evidence that they can cover minimum costs for living and studying. International students are permitted to earn money through part-time work. Student visa holders can work a maximum of 40 hours per fortnight once classes have begun and are in session, and unlimited hours during scheduled breaks. Masters by research (MRes) and doctorate (PhD) students can work unlimited hours once their program of study has begun.

The living costs requirement is meant to ensure that students (and any family members) have sufficient funds to cover their expenses while studying. Prospective student visa applicants and their accompanying family members must demonstrate access to minimal funds during their stay. Figures and conversions for July 2019 were:
- $AUD 20,290 (12,442 €) a year for the main student;
- $AUD 7,100 (4,364 €) a year for the student's partner;
- $AUD 3,040 (1,895 €) a year for a dependent child.

This figure is the minimum required by law and does not take into account lifestyle and location of study.

Further details and up-to-date information on student visas and the living costs requirement are available from the Department of Home Affairs (http://immi.homeaffairs.gov.au).

Accommodation and Living Costs for International Students

Costs of living in Sydney, Melbourne, and Brisbane approach that of Paris. The other state capital and regional cities are cheaper. The Study in Australia website provides ample information on accommodation and living costs (www.studyinaustralia.gov.au). To get a personalized estimate of the costs in a particular city, Study in Australia recommends using the Insider Guides Cost of Living Calculator (insiderguides.com.au/cost-of-living-calculator).

Australian cities are similar to many in the US: a small city or suburban center with high-rise buildings surrounded by low-density sprawling suburbs. Public transport systems are inadequate and expensive compared to those in Europe; therefore it is essential outside the centers of the major state capital cities to own a car. Remember that as in the UK, one drives on the left.

Conclusion

Australia offers a quality education at a reasonable cost and in a pleasant environment. Its geographic location offers a career gateway to Asia and the international recognition of its degrees and diplomas makes Australia an attractive option for the global-minded student.

References and Resources

- Department of Education and Training: www.education.gov.au
  - Data on international students: https://internationaleducation.gov.au/research/International-Student-Data/Pages/default.aspx
  - Information for international students: www.education.gov.au/international-students
- Group of 8 (Go8): http://go8.edu.au/about/the-go8
- Austrade (Australian Trade and Investment Commission) / Study in Australia: www.studyinaustralia.gov.au
  - Student Visa: www.studyinaustralia.gov.au/english/apply-to-study/visas
- Commonwealth Register of Institutions and Courses for Overseas Students (CRICOS): http://cricos.education.gov.au
- Tertiary Education Quality and Standards Agency (TEQSA): www.teqsa.gov.au
- Australian Qualifications Framework (AQF): www.aqf.edu.au
  - AQF review: www.education.gov.au/australian-qualifications-framework-review-0
- Australian Skills Quality Authority (ASQA): www.asqa.gov.au
- Academic Qualification Recognition Agreement between Australia and France: http://au.ambafrance.org/IMG/pdf_Qualification_recognition_agreement.pdf
- ENIC-NARIC (European Network of Information Centres - National Academic Recognition Information Centres): www.ciep.fr/en/enic-naric-france
- Vocational Education: www.studiesinaustralia.com/studying-in-australia/what-to-study-in-australia/types-of-education/vocational-education
- Bachelor of Advanced Computing, University of Sydney, "Data Analytics: Learning from Data": https://sydney.edu.au/courses/units-of-study/2019/data/data2002.html
- Universities Admissions Centre (UAC): www.uac.edu.au
- Scholarships for International Students: www.studyinaustralia.gov.au/english/australian-education/scholarships
- Australian Department of Home Affairs: http://immi.homeaffairs.gov.au
  - Student Visa: http://immi.homeaffairs.gov.au/visas/getting-a-visa/visa-listing/student-500
  - Financial capacity requirements: www.legislation.gov.au/Details/F2018L00032
- Insider Guides Cost of Living in Australia: http://insiderguides.com.au/cost-of-living-calculator
- Currency conversions: www.xe.com
- French Embassy in Australia: www.au.ambafrance.org
- Information in French: www.australiemag.com and www.australiemag.com/AustralieMag/australiemag-centre-officiel-des-universites-australiennes-en-france

Endnotes

1. In this context, the term "course" in Australian English is the same as "program" in American English.
2. https://data.worldbank.org/indicator/SP.URB.TOTL.IN.ZS?locations=AU, and www.population.net.au
3. https://internationaleducation.gov.au/research/International-Student-Data/

About the Authors

Elyse Michaels-Berger is an executive and academic coach. She is founder and Director of the HEC Youth Leadership Initiative and the Director of the HEC Summer School, as well as the former Academic Director of the HEC MBA Program. She previously worked as a consultant with Accenture, where she specialized in coaching, training, and leadership development. Elyse earned her MA in Organizational Psychology from Columbia University, Teachers College, and an MBA from ESSEC. A graduate of Princeton University, she serves as co-president of its Alumni Association in France. Elyse obtained her Coaching Certificate from the Coaches Training Institute, as well as a College Counselor Advising Certificate from Columbia University, Teachers College. She regularly facilitates personal development and intercultural workshops for educators, students and parents.

Caroline Bouffard is an Independent Educational Consultant and founder of A+ College Coaching. Based in Paris, she helps families identify and evaluate options for college and universities abroad as well as navigate the admissions process with the goal of finding the best academic, social, and financial fit for their child. Having raised her own children in Germany, Japan, and now France, she is particularly sensitive to the needs of 'global nomad kids'. Caroline holds a BA from the American University of Paris, an MBA from the University of Hartford, and a Certificate in Independent Educational Consulting from UC Irvine. She stays on top of college admission trends by regularly visiting college campuses, attending conferences and webinars, and is a Professional member of IECA and International ACAC.

Sallie Chaballier is the mother of two children who took time off before college: one took a gap year on a Work and Holiday Visa in Australia and the other took a semester to work on a political campaign in the US. She was co-editor for the 7th edition of the *AAWE Guide to Education in France,* longtime AAWE liaison for Paris College Day, President of AAWE from 2008 – 2010, and President of FAWCO from 2017 – 2019. Sallie holds degrees in Russian and Soviet Studies from Yale and Harvard Universities.

Kathleen Choiset is a graduate of UC Berkeley (Anthropology) and worked in Paris for nine years in an international film production syndicate. As a certified EFL teacher of English, she worked for over twenty years in French public schools (including preschool, primary, *lycée*, BTS, and adult education - Greta). Kathleen is the mother of four who as a parent has experienced a total of eight years of CPGE and five years of *concours*!

Noémie Choiset lives in Vienna, Austria, and works for an international organization, covering human resources and finance topics. She previously lived for nearly six years in Washington D.C., working for the International Monetary Fund (IMF). Before that, she worked for over eight years as an Artistic Administrator in Paris, handling contracts, budgets, and logistics for international symphony and opera productions. She holds a Master of Science in Management from ESSEC Business School in Paris, a Master of Science in Arts Administration from Paris-Dauphine University, and a Bachelor of Arts in Musicology from the Sorbonne University. Noémie is a mother of three young children who attend the Lycée Français in Vienna.

Henrietta Flinn moved to Australia from England with her family at the age of seven. She completed her primary, secondary, and higher education studies in Melbourne and has a B.A. in Media Studies and Philosophy from Swinburne Institute of Technology (now Swinburne University). Her three Australian-born children have attended a variety of secondary schools and higher education institutions in Australia, Canada, France, Spain, and the US. She currently teaches English to secondary school students in the Paris area and at the Extension Program of the American School of Paris.

Lisa Fleury is Assistant to the Director of the Vassar-Wesleyan Program in Paris. She studied at Wellesley College and Université Denis Diderot – Paris VII and worked as a lecturer in English for the Human Resources Management *Master 2* program at the Université de Paris Dauphine.

Catherine Godard holds degrees from Arizona State University (B.A., M.A.). She retired as college counselor from the École Jeannine Manuel and currently works as an international education consultant in the Paris area. An active member of organizations that promote ethical college admissions practices (NACAC, IACAC, and CIS), she actively participates in conferences and college tours, and lectures frequently on international college counseling.

Marine Halbron has practiced medicine since 1989 after pursuing her medical studies at the University of Paris VI. She is a full-time senior physician in Diabetology at Hôpital La Pitié Salpêtrière in Paris, where she also teaches medical students of Paris Sorbonne University.

Joumana Ordelheide is a Paris-based higher education expert specialized in international counseling. After spending ten years as an admissions counselor and manager at The American University of Paris, she co-founded an educational consulting company that allowed her to take her expertise abroad and advise students from over a dozen countries on their university and career choices. Joumana currently is Manager of International Counseling at the École Internationale Bilingue (EIB), where she oversees the counseling curriculum and international university applications.

Anne-Laure Moya-Plana is registered at the Paris Bar since 2010. Her areas of expertise are copyright, patent, and trademark law as well as IT and digital law, including compliance with the management of personal data (GDPR). Anne-Laure teaches at ESG as part of the Startup program, and at Paris-Dauphine University in the area of digital law.

Céline Ouziel has been educational adviser at the Franco-American Fulbright Commission since 2001. She advises students living in France who wish to study or conduct research in the United States for every level of study and any kind of discipline. She is affiliated with Education USA, a global network of information centers connected with the US State Department. Ms. Ouziel holds degrees in English and American civilization from the Université de Paris XII Créteil and pursued graduate studies at Portland State University where she also worked as a Teaching Assistant.

Laura Paget is registered at the Paris Bar since 1999. She provides counsel in commercial and corporate law and has wide experience negotiating, advising on and drafting corporate documentation, joint ventures, and commercial agreements of all kinds. She also gives advice in relation to compliance programs within the scope of anti-corruption laws in France. Laura is a Franco-American dual national.

Robynne Pendariès has lived and worked in France for the past 30 years. Both her husband and son have attended university in the US (and soon her daughter as well) on sports scholarships. Robynne and her husband, Marc, a golf professional, assist junior golfers in their pursuit of a sports scholarship in the US.

Mariët Robert is an independent higher education specialist for university applications to the UK and the Netherlands and is founder of the independent agency, ULYSSES International Studies (UIS) in Paris. UIS organizes the annual Dutch University Fair, "Étudier aux Pays-Bas", in partnership with the Dutch Embassy and numerous Dutch research universities and University Colleges. A dual Dutch/French citizen, Mariët's approach has also been informed by her personal experience as mother to three daughters, all of whom have studied abroad in English. She is a British Council Education Agent and a CIS Affiliated Consultant.

Elaine Rothman has lived and worked in France for the past 25 years and has two sons who both chose to leave France for higher education (US and Scotland). Having experienced corporate France firsthand and observed hiring practices and how a *grande école* can affect careers, she wanted to get an in-depth view of the CPGE and *grande école* process. Elaine holds both a master's and a doctorate from MIT and was a postdoctoral fellow at Harvard Business School.

Laura Vincens was the University Admissions Counselor at the American School of Paris for 24 years. She began working at ASP in 1974 as a Middle School teacher and counselor, and joined the Upper School as College Counselor in 1993. In the course of her career, Laura assisted thousands of students with admission to universities in the United States, Canada, the UK, Europe, and elsewhere in the world. Since retiring from ASP in 2017, Laura works as an independent University Admissions Consultant, providing students without access to a college adviser at their school, with guidance and support in applying to universities. Laura considers herself fortunate to have such a gratifying career, which allows her to aid so many diverse, exciting, and promising young people to fulfill their ambitions.

Fred Weissler is Professor Emeritus of Mathematics at Université Paris 13, where he taught from 1992 to 2015. He hails from Washington D.C. and holds a B.A. in

Mathematics and Physics from Yale, and an M.A. and PhD in Mathematics from UC Berkeley. Fred taught at Brown University, University of Texas - Austin, and Texas A&M before moving to France in 1987. He taught at Université Paris 6, Université de Nantes, and Université Paris 12 prior to joining the faculty of Université Paris 13.

Printed in Poland
by Amazon Fulfillment
Poland Sp. z o.o., Wrocław